THE SOUND PATTERN
OF ANCIENT GREEK

PUBLICATIONS OF THE PHILOLOGICAL SOCIETY
XXIII

THE SOUND PATTERN
OF
ANCIENT GREEK

by

ALAN H. SOMMERSTEIN

King's College, Cambridge

PUBLISHED FOR THE SOCIETY BY
BASIL BLACKWELL, OXFORD
1973

© THE PHILOLOGICAL SOCIETY, 1973
ISBN 0 631 14770 5
Library of Congress Catalog Card Number: 72-96836

_____

To
Rebecca

_____

PRINTED IN ENGLAND BY
STEPHEN AUSTIN AND SONS, LTD., HERTFORD

PREFACE

This book is based on a doctoral dissertation entitled *Phonological Theory and Ancient Greek*, which I submitted to the Degree Committee of Classics, University of Cambridge, in 1971. It is a revised and expanded version of Part II of that work; Part I, which dealt with the theory of stratificational grammar, has been omitted.

Of the people whose advice and assistance I gratefully acknowledge, W. Sidney Allen and Pieter Seuren must come first, my successive supervisors over the two years I was working in Cambridge on Greek phonology. Even after he ceased officially to direct my work, Professor Allen has always been ready with good advice; and to Dr. Seuren it was mainly due that my dissertation was capable of being made into a book at all and was not a sheer miscellany. My especial thanks also go to those who read, and made valuable suggestions upon, earlier drafts of my dissertation: in addition to Professor Allen and Dr. Seuren these kind people are Bernard Comrie, P. H. Matthews, Calvert Watkins, and Andrew Carstairs (of MIT).

It was Professor Allen who recommended Indiana University to me as the place where I could continue my linguistic training, at a time when I had much enthusiasm for the subject but little knowledge of it. I shall always be grateful to him for the recommendation, and to the English-Speaking Union, the U.S.-U.K. Educational Commission, and Indiana University itself for making it possible for me to act upon it, as well as to all those who made my stay so profitable – in particular, Fred W. Householder, who has both then and since used for my great benefit his knowledge and insight both in linguistics and in Greek, and Richard Carter, who in his seminar in the first half of 1969 tried to teach me something of what phonology, particularly generative phonology, is about. I need hardly say that none of these people is in any way responsible for any defects or shortcomings in this work.

Next I must thank the Council and Publications Secretary of the Philological Society for permitting me to become a contributor to their Publications Series, and Bob Coleman for taking off my shoulders the task of approaching the Society in the first place, at a time when I had many other preoccupations.

My thanks go also to all the others who have helped this work in many different ways, and especially to King's College, for whom nothing has ever been too much; but my greatest debt of all has been to the constant encouragement of my wife, to whom, with all love and gratitude, I dedicate this book.

ALAN H. SOMMERSTEIN

King's College,
Cambridge,
November, 1971

CONTENTS

CHAPTER ONE

ORIENTATION

1.0. *GENERAL*

This book is about the phonology of Ancient Greek. It consists of an account of the most important rules (so far as they are known) governing the pronunciation of sentences in that language, and a consideration of some of the implications of evidence from Greek for general phonological theory. Interest will be concentrated primarily on the rules themselves rather than on the actual pronunciation; the reader seeking more detailed information about the latter is referred to Allen (1968), whose well documented and argued conclusions I have followed except where I indicate disagreement.

The variety of Greek being described is ' classical Attic ', that is the dialect of Athens as it was spoken between about 480 and 320 B.C., particularly around the midpoint of this period. In various places I use evidence from the Greek of other places and periods; this is when direct Attic evidence is not available, and is done with the object of determining the probable Attic pronunciation in the period mentioned.

The phonological theory on which my work is based is that of Chomsky and Halle (1968), in which, however, I have certain revisions to propose. Some of these will arise in the course of the discussion of Greek segmental phonology (the phonology of the consonant and vowel systems) in Chapter II; two of the most important are treated separately in Chapters III and IV. After this, in Chapter V, I give a full account, in the framework of the revised theory, of the Greek accentual system, in the course of which some further theoretical modifications are proposed. The final chapter, Chapter VI, contains a summary, in order,[1] of the rules of the part of Greek phonology that I have investigated, a stretch of text written in the form it would have before the application of these rules, and a number of illustrative derivations of particular words.

---

[1] That is, in one possible order: not every pair of rules is crucially ordered.

1.1. *THE PHONOLOGICAL INVENTORY*

An autonomous phonemic description of classical Attic would probably [2] require eighteen consonant phonemes and twelve vowel phonemes, as follows: [3]

$$
\begin{array}{llllllll}
(1) & /\text{p}^\text{h} & \text{t}^\text{h} & \text{k}^\text{h} & \bar{\text{\i}}\ \text{i} & [\ddot{\bar{\text{u}}}]\ \ddot{\text{u}} & \bar{\text{u}} \\
& \text{p} & \text{t} & \text{k} \\
& \text{b} & \text{d} & \text{g} & \bar{\text{e}} \\
& & \text{s} & & \text{e} & & \text{o} \\
& \text{m} & \text{n} & \text{ŋ} & \bar{\text{ę}} & \bar{\text{ǫ}} \\
& & \text{l} & \text{r} \\
& \text{w} & \text{y} & \text{h} & \bar{\text{a}}\ \text{a} & & /
\end{array}
$$

As Allen points out, even in an autonomous system the phonemic status of /ŋ/ is dubious, and it can easily be shown to be a conditioned variant of /n/ in some contexts and of /g/ in others. All the other consonants in (1) will also appear in the underlying representations of a generative phonological description. As to the vowels, it will be shown in Chapter II that there is underlyingly a system of five short vowels, /a i u ę ǫ/, and five corresponding long vowels; the complicated and asymmetrical system of (1) results from various rules which interfere with this underlying pattern.

In this study I assume the system of phonological-phonetic features described by Chomsky and Halle (1968), with certain modifications which will be mentioned when they become relevant. In tables (2) and (3) there are described, using this feature system, all the segment types of (1), all others which are needed in underlying or intermediate representations for Greek, and one or two which are known to have occurred as low-level conditioned phonetic variants.

Tables (2) and (3) are not intended as a classificatory matrix, but as a display of the features relevant to the part which the segment types in question play in Greek phonology.

---

[2] On the maximum assumptions of Allen (1968, 8 and 59).

[3] Throughout, the symbols [ę] and [ǫ] refer to low or lower-mid vowels, respectively front unrounded and back rounded; [r̥] to a voiceless [r]; and [c] and [ʒ] to dental affricates, respectively voiceless and voiced.

(2) Vowels and Glides

	ī	ē	ę̄	ā	ǭ	ō	ū	ů̃	i	e	ę	a	ǫ	o	u	ü	w	y	h
syllabic	+	+	+	+	+	+	+	+	+	+	+	+	+	+	+	+	−	−	−
consonantal	−	−	−	−	−	−	−	−	−	−	−	−	−	−	−	−	−	−	−
sonorant	+	+	+	+	+	+	+	+	+	+	+	+	+	+	+	+	+	+	+
long	+	+	+	+	+	+	+	+	−	−	−	−	−	−	−	−	−	−	−
high	+	−	−	−	−	−	+	+	+	−	−	−	−	−	−	+	+	+	−
low	−	−	+	+	+	−	−	−	−	−	+	+	+	−	−	−	−	−	+
back	−	−	−	+	+	+	+	−	−	−	−	+	+	+	+	−	+	−	−
round	−	−	−	−	+	+	+	+	−	−	−	−	+	+	+	+	+	−	−
heightened subglottal pressure (h.s.p.)																	−	−	+

(3) True Consonants (including liquids)

	l	r	ṛ	m	n	ŋ	s	z	b	d	g	p	t	k	pʰ	tʰ	kʰ	c	ȝ
syllabic	−	−	−	−	−	−	−	−	−	−	−	−	−	−	−	−	−	−	−
consonantal	+	+	+	+	+	+	+	+	+	+	+	+	+	+	+	+	+	+	+
nasal	−	−	−	+	+	+	−	−	−	−	−	−	−	−	−	−	−	−	−
sonorant	+	+	+	+	+	+	−	−	−	−	−	−	−	−	−	−	−	−	−
low	−	−	−	−	−	−	−	−	−	−	−	−	−	−	−	−	−	−	−
high	−	+	+	−	−	+	−	−	−	−	+	−	−	+	−	−	+	−	−
back	−	−	−	−	−	+	−	−	−	−	+	−	−	+	−	−	+	−	−
voice	+	+	−	+	+	+	−	+	+	+	+	−	−	−	−	−	−	−	+
h.s.p.	−	−	?	−	−	−	−	−	−	−	−	−	−	−	+	+	+	−	−
anterior	+	−	−	+	+	−	+	+	+	+	−	+	+	−	+	+	−	+	+
coronal	+	+	+	−	+	−	+	+	−	+	−	−	+	−	−	+	−	+	+
continuant	+	+	+	−	−	−	+	+	−	−	−	−	−	−	−	−	−	−	−
delayed release							−	−	−	−	−	−	−	−	−	−	−	+	+
strident	−	−	−	−	−	−	+	+	−	−	−	−	−	−	−	−	−	+	+
lateral	+	−	−	−	−	−	−	−	−	−	−	−	−	−	−	−	−	−	−

The order in which features are given therefore has no significance, and the presence of blanks signifies only that segments of
a certain class can never be distinguished by the features in
question (thus ' heightened subglottal pressure ' is relevant
only for consonants, and ' delayed release ' only for oral stop
consonants).

In generative phonology, the phonological part of the
grammar of a language is regarded as a system of operations,
usually termed ' rules ', whereby the ' phonological representation ' of a sentence of the language is converted into a ' phonetic
representation ' specifying the actual pronunciation of that
sentence. The phonological representation is arrived at by the
criteria of maximizing simplicity and generality in the rules

required, and minimizing the number of differing phonological forms that need to be assumed for any single lexical or grammatical element.[3a]

Each rule is of the form

(3a) A → B / X —— Y

which is interpreted ' If in the input string there is an A preceded by X and followed by Y, then give this A the feature specifications B.' For example:

$$(3b) \quad [-\text{cont}] \rightarrow \begin{bmatrix} +\text{voice} \\ +\text{nas} \end{bmatrix} / \ [+\text{syll}] \text{——} [+\text{nas}]$$

(3b) is an instruction to take any non-continuant segment that is preceded by a vowel and followed by a nasal, and make it voiced (if it is not voiced already) and nasal (if it is not nasal already). If in the input to a rule of the form (3a) there is a string XAY in which the A already has the features B, then A is unchanged by the rule, and we say the rule applies vacuously.

Neither X nor Y (which together are said to constitute the *environment description* of the rule) need be a single segment. Either or both may be a sequence of two or more segments, or of segments interspersed with boundary symbols (for which see below); either or both may be blank. If X or Y is blank, then the rule operates regardless, respectively, of preceding or following context. A and B may not contain more than one segment each, but each may contain any number of features. A may be a blank pair of brackets without any features at all; in that case the rule applies to any segment in the given environment, regardless of what kind of segment it is. Either A or B, again, may be zero (∅); if B is zero we have a *deletion*, if A is zero we have one variety or another of *epenthesis*.

Boundary symbols play a very important role in generative phonology. Each morpheme has the boundary symbol + at

---

[3a] Such single lexical or grammatical elements are usually termed *morphemes* or *formatives*.

beginning and end, and each syntactic unit (constituent), roughly speaking, has at beginning and end the word boundary symbol ⧣. We shall also later on be meeting a third, intermediate boundary symbolized by =, found typically between the parts of compound words. From time to time we will be referring to boundaries in feature terms; the features used by Chomsky and Halle to define boundaries are 'formative boundary' (FB) and 'word boundary' (WB). The boundary = is represented as [−FB, −WB].

As has been mentioned, boundaries may figure in the environment of a rule. Formative boundary, moreover, figures by implication in the environment of every rule. This is because, in determining whether a string satisfies the environment description of a rule, the presence in the string of morpheme boundaries not mentioned in the rule is ignored. Thus the t of the string *patnak* meets the environment description of (3*b*), but so does the t of such strings as *pa+tnak*, *pat+nak*, *pa+t+nak*, etc. On the other hand, if the environment description of a rule specifically mentions a morpheme boundary, the rule will *not* apply to a string not containing a morpheme boundary in the place where the rule requires one.

It is also possible for a rule to change one kind of boundary into another, or to insert or delete a boundary. I know of no rule in any language, however, that changes a boundary into a segment or vice versa.

Phonological rules are ordered: starting with the first rule, each rule is tested for applicability and applied if appropriate, after which the output of the nth rule (which may be the same as its input, if the rule has not applied or has applied vacuously) becomes the input to the $(n+1)$th. In Greek and possibly in other languages it is necessary to superimpose on this linear ordering other ordering principles, which will be discussed later (pp. 128 ff.).

Finally, a note about one or two important notational conventions. The brace symbol { } marks the 'collapsing' of two rules into one: the resulting schema is to be read first as if only the first of the strings enclosed by the braces were present (reading from top to bottom), then as if only the second were present, etc. Otherwise put, a schema

$$(3c) \quad Z \begin{Bmatrix} Q_1 \\ Q_2 \\ : \\ . \\ Q_n \end{Bmatrix} W$$

is an abbreviation for the sequence of rules

$$(3d) \quad ZQ_1W, ZQ_2W, \ldots, ZQ_nW$$

Another means of collapsing rules is the parenthesis notation, which denotes the optional absence of an element or elements. Again a schema with parentheses abbreviates a sequence of rules with and without the parenthesized elements, the longest first. It is possible to have parentheses within parentheses; thus an environment description

$$(3e) \quad \text{——} VC(VC(VCC(V)))\#$$

abbreviates four environment descriptions in the following order:

$$(3f) \quad \begin{aligned} &\text{(i)} \text{——} VCVCVCCV\# \\ &\text{(ii)} \text{——} VCVCVCC\# \\ &\text{(iii)} \text{——} VCVC\# \\ &\text{(iv)} \text{——} VC\# \end{aligned}$$

It has been found to be a characteristic of the parenthesis notation that rules abbreviated by it apply ' in disjunctive order ', i.e. once any one of such a set of rules as $(3f)$ has found a match and applied, no subsequent rule in the set may apply.

Certain phonological phenomena, such as metathesis or loss of consonants with compensatory lengthening of vowels, involve simultaneous changes in more than one segment. Such phenomena cannot be stated in the form $(3a)$, and rules for them are given in a ' transformational ' format, so called because it resembles the customary format for syntactic transformations. An example of such a rule might be:

(3g) [+syll] [+nas] [+strid]
        1   2   3   ⇒

$$\begin{bmatrix} 1 \\ +\text{long} \end{bmatrix} \quad \emptyset \quad 3$$

(3g) has the effect of simultaneously deleting the nasal and lengthening the preceding vowel.

The abbreviations V and C stand, of course, for vowel and consonant, that is [+syllabic] and [−syllabic] respectively. In several rules will be found expressions like C_0 and C_1; these are instances of a notation whereby X_n means 'not less than n successive occurrences of X'. Thus C_1 means 'one or more consonants'; C_0 means 'one or more consonants, or zero'; $\#_1$ means 'at least one word boundary'; etc.

In the use of obliques (/ . . . /) and square brackets ([. . .]) to enclose phonological and phonetic representations I follow the practice of Chomsky and Halle, who say (1968, 65) that they use obliques ' for representations in which the features are functioning as classificatory devices . . . and square brackets for representations in which they function phonetically '; like them, however, I ' cannot adhere to this convention rigidly ', and intermediate representations (where some but not all rules have applied) have been shown in one or the other way according as their remoteness from, or their relative nearness to, the phonetic output needed to be emphasized.

I generally quote Greek words in Greek script, followed by either a phonetic representation, where the exact pronunciation is of importance, or a conventional transliteration (printed in italics). It should be noted that in transliterations, ¨ serves as a diaeresis, and a sequence of vowel plus *i* or *u* without such a diaeresis (e.g. *ai*, *eu*, *ou*, *yi*) is pronounced (either as a long vowel or a diphthong) in a single syllable.

CHAPTER TWO

THE SEGMENTAL PHONOLOGY OF GREEK

2.1. *RULES RELATING TO CONSONANTS*

2.1.1. WEAKENING RULES

There is a great deal of evidence that many Greek words contain, in their underlying representations, consonants and glides which in the phonetic output are represented either by [h] or by nothing at all; also that phonetic [s] often represents underlying /t/. The phenomena in question can be accounted for by five rules which it is the purpose of this section to present and justify.

The neuter noun γένος [génos] ' kind ' is inflected, in the singular, in the following manner; the declension of another third-declension neuter noun, ὄμμα [ómma] ' eye ', is set beside it for comparison:

(4) Nominative &   γένος [génos   ὄμμα   [ómma
      accusative
      Genitive   γένους génūs   ὄμματος ómmatos
      Dative   γένει   génē]   ὄμματι ómmati]

The genitive and dative case-endings appear to be quite different. Indeed, while ὄμμα [ómma] forms its oblique cases by additions to the stem, γένος [génos] appears to form them by mutations.

The difference between the two paradigms diminishes considerably once we take into account the possibility that the independently needed rules of vowel contraction (discussed later in this chapter) have operated in the derivation of γένους [genūs] and γένει [genē]. For these forms could by those rules be analysed as derived from forms which for the time being we will represent as [géneos] and [génei].[4] Here we seem to have the same endings as in ὄμματος [ómmatos] and ὄμματι [ómmati], added to a stem [géne-]. But we are still left with the nominative-accusative. The [-o-] in its second syllable does not bother

---

[4] As we shall see in section 2.2, the vowels represented as [e o] should really be [ẹ ọ].

us overmuch: we can easily recognize the /o/-/e/ ablaut alternation, very common in Greek – there is another example of it within the sphere of noun declension, viz. second-declension non-neuter nouns such as ἀδελφός [adelpʰós] ' brother ', which have [-o-] (sometimes contracted with another vowel) in all cases except the vocative singular, which has [-e] (ἄδελφε [ádelpʰe]). There remains, however, the apparent [-s] ending. This would be almost unique among neuter nouns, which regularly [5] avoid [-s], the standard nominative-singular ending in non-neuter nouns, and in the third declension usually add no ending at all to the stem in the nominative-accusative singular.[6] One way out would be to regard the [-s] as belonging to the stem, and as being deleted (by a rule earlier than the vowel contraction rules) when it occurs between vowels. Other facts suggest that this decision is by no means ad hoc.

(1) There is a productive suffix -τηριο- [tērio-] which forms adjectives from verb stems; e.g. from λύω [lũǭ] ' release, dissolve ' comes λυτήριος [lütḗrios] ' releasing ', and from ὀσφραίνομαι [ospʰráynomay] ' smell ' comes ὀσφραντήριος [ospʰrantḗrios] ' having a good sense of smell '. But from δρῶ [drǭ] ' do ' (contracted from [dráǭ]) we have not *[drātḗrios] but δραστήριος [drāstḗrios] ' active ', with an apparently intrusive [s]. Similarly with various other suffixes: ἄλυτος [álütos] ' indissoluble ' from λύω [lũǭ], but ἄτρεστος [átrestos] ' intrepid ' from τρέω [tréǭ] ' tremble '; κυβερνήτης [kübernḗtēs] ' steersman ' from κυβερνῶ [kübernǭ] ' steer ', but χρήστης [kʰrḗstēs] ' creditor ' from χρῶ [kʰrǭ] [7] ' lend '. Many

---

[5] Apart from γένος [génos] itself and the nouns declined exactly like it (a large but homogeneous class) there are some half-dozen other neuter nouns whose nom. sing. ends in [-s]; in some of these there is justification for an analysis with a stem ending in /s/, but in others – τέρας [téras] ' prodigy ', πέρας [péras] ' boundary ' and οὖς [ûs] ' ear ', which have genitive sing. τέρατος, πέρατος, ὠτός [tératos pératos ǭtós] – there is not.

[6] Often, as a result of the dropping of certain final consonants (for which see 2.1.3), the nom.-acc. sg. is apparently shorter than the stem; cf. ὄμμα [ómma].

[7] This form of the present was actually used only in the sense ' give an oracular response '.

B

of these forms ⁸ would be neatly explained by an /s/-deletion rule, such as that postulated, operating between vowels.

(2) Greek verbs have, in their past tenses, a prefix known as 'the augment'. The general rule is that where the verb stem begins with a consonant the prefix consists of the vowel [e], and where the verb stem begins with a vowel the prefix is realized by a lengthening of the vowel.⁹ (For the purpose of this rule [h] does not count as a consonant.) In particular, verbs whose stems begin with [e-] (or [he-]) regularly have initial [ẹ-] (or [hẹ-]) in their augmented tenses; e.g. present ἐθέλω [etʰélọ] 'be willing', imperfect ἤθελον [ẹ̄tʰelon]; present ἑτοιμάζω [hetoymázdọ] 'make ready', imperfect ἡτοίμαζον [hẹtóymazdon]. A fair number, however, have initial [hē-] instead of the expected [hẹ-], or [ē-] instead of [ẹ-]; e.g. present ἔχω [ékʰọ] 'have', imperfect εἶχον [ẹ̄kʰon]; present ἕπομαι [hépomay] 'follow', imperfect εἱπόμην [hēpómẹn]. These irregularities could be eliminated if it is assumed that verbs of the type just mentioned should be represented in the lexicon with an initial consonant which is dropped after the form of the augment has been determined. In the case of the two verbs used as examples, not only the existence but also the particular nature of this consonant is revealed when we take other forms of the verb into consideration: for in both of them an [s] appears in the stem in the aorist tense – the forms are ἔσχον [éskʰon] and ἐσπόμην [espómẹn] respectively, and point to stems /sekʰ/ and /sep/ with loss of vowel in certain tenses.

From these verbs it appears that our earlier description of the rule we need as 'an /s/-deletion rule . . . operating between vowels' is not quite correct. What happens to the /s/ of the verb-stem /sep/ is a little more complicated. Initially before a vowel,

---

⁸ There are some inconsistencies; for instance, the perfect mediopassive of δρῶ [drọ̄] is not *[dédrāzmay] analogous to δραστήριος [drāstẹ́rios] but δέδραμαι [dédrāmay]. The aorist passive, on the other hand, does contain a sibilant.

⁹ The augmented vowel is not generally identical in quality with the unaugmented; the differences are a function of general rules which will be discussed in the section on vowels.

it is weakened to [h].   Medially between vowels, it disappears, but instead an [h] shows up at the beginning of the word.[10]

This might suggest a complication of our rule (which we shall henceforward call FRICATIVE WEAKENING) to carry out this double task. Fortunately, however, other evidence shows that this is not necessary. Suppose for the time being that we assign the least possible work to Fricative Weakening, simply letting it weaken /s/ to [h] when a vowel follows and either a vowel or a major boundary precedes, so that the rule will provisionally be of the following form: [11]

$$(5) \quad \begin{bmatrix} -\text{son} \\ +\text{cont} \end{bmatrix} \rightarrow \begin{bmatrix} -\text{strid} \\ -\text{ant} \\ -\text{cor} \\ +\text{back} \\ +\text{low} \\ +\text{son} \\ -\text{cons} \end{bmatrix} / \left\{ \begin{bmatrix} [-\text{cons}] \\ \begin{bmatrix} -\text{seg} \\ -\text{FB} \end{bmatrix} \end{bmatrix} \right\} \underline{\hspace{1cm}} [-\text{cons}]$$

It will then be necessary to add another rule (call it H-PROMOTION) whereby when an initial vowel is followed by an aspirate, the two change places. Since this rule moves segments around, it must be stated in transformational form:

$$(6)^{12} \quad \begin{array}{cccc} [+\text{WB}] & \text{V} & (=) & \text{h} \\ 1 & 2 & 3 & 4 \Rightarrow \\ 1 & 4+2 & \emptyset & \emptyset \end{array}$$

Now it so happens that the only forms in Greek that will meet the structural description of this rule are the types of augmented verbs that we have been discussing. Nevertheless, the

[10] There is no initial aspirate in ἔχω [ékʰǭ]; this is due to Grassmann's Law, discussed in 2.1.4. Note that in the future tense, where the medial consonant has had its aspiration assimilated away, the initial aspirate duly reappears; the form is ἕξω [héksǭ].

[11] The application of Chomsky and Halle's theory of markedness would considerably simplify the output description of this and several other rules. See the discussion of the theory in Chapter III.

[12] The boundary =, neither formative boundary (+) nor word boundary (#), and hence included in the class [−seg, −FB] referred to in (5) and elsewhere, is required in Greek for the following reason. Prepositions, being proclitic, are separated from the following word by a single # boundary. But when they occur as prefixes in compound nouns, adjectives and verbs

rule is not ad hoc. For it makes no specific reference to the augment and uses no special features; it applies without any exceptions; [13] and it fits in well with the general phonological pattern of Greek, which does not tolerate intervocalic [h] in the phonetic output.[14]

H-Promotion accounts for forms like εἱπόμην [hēpómęn] satisfactorily, but we have not yet accounted for the failure of the expected [h] to show up in the declension of words like γένος [génos]. Some rule of the grammar must delete this aspirate. There seem to be two possibilities.

As we shall see, a rule is necessary in any case to delete /y w/ between vowels and in certain other positions. These glides share with /h/ the feature specifications [—consonantal, —syllabic], and thus /y w h/ form a natural class, which we may call the class of glides; [15] if the environments in which deletion occurs are similar, it should be possible, with an actual gain in

they are more closely linked with the stem; for example, they can then take the accent. Contrast κατὰ λόγον *kata lógon* ' in proportion ' (preposition-noun) with κατάλογος *katálogos* ' catalogue ' (prefix-stem). Thus the boundary separating prepositional prefixes from stems cannot be word boundary. Neither, however, can it be formative boundary. Vowels in contact across formative boundary undergo contraction: thus Homer's κακοεργός [kako-ergós] ' evil-doing ' appears in Attic as κακουργός [kakūrgós]. The final vowel of a prepositional prefix, on the other hand, is elided before a vowel, as that of κατά *kata* is elided in κατεργάζομαι *katergázomai* ' accomplish '. We therefore set up, as do Chomsky and Halle for English, a third type of boundary, =. This has various special effects: one is that the accent cannot be separated by more than one occurrence of = from the end of the word – that is, if there is more than one prepositional prefix, the accent, if it falls on one of them at all, may only fall on the last (so παρένθες, *par-én-thes* ' interpolate ' (imperative) not *πάρενθες *párenthes). With respect to this rule the augment behaves exactly like a prepositional prefix (e.g. παρῆν, *par-ên* ' he was present ' not *πάρην *párēn), and we therefore suppose it too to be separated from the stem by a = boundary.

In the output description of (6), ' 4+2 ' means ' Insert a copy of item 4 ' (viz. [h]) ' to the left of item 2 ' (viz. the vowel).

[13] The only possible exception is the interjection εἷέν [ēhen] ' all right, well then '; but this, like English *uh-huh*, may well be almost completely outside the phonological pattern of the language.

[14] Except, it would appear, in ταῶς [tahôs] ' peacock ', in this unique in Greek, as far as we know, even among loanwords.

[15] As Householder (1971) points out, the term ' glide' is less than satisfactory, particularly since the class also includes the glottal stop; *faute de mieux*,

simplicity, to extend the rule to cover the aspirate as well as high glides. The other possibility is that (6) could be reformulated so that the aspirate was deleted when neither initial nor in a position to be promoted. In view, however, of the 'transformational' form of (6), such reformulation will be difficult, and the deletion of the aspirate should therefore be combined into one rule with the deletion of high glides.

The rule of Fricative Weakening should take into account not only the weakening of underlying /s/ in vocalic environments, with which we have so far been concerned, but also certain changes that it undergoes in other environments. These are as follows.

(a) Between two consonants, /s/ drops. The infinitive ending in all medio-passive tenses is /-sthay/; so, for example, the infinitive corresponding to κέχυται [kékʰütay] ' (it) has been poured ' is κεχύσθαι [kekʰústʰay]. But when the stem ends in a consonant, the /s/ of the ending disappears: the infinitive to ἔσταλται [éstaltay] ' (he) has been sent ' is ἐστάλθαι [estáltʰay] Nowhere in Greek do we find the sequence [CsC] at the phonetic level, except when a word boundary intervenes; and even then the boundary must be between accentual units. The preposition /eks/ loses its final consonant when the next word begins with a consonant. Since the preposition will be separated from the next word by a single # boundary (see note 12), our rule must provide for the deletion of /s/ except when followed [16] by *two* or more # boundaries. This can be done by incorporating an optional single boundary in the environment, which will look like this:

(7) / [+cons] —— ([−seg]) [+cons]

When incorporating this rule into Fricative Weakening, we

however, I continue to use it. A *natural class* is defined as a class of sounds which can be referred to with fewer features than can any of its individual members; thus the class of glides is definable with two features, while each of its members requires at least three.

[16] A single such boundary *preceding* the sibilant appears to be sufficient to block deletion; e.g. ἐκ στρατοῦ [ek stratû] ' out of an army ', not *ἐκ τρατοῦ *[ek tratû].

can achieve a simplification by having the rule convert /s/ to [h] between consonants, instead of deleting it; the aspirate will subsequently be removed by the Glide Deletion rule already referred to (p. 12).

(b) The cluster /sn/ is assimilated to [nn]. This cluster does not normally occur within words, so the rule can be seen at work only when two words coalesce into one; for example, [müos nḛsos] ' mouse's island ', when it is used as a proper name and accented like a single word, takes the form Μυόννησος [müónnḛsos].[17]

The form of the Fricative Weakening rule will therefore be:

$$(8) \quad \begin{bmatrix} -\text{son} \\ +\text{cont} \end{bmatrix} \rightarrow \left\{ \begin{matrix} \begin{bmatrix} -\text{strid} \\ -\text{ant} \\ -\text{cor} \\ +\text{back} \\ +\text{low} \\ +\text{son} \\ -\text{cons} \end{bmatrix} \Big/ \left\{ \begin{matrix} \begin{bmatrix} [-\text{cons}] \\ \begin{bmatrix} -\text{seg} \\ -\text{FB} \end{bmatrix} \end{bmatrix} \end{matrix} \right\} \text{---} [-\text{cons}] \\ [+\text{cons}] \text{---} ([-\text{seg}])[+\text{cons}] \\ \begin{bmatrix} -\text{strid} \\ +\text{voice} \\ +\text{nas} \\ -\text{cont} \\ +\text{son} \end{bmatrix} \Big/ \quad \text{---} \begin{bmatrix} +\text{nas} \\ +\text{cor} \end{bmatrix} \end{matrix} \right\}$$

[17] Although the operation of this rule is in point of fact confined to Μυόννησος Myónnēsos, Πελοπόννησος Pelopónnēsos and other names of islands and peninsulas, nevertheless, at the period we are dealing with, it was a living, potentially productive rule. Two pieces of evidence may be noticed. On the one hand, such place-names never have the [-nn-] where derivation from an underlying /-sn-/ is impossible, e.g. Χερρόνησος Kherrónēsos, where the first element is the noun stem /kʰerro-/ ' dry land ', and not a genitive case form ending in /-os/. On the other, names such as Πελοπόννησος Pelopónnēsos could still in the fifth century be separated into their component parts in a way that names like Χερρόνησος Kherrónēsos could not : so a tragic poet, who found difficulty in fitting the name into his verse, could use an expression like Πέλοπος ἐν τόποις Pélopos en tópois ' in the regions of Pelops ' (Aeschylus, Eumenides 703), or even ἐν τᾷ ... νάσῳ Πέλοπος en

[continued on next page]

One process affecting underlying fricatives has not yet been mentioned, and it might be thought that it should be included in the Fricative Weakening rule. Underlying /ss/ is simplified to [s]. For example, the third-declension dative plural ending is /si/, as in φύλαξι [pʰülaksi], dat. pl. of the stem [pʰülak-] ' guard '; but the dat. pl. of γένος [génos], whose stem as we have seen ends in /s/, is γένεσι [génesi]. Again, the future active of verbs is ordinarily formed by the addition of /-s-/ to the stem; e.g. φυλάξω [pʰülák-s-ǫ] ' I shall guard '. From the stem /drās/, however (see p. 9), the future is δράσω [drásǫ]. Should we not add a further subrule to Fricative Weakening, deleting /s/ (or perhaps converting it to an aspirate) when preceded (or should it be followed ? [18]) by another /s/ ?

The answer is no; FRICATIVE GEMINATE SIMPLIFICATION must be a separate rule from Fricative Weakening. The reason is as follows.

There are certain environments in which underlying dental stops are realized as fricatives. These are: (a) before obstruents; e.g. from πείθω [pétʰǫ] ' persuade ' comes the perfect passive πέπεισται [pépēs-tay] ' (he) is convinced '; (b) before /m/, exemplified by the first person singular of the same perfect passive, πέπεισμαι [pépēzmay] (with voicing assimilation); (c) before /i/ followed by another vowel, provided the dental is also preceded by a vowel ;[19] e.g. from πλοῦτος [plûtos] ' wealth ' is formed the adjective πλούσιος [plûsios] ' wealthy '. All this we may bring under a rule of FRICATIVIZATION. In case (c) the fricative does not weaken; this will be accounted for if we order Fricativization after

tâi ... nâsōi Pélopos ' in the isle of Pelops ' (Sophocles, Oedipus at Colonus 695—the latest Athenian tragedy we possess).

[18] There seems to be nothing to choose between these two ways of stating the rule. Choose, however, we must; if we allow weakening to take place in both environments we shall end up not simplifying the underlying geminate but removing it altogether.

[19] The application of case (c) is restricted to adjectives ending in /-ios/, nouns ending in /-iā/, and derivatives of these.

Fricative Weakening.[20]   The form of the Fricativization rule is:

$$
(9) \quad
\begin{bmatrix} -\text{son} \\ +\text{cor} \end{bmatrix}
\rightarrow
\begin{bmatrix} +\text{del rel} \\ +\text{cont} \\ +\text{strid} \end{bmatrix}
\Big/
\left\{
\begin{array}{ll}
\left\{
\begin{bmatrix} -\text{son} \end{bmatrix} \\
+\begin{bmatrix} +\text{nas} \\ -\text{cor} \end{bmatrix}
\right\} & (a) \\
 & (b) \ 21 \\
V \underline{\quad} iV & (c)
\end{array}
\right.
$$

Now consider the dative plural of the third-declension noun πούς [pŭs] ' foot ', whose stem is /pod-/. The underlying form for the dative plural will be /pod+si/; the phonetic form is ποσί [posí]. If Fricativization applies before Fricative Geminate Simplification, but not otherwise, a derivation can be constructed to take us from one to the other, without positing any rules not independently necessary:

(10)   pod+si → (Fricativization)
  poz+si → (Manner Assimilation)
  pos+si → (Fricative Geminate
     Simplification)
  posi

Thus the order of rules must be Fricative Weakening, Fricativization, Fricative Geminate Simplification. Since a single rule cannot be split so that some of its subrules apply before another rule and the rest apply after, Fricative Geminate Simplification

[20] This is the same as the historical order of the sound changes which these rules reflect.

[21] Note that Fricativization before /m/ applies only across a morpheme boundary. This provision is necessary because there are words, such as ἀριθμός [aritʰmós] ' number ', in which clusters of dental stop plus [m] do occur at the phonetic level. It turns out that, with one possible exception, in the words of this kind which are found in Attic prose the cluster is always part either of the stem or of the noun-forming suffix /tʰmo/; so at least it would appear from the lists in Buck and Petersen (1944). The possible exception is ἠθμός [ę̄tʰmós], ' sieve ', derived from the verb ἠθῶ [ę̄tʰǭ] ' strain ', which may be regarded as having had its internal morpheme boundary deleted by an ad hoc readjustment rule. The very large and open classes of deverbal nouns ending in -μα -ma and -μος -mos show no other exception to Fricativization, nor do any other words in which there is any reason to posit a morpheme boundary between the dental and the /m/.

must be treated as a separate rule.[22] Here is the rule; we arbitrarily choose to present it as deleting the first of the two identical consonants.

(11) $\begin{bmatrix} -\text{son} \\ +\text{cont} \end{bmatrix} \rightarrow \emptyset \ / \ \underline{\qquad} \begin{bmatrix} -\text{son} \\ +\text{cont} \end{bmatrix}$

We have mentioned (p. 12) that a rule will be needed to delete the high glides /y w/ in various positions, and suggested that it could be used to delete the non-high ' glide ' /h/ also. Let us look at the evidence for positing this rule of GLIDE DELETION.

(1) Certain paradigmatic alternations suggest that the stems in question contain an underlying glide which is deleted between vowels and retained elsewhere. There is a verb stem meaning ' flow ' which has a rounded vowel or glide in all its forms and derivatives – the aorist active ἔρρευσα [érrewsa], the derived adjective ῥυτός [r̥útós] ' flowing ', the derived nouns ῥοῦς [r̥ûs] ' flow ', ῥεῦμα [rêwma] ' stream ' and ῥυθμός [r̥út ʰmós] ' rhythm ', etc. – with the exception of those whose suffix begins with a vowel, in particular the present tense ῥέω [r̥éǫ]. There is a large class of nouns ending, in the nominative singular, in -εύς [-éws] (e.g. βασιλεύς [basiléws] ' king ') which have a stem-final [w] when a consonant follows (in the nom. sg. and in the dative plural βασιλεῦσι [basilêwsi]) or when there is no ending (in the vocative singular βασιλεῦ [basilêw]), but no sign of it when the case ending begins with a vowel (accusative singular βασιλέα [basiléā], genitive singular βασιλέως [basiléǫs], etc.) As far as /y/ is concerned, there is a class of nouns with stems apparently ending in /i/ which show no sign of this /i/, either as vowel or glide, before endings beginning with a vowel:

(12) nom.sg. πόλις [pólis   ' city '
       acc.   πόλιν   pólin
       gen.   πόλεως   póleǫs
       dat.   πόλει   pólē]

---

[22] It is interesting that Fricative Weakening and Fricative Geminate Simplification are also quite unrelated historically, the former being of very early date and operative throughout Greek, the latter almost confined to Attic-Ionic.

(2) Not all the verbs which take an apparently irregular form of the augment (see p. 10) can be accounted for by Fricative Weakening. For example, neither ἐργάζομαι [ergáz-domay] (imperfect εἰργαζόμην [ērgazdómēn]) ' work ' nor ἐῶ [eǭ] (imperfect εἴων [éǭn]) ' allow ' can be analysed as having an underlying initial /s/. An underlying initial glide, deleted after the form of the augment was fixed, would account for the past forms of these verbs.[23]

(3) Fricative Weakening has produced instances of [h] between vowels and between consonants, and [h] will need to be deleted in these environments. The only other instances of non-initial [h] at this stage will be in compound words; these cannot be deleted yet, since (as will be seen in Chapter V) they form part of the environment for Aspiration Shift, which follows the late rule of Elision.

We thus require a rule to delete high glides between vowels and initially, and [h] between vowels and between consonants. If we also allow the rule to apply vacuously to high glides between consonants (which do not occur anyway) we can state it in the following simple form, using variable feature coefficients (for which see Chomsky and Halle 1968, 83) and the angled bracket convention (ib. 76–7): [23a]

[23] So, however, would the postulation of an underlying initial consonant of any type that happens not to occur in Greek. There is no other evidence for underlying initial high glides in classical Attic, and it will be observed that if such glides were *not* postulated for the few verbs in question, (13) could be further simplified, and the generalization could be stated that no Greek lexical matrix began with a high glide. On the other hand, six verbs would become exceptions to the rule about the augment – but they were exceptions anyway, namely exceptions to the lexical generalization just stated.

[23a] The principles of these two conventions should perhaps be explained here. A feature coefficient may either be +, meaning that the segment has the feature in question, or –, meaning that it has the contrary feature. It is permitted in stating a rule to give a feature a variable coefficient (represented by a Greek letter); such a coefficient may have either the value + or the value –, but the same variable coefficient must have the same value wherever it occurs, and such pairs of variables as ' αF ' and ' – αF ' (where F is a feature) must always have mutually opposite values. Thus (13) deletes all glides on condition that the preceding and following segments

(13)
$$\begin{bmatrix} -\text{cons} \\ -\text{syll} \end{bmatrix} \rightarrow \emptyset \ / \ \left\{ \begin{matrix} [a \ \text{syll}] \\ \left\langle \begin{bmatrix} -\text{seg} \\ -\text{FB} \end{bmatrix} \right\rangle \end{matrix} \right\} \begin{bmatrix} \overline{\langle +\text{high} \rangle} \end{bmatrix} [a \ \text{syll}]$$

This rule first deletes intervocalic, interconsonantal and initial high glides, and then (read with the angled material ignored) deletes [h] between vowels and between consonants: the desired result.

2.1.2. CONSONANTS IN CLUSTERS

2.1.2.1. *Clusters with nasals*

In Greek, as in many languages, nasals assimilate in point of articulation, and sometimes in other respects, to a following consonant. Two common prepositions, ἐν *en* ' in ' and σύν *syn* ' with ', end in nasals, and the alternations of the latter exemplify all the various kinds of nasal assimilation which operate in Greek.

(14) *Following*

Segment	Result	Example
(*a*) Vowel	No assim.	συναίτιος [sünáytios] ' sharing responsibility '

have the same value for the feature ' syllabicity ', i.e. are both vowels or both consonants.

A series of expressions in angled brackets in a rule are treated as though they were a single discontinuous parenthesized expression. Thus in (13) we must read the rule first with both angled expressions present (in which case it applies to initial glides, but only if they are high) and then with both absent (in which case it does not apply to initial glides). Hierarchies of angled expressions one within the other are expanded in the same way as hierarchies of parenthesized expressions (see p. 6). And rules abbreviated by this convention, just like rules abbreviated by the parenthesis convention, are applied in disjunctive order (ib.).

Note also that (13) has a *simultaneous environment*, i.e. that part of the feature composition of the input segment is stated in the environment description instead of the input description. This is done by giving the rule the form

$$A \rightarrow B \ / \ X \begin{bmatrix} \overline{Z} \end{bmatrix} Y$$

which means the same as

$$\begin{bmatrix} A \\ Z \end{bmatrix} \rightarrow B \ / \ X \text{——} Y$$

Following Segment	Result	Example	
(b) Labial stop	m	σύμβουλος	[sŭmbūlos] ' adviser '
(c) Dental stop	n	συνθήκη	[sünthękę] ' agreement '
(d) Velar stop	ŋ	συγχωρῶ	[süŋkʰǫrǭ] ' agree '
(e) Fricative or liquid	Complete assim.	συσσιτία	[süssitíā] ' common meal '
		συλλέγω	[süllégǭ] ' collect '
(f) Fricative plus stop	Zero	σύστημα	[sŭstęma] ' a complex whole '

All these cases except (f) can be brought under the generalization that a nasal assimilates completely to a following continuant consonant, and in point of articulation to any other following consonant. Ignoring (f) for the moment, we can express this by the following rule:

(15) NASAL ASSIMILATION [24]

$$[+\text{nas}] \rightarrow \begin{bmatrix} \alpha \text{ ant} \\ \beta \text{ cor} \\ \langle +\text{cont} \\ \gamma \text{ features} \rangle \end{bmatrix} / \underline{\hspace{1cm}} \begin{bmatrix} -\text{seg} \\ \langle -\text{FB} \rangle \end{bmatrix} \begin{bmatrix} +\text{cons} \\ \alpha \text{ ant} \\ \beta \text{ cor} \\ \langle +\text{cont} \\ \gamma \text{ features} \rangle \end{bmatrix}$$

This will give the correct results except in case (f), where it will send /VnsC/ to [VssC], whereas the desired output is [VsC]. This at once suggests ordering (15) before Fricative Geminate Simplification, and using that rule to simplify the [ssC] cluster. Our present version of Fricative Geminate Simplification will not, however, do the job. Assimilating nasals are almost always

---

[24] ' Features ' in (15) means ' all features not expressly mentioned in this column ', and so directs complete assimilation in case (14e). Note that case (14e) applies *only* across a boundary stronger than formative boundary, i.e. only in compounds and looser groups; within simple words different rules apply, the Resonant Aorist Rule and Nasal Dropping, discussed later in this section. The form of (15) ensures that case (14e) will apply only in these circumstances.

to be found on the boundary between the elements of a compound – a = boundary (see note 12); and the structural description of (11) does not allow for such a boundary. We must therefore modify (11) so that a boundary may be present just in case the two adjacent fricatives are followed by another consonant (for we don't want the output of case (14*e*) to undergo simplification); that is, the rule must be:

(16) $\begin{bmatrix} -\text{son} \\ +\text{cont} \end{bmatrix} \rightarrow \emptyset \ / \ \underline{\quad} \ \langle\!\langle [-\text{seg}] \rangle\!\rangle \begin{bmatrix} -\text{son} \\ +\text{cont} \end{bmatrix} \langle [-\text{syll}] \rangle$

With this modification to Fricative Geminate Simplification, (15) now gives a fully adequate account of Nasal Assimilation.

When a labial or velar stop directly precedes a nasal, it is often itself realized as a nasal. Thus in the first person singular of the perfect medio-passive, in which the ending /may/ is added directly to the verb stem, we find the following forms:

(17) Present active | Perfect medio-passive
λείπω [lépọ̄] 'leave' λέλειμμαι [lé-lēm-may]
γράφω [gráphọ̄] 'write' γέγραμμαι [gé-gram-may]
ἄγω [ágọ̄] 'lead' ἦγμαι [ệ̄ŋ-may] [25]
φυλάττω [pʰüláttọ̄] 'guard' πεφύλαγμαι [pe-pʰülaŋ-may]
(cf. φυλακή
[pʰülakẹ̄]
'custody')

Deverbal nouns ending in -μα -*ma* and -μος -*mos* generally have analogous forms. In many words, however, velar stops before /m/ do not assimilate. It turns out, as in the case of Fricativization (see note 21), that these words are those in which there is no formative boundary directly before the nasal.[26] If there

[25] The letter gamma in this environment stands for a velar nasal; evidence in Allen (1968, 34).

[26] The lists in Buck and Petersen (1944) contain only four words with -κμ- [km] or -χμ- [kʰm] clusters in which there is any reason to suppose a formative boundary before the nasal; and all of these are semantically distinct enough from their congeners to have been reanalysed as unit formatives. They are ἀκμή *akmḗ* 'peak' (remotely connected with ἄκρος, *ákros* 'extreme'); δοχμή *dokhmḗ* 'handbreadth' (from δέχομαι *dékhomai*

were ever any words containing intramorphemic clusters /pm bm pʰm/, they all, historically, underwent assimilation long before the period with which we are concerned, and will be represented in the lexicon of classical Attic with /mm/. In classical Attic, therefore, NASALIZATION need apply only across formative boundary, and will thus have the following form (restricting ourselves for the moment to what happens when the nasal is /m/):

$$(18) \quad \begin{bmatrix} -\text{cont} \\ -\text{cor} \end{bmatrix} \rightarrow \begin{bmatrix} -\text{hsp} \\ +\text{voice} \\ +\text{son} \\ +\text{nas} \end{bmatrix} / - + \begin{bmatrix} +\text{nas} \\ -\text{cor} \end{bmatrix}$$

What if a labial or velar stop precedes /n/ ? In this case there are no large classes of alternating forms to guide us, no inflexional endings or productive suffixes. The evidence in fact is very scanty. It will be best to consider it for labial and velar stops separately.

Voiceless labial stops do not assimilate to a following /n/ (ὕπνος [húpnos] ' sleep ' and ἐξαίφνης [eksáypʰnēs] ' suddenly ' are typical); with voiced stops the position is less clear. There are no good alternations,[27] but there is some evidence from what used to be called ' pattern congruity '. With one exception, every obstruent can form a word-initial cluster with /n/; and with one exception, every word-initial cluster of two or more consonants must begin with an obstruent. The exception is that we don't find [bn], and we do find [mn], as an initial cluster. It would therefore regularize the underlying phonological pattern of the language if we were to derive [mn] from

' receive ') ; λοχμή lokhmḗ ' thicket ' (connected with λόχος lókhos ' military company ', in Homer ' ambush '); and δραχμή drakhmḗ ' drachma ' (from δράττομαι dráttomai ' grasp '). With the last, contrast δράγμα drágma ' sheaf' and δραγμός dragmós ' act of grasping ', which do undergo (18). In this survey, as in that discussed in note 21, only words found in Attic prose were taken into consideration.

[27] One that might be suggested is that of σέβομαι sébomai ' revere ' and σεμνός semnós ' holy '; but there is no sign that these words were still felt to be related in the fifth century.

/bn/. It would also, however, complicate the Nasalization rule considerably, and one is reluctant to do this solely for the sake of the underlying pattern. Sometimes underlying patterns are irregular. In Greek the initial cluster /bd/ occurs (e.g. in βδελυρός *bdelyrós* ' loathsome '), but */gd/ does not; we do not consider this to be justification for adding a rule to the grammar to convert initial /gd/ into something else, even though this would make the underlying pattern more symmetrical.

As for velar stops before /n/, voiceless ones do not assimilate. The underlying cluster /gn/ is realized as something that is noted orthographically as *gn*, but its pronunciation is disputed. The evidence seems to me to be against the hypothesis of a nasal pronunciation.[28] If, however, that hypothesis is correct – and it could be that some day inscriptional evidence will turn up showing that it is – it would then be necessary to extend Nasalization to apply to /g/ before /n/, and in that case it would be simplest to derive phonetic [mn] in a parallel way from /bn/. It is, though, very difficult to state this extended version of Nasalization, using established notational conventions, in a way that brings out clearly the fact that Nasalization is one process, not two processes that happen to have a lot in common; which suggests that either a new notational convention is needed (for which there is no other evidence), or Nasalization did not apply to the cluster /gn/.

For these reasons I consider that Nasalization should be left in the form (18).

We excluded from the domain of Nasal Assimilation (see note 24) clusters of the form /n+s/, where /+/ is morpheme boundary. These clusters are treated in two quite different, indeed opposite, ways.

The aorist tense in all regular verbs is formed by the addition to the verb stem of a suffix /s/; e.g. the aorist of βλέπω [blépǭ]

---

[28] For arguments and evidence on both sides of this question, see Sturtevant (1968, 64–5) and Ward (1944). Ward omits to mention the form γιννόμενον *ginnomenon* (for γιγνόμενον *gignómenon*) found at Gortyn in Crete (Schwyzer 1959, 215); this, however, can at most be evidence for a local Cretan pronunciation, and Ward's own evidence (especially from modern Greek) is very strong.

' look ' is ἔβλεψα [éblepsa]. One phonologically defined class of verbs, however, superficially forms its aorists in a quite different way.[29] These are the verbs whose stems end in a nasal or a liquid. They form their aorist by lengthening the stem vowel (if it is not long already) and do not add any suffix; e.g.

(19) *Present*   *Aorist*

αἰσχύνω	[ayskʰū̆nǭ]	ἤσχυνα	[ę̄yskʰū̄na]	' put to shame '
ἀγγέλλω	[aŋgéllǭ]	ἤγγειλα	[ę̄ŋgēla]	' report '
σπείρω	[spérǭ]	ἔσπειρα	[éspēra]	' sow '
μένω	[ménǭ]	ἔμεινα	[émēna]	' remain '

This points to a special, minor [29a] rule sending /Vns/ to [Ṽn]. It is minor because it applies *only* where the /s/ is the aorist morpheme; where the /s/ is some other morpheme, such as that for the nominative singular, it is the nasal that is deleted (by Nasal Dropping, to which we shall come in a moment) – for example, the nom. sg. of the noun for ' nose ' (genitive ῥινός [r̥īn-ós]) is not *[r̥ín] but ῥίς [r̥ís]. But for the aorists the rule is undoubtedly needed: any other analysis [30] would merely result in an increase in suppletion. Suppletion, of course, is sometimes unavoidable; but in this case it would be very undesirable, since we are dealing with a large and phonologically definable class of verb stems which form their aorist in a phonologically regular way.

The rule must be a relatively early one. In particular, it must be earlier than the Low Vowel Rule (q.v. in section 2.2), since when /a/ is lengthened in the aorist, the result is not [ā] but [ę̄]; e.g. from the stem /pʰan/ ' reveal ' (present φαίνω [pʰáynǭ]) is formed the aorist ἔφηνα [épʰę̄na]. This is what would result if /ā/ resulting from the rule we are now con-

---

[29] The few verbs of this form that do have [-s-] in their aorist are found only in poetry.

[29a] Most phonological rules apply whenever their environment description is met, except for morphemes specially marked as not undergoing them. A minor rule is one that applies *only* to morphemes specially marked to show they *do* undergo it.

[30] There is, in any case, no other analysis possible that would account for the forms of all the aorists in question without recourse to ad hoc rules.

sidering (the RESONANT AORIST RULE) were then to become input to the Low Vowel Rule.

(20) RESONANT AORIST RULE [31]

$$
V \quad \begin{bmatrix} +\text{cons} \\ +\text{son} \end{bmatrix} \quad [+\text{FB}] \quad \begin{bmatrix} +\text{strid} \\ \text{Aorist} \end{bmatrix}
$$

$$
\begin{array}{cccc}
1 & 2 & 3 & 4 \\
\begin{bmatrix} 1 \\ +\text{long} \end{bmatrix} & 2 & 3 & \emptyset
\end{array} \Rightarrow
$$

An example has already been given (p. 24) of what happens to those /ns/ clusters which are not subject either to Nasal Assimilation or to the Resonant Aorist Rule: the nasal is deleted, and the preceding vowel lengthened. Various other forms can also be accounted for by this NASAL DROPPING rule; in some of them, it should be noted, the /ns/ cluster is not present in the underlying form, but is derived by rules still to be given.

(1) Participles and other words whose stems end in /-nt/ mostly have several forms in which this /nt/ is replaced by [s] with lengthening of the preceding vowel; with the help of Nasal Dropping and other rules to be discussed in the next section, these forms can be analysed as containing underlying /nt+y/ or /nt+s/. Consider these forms from the stem /pant-/ ' all '.

(21)
Masc. nom. sg.	πᾶς	[pâs	from	/pant+s
acc. sg.	πάντα	pánta		pant+a
gen. sg.	παντός	pantós		pant+os
dat. pl.	πᾶσι	pâsi		pant+si
Fem. nom. sg.	πᾶσα	pâsa]		pant+ya/

(2) Nouns and adjectives of the first and second declensions have an accusative plural ending in -ας -[ās] (1st decl.), -ους

---

[31] This statement of the rule is a slight oversimplification; when we come to discuss vowels we shall see that it would incorrectly give *ἔμηνα *[émẹna] as aorist to μένω [ménọ]. See the Summary of Rules for a corrected version. The use of the feature ' length ' instead of ' tenseness ' for vowels will be justified in Chapter III.

C

[-ūs] (2nd). Both could be neatly accounted for on the assumption of a uniform acc. pl. ending /ns/ for vowel-stem nouns and adjectives; compare for the 1st-decl. ending πᾶς [pâs], and for the 2nd-decl. ending ὀδούς [odûs] (stem /odont-/) ' tooth '.[32]

(3) The third person plural present active of verbs ends in [-V̄si], e.g. φέρουσι [pʰérūsi] ' they bear ', εἰσι [ēsi] ' they are ', φασι [pʰāsi] ' they say ', whereas in the other persons the ending is usually preceded by a short vowel (e.g. 1st pl. φέρομεν [pʰéromen] ἐσμεν [ezmen] φαμεν [pʰamen]). The long vowel and the retention of [s] would both be accounted for if we assumed an immediately underlying /Vnsi/. Whether /nsi/ is to be considered as the base form of this termination, or as itself derived from some other form, is a question not fully decidable by any evidence we have. In view, however, of the other third-person-plural endings – medio-passive /ntay/ and /nto/ and past active [n], which could be treated as derived from /nt/ but not as derived from /ns/ – the only base form that will allow us to posit a third-plural morpheme with a single underlying shape in all its appearances in /ntsi/.[33] What is not clear is whether there is any point in setting up such a morpheme.[34]

On dropping of the nasal, the vowels change as follows:

---

[32] First and second declension noun stems end in /a/ or /ā/ and in /o/ respectively; vowel-stem adjectives follow the first declension in the feminine (if any) and the second in the other genders.

[33] Not, be it noted, /nti/, although this was the form from which /nsi/ historically developed and which survived in the West Greek dialects. In Attic, synchronically speaking, /nti/ remains unchanged; the dative singular of /pant-/ is παντί [pantí], and the preposition ἀντί [anti] ' in return for ' has the same form in Attic as in West Greek. The derivation of [n] from /nt/ is by Obstruent Dropping, for which see 2.1.3.

[34] Except in the dual, the only other such person-number morpheme one might be tempted to set up would be /me/ for the 1st plural, which in the active has the ending /men/, in the medio-passive /metʰa/. In both cases there is the problem of what to do with the residue: ' voice morphemes ' would be even more dubious and suppletionful than person-number morphemes. It seems better to treat all these verbal endings as portmanteau morphemes combining person, number and voice indications.

(22) *Underlying Vowel* *Long Vowel after*
                         Nasal Dropping

i	ī
e	ē
a	ā
o	ū
ü	ǖ

It is obvious from (22) that Nasal Dropping, unlike the Resonant Aorist Rule, should be ordered after the Low Vowel Rule: indeed, that it should be ordered after all the main rules modifying the quality of long vowels, with one exception. The exception must be a rule that will account for the fact that the long vowel corresponding to [o] is not *[ō] but [ū]. Since [ō] does not occur at all phonetically in Greek, this rule can be context-free:

(23) Ō-RAISING

$$\begin{bmatrix} V \\ +\text{long} \\ +\text{back} \\ -\text{low} \end{bmatrix} \rightarrow [+\text{high}]$$

And Nasal Dropping, ordered before it, will also be very simple:

(24)   V   [+nas]   [+strid]
          1   2   3   ⇒

$$\begin{bmatrix} 1 \\ +\text{long} \end{bmatrix} \quad \emptyset \quad 3$$

2.1.2.2. *Postconsonantal Glides*

Several morphological categories in Greek are frequently marked, in addition to suffixes, by changes in the final consonant of the stem or in the preceding vowel. The consonant may become a geminate, and may change its point of articulation as well; or it may appear as [zd]. The vowel may be lengthened, or it may be diphthongized. These alternations occur in the present tense of verbs, in the comparative of adjectives and adverbs, and in feminine adjectives and some feminine nouns. Examples are given in (25–7).

(25)	Present		Stem
ἐλπίζω	[elpízdǭ]	' hope '	/elpid/, cf. ἐλπίς, -ίδος elpis, -idos ' hope '
φυλάττω	[pʰüláttǭ]	' guard '	/pʰulak/, cf. φύλαξ -ακος phýlaks, -akos ' guard '
βάλλω	[bállō]	' cast '	/bal/, cf. aorist ἔβαλον ébalon
χαίρω	[kʰáyrǭ]	' rejoice '	/kʰar/, cf. aorist ἐχάρην ekhárēn
διαφθείρω	[diapʰtʰérǭ]	' destroy '	/-pʰtʰer/, cf. future διαφθερῶ diaphtheró

(26)	Comparative [35]		cf. Superlative	
μείζων	[mézdǭn]	' greater '	μέγιστος	[mégistos]
κρείττων	[kréttǭn]	' superior '	κράτιστος	[krátistos]
μᾶλλον	[mållon]	' more '	μάλιστα	[málista]

(27)	Feminine		Stem
μέλιττα	[mélitta]	' bee '	/melit/, cf. μέλι μέλιτος méli, mélitos ' honey '
Κρίτυλλα	[krít-ülla] (woman's name)		/-ul-/, cf. Κράτυλος Krátylos (man's name)
μέλαινα	[mélayna] (f.)	' black '	/melan/, cf. neuter μέλαν mélan

These clusters, lengthenings, etc., are historically the reflex of clusters of consonant plus [y]: originally the presents of (25) were formed with a suffix /ye/ or /yo/, the comparatives of (26) with a suffix /yon/, and the feminines of (27) with a suffix /ya/. And in classical Attic also, there must be some one element behind the alternations: if there is not, we are left with an extraordinary series of consonant mutations, not formally related, which nevertheless, as if by coincidence, constantly

[35] For the long vowel in these comparatives, which is in addition to, not instead of, a consonantal modification, see section 2.2 (' Lengthening in Irregular Comparatives ').

appear in connexion with the same suffixes to express the same grammatical categories.

History, of course, is not evidence that this common underlying element in classical Attic was the palatal glide /y/. However, there is no reason not to postulate that it was /y/, and various bits of evidence suggest that it was.

(1) In addition to the comparatives with consonant mutation seen in (26), there is another class of comparatives which are similar except that the suffix is disyllabic; and this suffix is [-īon-], e.g. ἡδίων [hēdíǫn], comparative of ἡδύς [hēdús] 'pleasant'. A suffix /yon/ could be derived from this by the mere reduction of the first vowel to a glide.

(2) In some nominal and adjectival feminines the suffix /ya/ is actually preserved, notably after an underlying /u/ or /w/: e.g. ἡδεῖα [hēdêyya] fem. to ἡδύς [hēdús], βασίλεια [basíleyya] 'queen' (cf. βασιλεύς [basiléws] 'king'), and perfect participles such as πεπωκυῖα [pepǫkûyya] 'having drunk' (fem.).

(3) In two of the forms of (25–7) a palatal glide also appears, but *before* the final consonant of the stem. This could be due to metathesis of a glide underlyingly *following* that consonant.

We therefore assume that in classical Attic the underlying representations of the present, comparative and feminine suffixes of the words in (25–7) were essentially the same as in older forms of the language.[36] We require, then, rules to

---

[36] One set of present tenses whose form is historically a reflex of an earlier form containing a /Cy/ cluster has not been considered here, namely those having [pt] from earlier /py/, such as κλέπτω [kléptǫ] 'steal' (stem /klep/: cf. κλοπή klopḗ 'theft'). This is because these forms could be regarded as containing, from the synchronic point of view, a different present-forming element /t/. There are no comparatives or feminines of parallel formation to support an analysis with /y/, whereas an analysis with /t/ could be supported by a small number of other verbs that show a dental stop in the present which there is no way of deriving from an underlying /y/. Such are τίκτω [tíktǫ] 'give birth to' (stem /tek/, cf. aorist ἔτεκον étekon) and ἀνύτω [hanútǫ] 'get (something) done' (cf. ἀνύω [hanúǫ] 'id.'). Moreover, the /y/ analysis would require extra machinery in the rules about to be given for /Cy/ clusters; the /t/ analysis requires neither new rules, nor complication of existing ones, nor (as we have just seen) a new shape for a morpheme which that morpheme would not sometimes have to assume in any event.

convert the clusters on the left side of (28) into their appropriate reflexes on the right side.

(28) *Underlying Cluster*   *Required Output*

Underlying Cluster	Required Output
gy, dy	zd
ky, ty	tt (/ V —); s (/C —)
kʰy, tʰy	tt (a vowel always precedes)
ly	ll
ny, ry:	
/ a —	yn, yr
otherwise	n, r, with lengthening of preceding vowel

This is quite a complex set of changes. Are there any motivated intermediate stages ?

Consider first the development of voiceless-stop-plus-/y/ clusters. The [tt] reflex following a vowel has been fully illustrated. After a consonant, however, as in feminine participles, the reflex is [s]; cf. the last line of (21). These two reflexes can most easily be referred to an intermediate /ts/. When this forms part of a three-consonant cluster, the cluster is simplified from /Cts/ to /Cs/ (which may then be further simplified, e.g. by Nasal Dropping); otherwise it is ultimately converted to a geminate stop.

If voiceless stop plus /y/ goes first to /ts/, the simplest thing to do with clusters of voiced stop plus /y/ is to treat them in a parallel way and send them first to /dz/; then we will need to metathesize this to [zd].

Thus for clusters of stop plus /y/ we appear to need four rules:

(29)   (i) Send all such clusters to dental stop + fricative.

      (ii) Delete /t/ between consonant and /s/.

      (iii) Send /ts/ to [tt].

      (iv) Metathesize /dz/ to [zd].

However, the last two of these can be collapsed, since they make the same changes to their inputs except that the first segment of the two-segment output is a stop in (iii) but a fricative in (iv). The rules, then, are:

(30) AFFRICATION

$$
\begin{bmatrix} -\text{son} \\ -\text{cont} \\ \alpha \text{ voice} \end{bmatrix} \quad \begin{bmatrix} -\text{cons} \\ -\text{syll} \\ -\text{back} \end{bmatrix}
$$

$$ 1 \qquad\qquad 2 \qquad \Rightarrow $$

$$
\begin{bmatrix} 1 \\ +\text{ant} \\ +\text{cor} \end{bmatrix} \quad \begin{bmatrix} 2 \\ +\text{cons} \\ -\text{son} \\ +\text{strid} \\ +\text{ant} \\ +\text{cor} \\ \alpha \text{ voice} \end{bmatrix}
$$

(31) RELEASE RETIMING [37]

$$
\begin{bmatrix} -\text{cont} \\ +\text{cor} \end{bmatrix} \rightarrow \emptyset \; / \; [+\text{nas}] \text{——} [+\text{strid}]
$$

(32) AFFRICATE RESOLUTION

$$
\begin{bmatrix} -\text{son} \\ -\text{cont} \\ \alpha \text{ voice} \end{bmatrix} \quad \begin{bmatrix} -\text{son} \\ +\text{cont} \end{bmatrix}
$$

$$ 1 \qquad\qquad 2 \qquad \Rightarrow $$

$$
\begin{bmatrix} 1 \\ \alpha \text{ cont} \\ -\text{hsp} \end{bmatrix} \quad \begin{bmatrix} 2 \\ -\text{cont} \\ -\text{hsp} \end{bmatrix}
$$

The treatment of /y/ after laterals requires a rule to itself:

(33) LATERALIZATION

$$
\text{y} \rightarrow \begin{bmatrix} +\text{lateral} \\ \alpha \text{ features} \end{bmatrix} / \; \text{V} \begin{bmatrix} +\text{lateral} \\ \alpha \text{ features} \end{bmatrix} \text{——}
$$

We are left with the treatment of clusters /ry ny/.[38] This has two different results, according to which vowel precedes. What they have in common, and in contrast with all the

---

[37] So called because the deletion of the /t/ would be equivalent to releasing the oral closure simultaneously with, instead of after, the closing off of the nasal passage. ' Would be ', not ' is ', because in the end the nasal also is deleted.

[38] There are no /my/ clusters in Greek.

other cases of (28), is that the /y/ is not consonantalized but is transferred to the preceding syllable, either as a postvocalic glide or as length on the vowel. This suggests a metathesis rule as the major one for these clusters; in its simplest form this will be:

(34) METATHESIS

$$\begin{bmatrix} +\text{cons} \\ +\text{son} \end{bmatrix} \quad \begin{bmatrix} -\text{cons} \\ -\text{syll} \end{bmatrix}$$

$$\begin{array}{cc} 1 & 2 \\ 2 & 1 \end{array} \Rightarrow$$

This statement of Metathesis assumes that it will follow Lateralization, so that there will be no clusters of resonant plus /y/ other than those to which Metathesis applies. The output of Metathesis will be as follows (R stands for ' resonant ', * denotes that the output will need adjusting by a subsequent rule):

(35)

Input	Output	Actual example	
aRy	ayR	χαίρω	[kʰáyrǭ]
eRy	*eyR	φθείρω	[pʰtʰérǭ]
iRy	*iyR	κρίνω	[krínǭ]
oRy	(not found [39])		
üRy	*üyR	αἰσχύνω	[ayskʰū̃nǭ] [40]

Clearly the output will need to be adjusted by a MONOPH-THONGIZATION rule like (36); we shall see in a moment why it is made not to apply before vowels.

(36)

$$\begin{bmatrix} \text{V} \\ -\text{low} \\ a \text{ back} \end{bmatrix} \quad \begin{bmatrix} -\text{cons} \\ -\text{syll} \\ +\text{high} \\ a \text{ back} \end{bmatrix} \quad \begin{Bmatrix} [+\text{cons}] \\ [+\text{WB}] \end{Bmatrix}$$

---

[39] The expected output, [oyR], is in fact found in several words which earlier had [oRy], but not in the three morphological categories which show the alternations we are discussing, and there is no reason to set up underlying /oRy/ for these words.

[40] For the stems /kri/ and /ayskʰun/ of the last two examples, cf. the perfect passive κέκριται [kékritay] and the future αἰσχυνῶ [ayskʰünǭ].

$$
\begin{array}{ccc}
1 & 2 & 3 \quad \Rightarrow \\
\left[\begin{array}{c} 1 \\ +\text{long} \end{array}\right] & \emptyset & 3
\end{array}
$$

Clearly Monophthongization must follow all rules changing the quality of long vowels. But is it independently motivated ?

Historically, what in early Greek had been the diphthongs [ey ow] had been monophthongized in most environments before the fifth century. Before vowels, however, they apparently retained a diphthongal pronunciation,[41] and even before consonants they alternated with [oy ew] which had retained their diphthongal pronunciation in all environments.[42] There is thus ample justification for deriving some instances [43] of [ē ū] [44] from underlying diphthongs, by Monophthongization. This independent motivation refers, it is true, only to diphthongs with mid vowels; to extend it to high vowels, though, not only accounts for everything still unaccounted for in (35) but also simplifies the statement of the Monophthongization rule. (36) is thus very highly motivated indeed.

These six fairly simple rules account for all the phenomena of (28).

2.1.2.3. *Clusters of Obstruents*

The most important characteristic of Greek obstruent clusters is that the obstruents in them are normally all alike as regards voicing and aspiration. There are no such clusters as */pd zt kʰd/. A stem ending in an obstruent changes its shape according to the opening consonant of the suffix; for example, the stem /krupʰ/ seen in κρύφα *krýpha* ' secretly ' undergoes one modification in κρύβδην *krýbdēn* ' id.' and another in κρυπτός *kryptós* ' secret '. The only real exception [45] is that of

[41] See Allen (1968, 77–80).

[42] So the perfect of λείπω [lêpǭ] ' leave ' is λέλοιπα [léloypa]; the verbal noun to σπεύδω [spéwdǭ] ' be eager ' is σπουδή [spūdę́] ' zeal '.

[43] Others are derived in other ways, e.g. by Contraction (see 2.2) or Nasal Dropping.

[44] From immediately underlying /ǭ/ (see p. 27).

[45] When the preposition ἐκ *ek* preceded a word or stem beginning with a voiced or aspirated consonant, it was pronounced [eg] or [ekʰ] respectively; see Allen (1968, 15).

two otherwise identical consonants in succession, the first is not aspirated even if the second is: so we have $\Pi\iota\tau\theta\epsilon\acute{\upsilon}s$ [pitt^{h}éws] (name of a hero) not *[-t^{h}t^h-]. We will keep the general rule simple, and add a late rule to cover the exception. Note that fricatives do not assimilate for aspiration, since (in Greek, at any rate) they cannot be aspirated.

(37) REGRESSIVE MANNER ASSIMILATION [46]

$$\begin{bmatrix} -\text{son} \\ \langle -\text{cont} \rangle \end{bmatrix} \rightarrow \begin{bmatrix} \alpha \text{ voice} \\ \langle \beta \text{ hsp} \rangle \end{bmatrix} / - ([-\text{seg}]) \begin{bmatrix} -\text{son} \\ \alpha \text{ voice} \\ \langle \beta \text{ hsp} \rangle \end{bmatrix}$$

(38) ASPIRATION ADJUSTMENT

$$\begin{bmatrix} -\text{cont} \\ \alpha \text{ ant} \\ \beta \text{ cor} \end{bmatrix} \rightarrow [-\text{hsp}] / - \begin{bmatrix} -\text{son} \\ -\text{cont} \\ \alpha \text{ ant} \\ \beta \text{ cor} \end{bmatrix}$$

The ordering of Regressive Manner Assimilation relative to other rules can be pretty closely established: as derivation (10), p. 16, shows, it must come between Fricativization and Fricative Geminate Simplification. Aspiration Adjustment must be later than Regressive Manner Assimilation, but it is not crucially ordered with respect to any other rules.

There is one set of underlying obstruent clusters whose behaviour is not accounted for by these rules. These are the clusters of the form /TsT'/, where T and T' are stops. For example, there is a verb $\H{\epsilon}\psi\omega$ [hépsǭ] ' boil ', and this, like many verbs, has a derivative adjective ending in -$\tau\acute{o}s$ [-tós], underlying form (as a first hypothesis) /hepstos/. We would expect the interconsonantal /s/ to be reduced to /h/ by Fricative Weakening, and subsequently to zero by Glide Deletion; (37), coming somewhere between these rules, would fail to apply, since the two stops, at the stage when (37) had a chance to apply, would be separated by another segment. The result

---

[46] Obstruents also assimilate in respect of whether they are partial exceptions to Grassmann's Law; see the discussion of that rule in 2.1.4.

would be *[heptós]. In fact, however, the word has the form ἐφθός [hepʰtʰós] ' boiled '.

Let us make two assumptions, and see if we can account for this anomaly. First assumption: this verb has an aspirated consonant in its underlying form; the verb stem is /hepʰs/. Second assumption: there is a rule preceding Fricative Weakening which (let us be as general as we can) assimilates stops in /TsT'/ clusters, rather like (37), but *in the reverse direction*. That is, it makes the cluster-final stop take on the same value for the voicing and aspiration features as the cluster-initial stop. With this rule (call it PROGRESSIVE MANNER ASSIMILATION) the derivation of ἐφθός *hephthós* will be as follows:

(39) /hepʰs+tós/   (Progressive M.A.)
    /hepʰs+tʰós/   (Fricative Weakening)
    /hepʰh+tʰós/   (Glide Deletion)
    [hepʰtʰós]

The new rule will also make it possible to construct derivations for some other forms which would otherwise have given trouble. The verb stem /patʰ/ ' suffer ' (aorist ἔπαθον *épathon*; derived noun πάθος *páthos* ' suffering ') makes a present tense πάσχω [páskʰǭ]. This cannot, without the help of Progressive Manner Assimilation, be derived in any motivated way from the verb stem, and a suppletive stem would seem to be needed. Yet the suffix does seem related to the /sk/ suffix found in many present tenses (e.g. εὑρίσκω *heurískō* ' find ', τιτρώσκω *titrōskō* ' wound '); and now it is possible to derive this present stem from /patʰ+sk+/, thus:

(40) /patʰ+sk+/   (Progr. M.A.)
    patʰ+skʰ+   (Fricative Weakening)
    patʰ+hkʰ+   (Fricativization) [47]
    pas+hkʰ+   (Glide Deletion)
    [paskʰ-]

[47] Which will have to be modified so that it ignores an /h/ between the two obstruents.

Another word whose phonetic form seems partly due to Progressive Manner Assimilation is μίσγω [mízgǭ] ' mix '. The stem here is /mig/, the most common form of the present actually being μείγνυμι [mēgnūmi].[48] However, a derivation along the lines of (39) or (40) would lead to an output form *[míggǭ]. We need, then, a further rule which will act on the intermediate form /mig+sg+/ and delete the first /g/, but will not interfere with either derivation (39) or derivation (40). Such a rule would be one that applied to a /TsT'/ cluster only in case T and T' were identical—a dissimilation rule, eliminating the repetition of an articulatory movement:

(41) DISSIMILATORY DELETION

$$
\begin{bmatrix} -\text{son} \\ -\text{cont} \\ \alpha \ \text{ant} \\ \beta \ \text{cor} \end{bmatrix} \rightarrow \emptyset \ / \ \underline{} \ s \ \begin{bmatrix} -\text{son} \\ -\text{cont} \\ \alpha \ \text{ant} \\ \beta \ \text{cor} \end{bmatrix}
$$

We can now construct a derivation for [mízgǭ]:

(42) /mig+sk+/   (Progr. M.A.)
       mig+sg+   (Dissimilatory Deletion)
       mi+sg+   (Regressive M.A.)
       [mizg-]

One other word which seems to undergo Dissimilatory Deletion presents some problems. This is διδάσκω [didáskǭ] ' teach '. The stem is /didakʰ/, as is shown by the derived noun διδάχη [didákʰę̄] ' teaching '. But from this stem plus the suffix /sk/ we would expect to derive a present *[didaskʰǭ]. One solution might be to make the stem /didakʰ/ an exception to Progressive Manner Assimilation; but although it has not yet been possible to give a principled account of which phonological rules can and which cannot have idiosyncratic exceptions, an assimilation rule of this type is not one that we would expect to have such exceptions: Regressive Manner Assimilation has none (the exception catered for by Aspiration Adjust-

---

[48] The vowel alternation is discussed in the section on Ablaut.

ment is phonologically conditioned). Another possibility would be to make the underlying form of the stem /didak/; but how could we then account for the form of the derived noun ? The best solution is to remove the verb from the operation of this group of rules altogether by taking the stem to be /dida/, extended in some forms and derivatives by a meaningless formative /kʰ/, and in others by /sk/.[49]

The rule of Progressive Manner Assimilation, then, is:

(43) [50]

$$
\begin{bmatrix} -\text{son} \\ -\text{cont} \end{bmatrix} \rightarrow \begin{bmatrix} \alpha\ \text{hsp} \\ \beta\ \text{voice} \end{bmatrix} \Big/ \begin{bmatrix} -\text{son} \\ -\text{cont} \\ \alpha\ \text{hsp} \\ \beta\ \text{voice} \end{bmatrix} [+\text{strid}] \underline{}
$$

2.1.2.4. *Other clusters*

There are no phonetic nasal-plus-liquid clusters in Greek. Where (generally as the result of the deletion of a vowel) we would expect to find one, we find that a voiced stop has been introduced, agreeing in point of articulation with the nasal. For example:

(44) ἄνδρα [ándra] ' man ' (acc. sg.), cf. ἀνήρ [anḗr] (nom. sg.)

μεσημβρία [mes-ẹmbriā] ' midday ', cf. ἡμέρα [hẹmérā] ' day '

The rule inserting this voiced stop (EXCRESCENCE) does not apply across a major boundary; there, as we have already seen (p. 20), the nasal assimilates completely to the liquid. We can represent this by simply not mentioning boundaries in the statement of the rule.

---

[49] This /sk/, as if further to emphasize the peculiarity of this verb, seems not to be the present-forming suffix ; for it appears in the derived noun διδάσκαλος *didáskalos* ' teacher ', and the present-forming suffix /sk/ does not appear in derivatives.

[50] As ἐφθός *hephthós* shows, stops which became aspirated by this rule were partial exceptions to Grassmann's Law ; cf. note 46 and see 2.1.4.

(45) EXCRESCENCE

$$\emptyset \to \begin{bmatrix} -\text{son} \\ -\text{nas} \\ \alpha \text{ features} \end{bmatrix} \Big/ \begin{bmatrix} +\text{nas} \\ \alpha \text{ features} \end{bmatrix} \underline{\quad\quad} \begin{bmatrix} +\text{cons} \\ +\text{son} \\ -\text{nas} \end{bmatrix}$$

In underlying representations there are various clusters consisting of glides, or glide plus /s/, or /s/ plus glide. Examples are:

(46) /wy/: /basilew+ya/ ' queen ', output βασίλεια [basíleyya] (see p. 29)

/ys/: /seys+ō̄/ ' shake ', output σείω [séyyǭ] (cf. σεισμός [sēzmós] ' earthquake ')

/sy/: /a+lāth+es+ya/ ' truth ', output ἀλήθεια [altę̄heyya] (cf. ἀληθέστατος [alętʰés-tatos] ' truest ')

Phonetically, as is seen in (46), almost all these underlying clusters have the same reflex, [yy]. Since the /ys/ and /sy/ clusters become /yh hy/ by Fricative Weakening, the clusters of (46) all at one stage consist of two glides, and their treatment implies a GLIDE ASSIMILATION rule sending certain glide-glide clusters to [yy].

Not all such clusters, however, go to [yy]. Two groups have the reflex [ww].

(47) /ws/: /gews+omay/ ' taste ', output γεύομαι [géwwomay] (cf. ἄγευστος [á-gews-tos] ' without taste ')

/wy/: /polīt+ew+y+omay/ ' engage in politics ', output πολιτεύομαι [polītéwwomay] [51]

Thus the treatment of glide clusters is as follows:

(48) *Input*   *Output*
    wh   ww
    hw   (not found)

---

[51] Stems in the large and open class of which this is a representative do not generally give any sign of an underlying stem-final /s/. Theoretically they could be regarded as having stems ending in /ew+w+/; but /w/ is not elsewhere found as a present-forming element, while /y/ is very common in this function (see 2.1.2.2).

Input	*Output*
wy	ww (in present tenses); yy (elsew.)
yw	(not found)
yh	yy
hy	yy

In view of the two divergent treatments of /wy/, both productive, we need two rules, one minor and one major.

(49) (i) When /y/ is the present tense formative and is preceded by /w/, assimilate it to that /w/.

    (ii) In all glide clusters, assimilate to [yy] if a /y/ is already present in the cluster, otherwise to [ww].

More formally:

(50) GLIDE ASSIMILATION, SPECIAL

Minor Rule for which only the present tense formative /y/ is marked plus.

$$\begin{bmatrix} -\text{cons} \\ -\text{syll} \end{bmatrix} \rightarrow [+\text{back}] \bigg/ \begin{bmatrix} -\text{cons} \\ -\text{syll} \\ +\text{high} \\ +\text{back} \end{bmatrix} \underline{\hspace{1cm}}$$

(51) GLIDE ASSIMILATION, GENERAL (Mirror-image [52])

$$\begin{bmatrix} -\text{cons} \\ -\text{syll} \end{bmatrix} \rightarrow \left\{ \begin{matrix} \begin{bmatrix} +\text{high} \\ -\text{back} \\ \alpha \text{ features} \end{bmatrix} \bigg/ \begin{bmatrix} -\text{cons} \\ -\text{syll} \\ +\text{high} \\ -\text{back} \\ \alpha \text{ features} \end{bmatrix} \underline{\hspace{1cm}} \\ \begin{bmatrix} -\text{low} \\ \beta \text{ features} \end{bmatrix} \bigg/ \begin{bmatrix} -\text{cons} \\ -\text{syll} \\ -\text{low} \\ \beta \text{ features} \end{bmatrix} \underline{\hspace{1cm}} \end{matrix} \right\}$$

[52] For mirror-image rules see Langacker (1969a; 1969b). A mirror-image rule stated with the environment XY——ZW (where X, Y, Z, W are arbitrary, possibly null, strings) applies not only in that environment but also in the environment WZ——YX.

2.1.3. FINAL CONSONANTS

2.1.3.1. ' Movable Nu '

This is the name given in traditional studies of Greek to a dental nasal which is inserted at the end of certain words that would otherwise end in a vowel, if the following word begins with a vowel or [h] (that is, with a non-consonantal segment), or if a major pause follows. The words in question are mainly verb forms, but they also include nominal and adjectival dative plurals ending in [-si] and even some adverbs like πέρυσι *pérysi* ' last year ' and one numeral, εἴκοσι *eíkosi* ' twenty '. The principle determining which words can have the nasal added is perfectly regular: as may be determined by comparing an index such as Kretschmer and Locker (1963) with LSJ, the non-verbal forms that can add the nasal are all and only those that end in [-si].[53] In verbal forms, in general, the same principle holds, but not in the case of third-person singular active forms. Many of these can add the nasal even though they do not end in [-si], namely:

(i) *esti* ' is '.

(ii) Almost all imperfect, aorist, perfect and pluperfect indicative forms.   Examples (from λείπω *leípo* ' leave '): imperfect, ἔλειπε(ν) *éleipe(n)*; aorist, ἔλιπε(ν) *élipe(n)*; perfect, λέλοιπε(ν) *léloipe(n)*; pluperfect, ἐλελοίπει(ν) *eleloípei(n)*. The pluperfect ending -ει *-ei* (pronounced [ē]) was contracted from /-ee/. Where, however, as a result of contraction, an *imperfect* form ended in a long vowel (e.g. ἐδόκει *edókei* ' it seemed '), the nasal could not be added.

(iii) One form of the aorist optative which ends in -ειε [-eyye]; e.g. εἰ οὕτως δόξειεν αὐτῷ *ei hoútōs dókseien autôi*, lit. if thus it-should-seem to-him, ' if that were to be his opinion '. Other forms of the 3rd sg. optative, which end in [-ay -oy -ē̦], cannot take [n] movable.

These three groups comprise *all* the third-person singular

---

[53] Except, as F. W. Householder points out to me, vocative case forms such as ξύνεσι [ksúnesi] ' (o) sagacity ' (Aristophanes, *Frogs* 893).

forms of verbs that end in a short front vowel; all the medio-passive forms, all the imperative and subjunctive forms, and all the optative forms except that mentioned in (iii), end either in a long vowel, or in a diphthong, or in a short back vowel. And, with the exception of the pluperfects, the three groups contain *only* third-person singular forms that end in a short front vowel. Disregarding the pluperfects,[53a] we may include in the grammar the following EPHELCYSIS [54] rule:

(52)

$$\emptyset \rightarrow n \; / \; \left\{ \begin{bmatrix} si \\ V \\ -back \\ -long \\ 3 \; Person \end{bmatrix} \right\} \underline{\qquad} [+WB]_1 \left\{ \begin{matrix} \% \\ [-cons] \end{matrix} \right\}$$

To ensure that contracted imperfects are excluded from the operation of the rule, it is only necessary to order it after Contraction. Note that it is not necessary to specifically exclude third-person plurals; where these do not end in [-si] they always end in a consonant (or, in the medio-passive, a diphthong or a back vowel), and where they do end in [-si] they do take [n] movable.

2.1.3.2. *Final obstruents and some related matters*

The only consonants that can end a word (other than a proclitic or a word whose final vowel has been elided) in Greek are [n r s]. Most of the other consonants are not present in word-final position in the underlying representation either; but one class of forms suggests that word-final /t kt rt nt/ must be regarded as occurring at that level.

Third declension neuter nouns, in all case-forms except the nominative-accusative singular, have for the most part (we

[53a] In which, incidentally, the nasal appears not to have been obligatory in the environment of (52); cf. καθειστήκει οὐδένι *katheistḗkei oudéni* (Demosthenes 49, 50) and ἐτεθνήκει ὁ πατήρ *etethnḗkei ho patḗr* (Lysias 19, 48).

[54] ' Ephelcystic ' is another name given to the movable *n*. In the statement of the rule, % denotes major pause.

D

do not speak here of irregular nouns) a constant stem, to which
the usual case endings are added. But the nominative-accusative singular is usually shorter than the stem ; and when this is
so, it is /t/ (in one case /kt/) that is missing from the stem. The
same is true of the neuter of those participles whose stem ends
in /nt/, and even of some masculine nouns and participles.
The nominative and genitive singular of some representative
examples of these classes are given in (53).

(53) Gen. sg.   Nom. sg.

ὄμματος	[ómmat-os]	ὄμμα	[ómma]	' eye '
δάμαρτος	[dámart-os]	δάμαρ	[dámar]	' wife ' (fem., not neuter; poetic)
γάλακτος	[gálakt-os]	γάλα	[gála]	' milk '
ὄντος	[ónt-os]	ὄν	[ón]	' being ' (neut.)
ὄντος	[ónt-os]	ὤν	[ọ̄n]	' being ' (masc.)
λέοντος	[léont-os]	λέων	[léọ̄n]	' lion ' (masc.)

With an alternation of this kind there are two things we can
do. We could take the nominative as the base form and add /t/
to the stem in the oblique cases and in derivatives. To this
there are three objections. First, γάλα gála would have to be
subject to a unique rule which added not simply /t/ but /kt/;
secondly, and more important, there are many nouns and
adjectives whose nom. sg. ends in /r/ or /n/ that do *not* show a
/t/ in the stem in the oblique cases, and so a new, arbitrary
lexical differentiation would have to be set up; thirdly, nouns
(such as ὄμμα ómma would be under this proposal) whose
stems end in /a/ are normally first declension, not third.

I have given these reasons in full to show that the decision to
choose the second alternative and take the form of the stem
shown in the oblique cases as the base form is based solidly on
considerations related directly to the description, and not on
historical priority. This decision means that we shall need a
rule to delete stops in word-final position – or rather (because of
γάλα gála) in word-final clusters of one or more stops.

(54) OBSTRUENT DROPPING (First Version) [55]

$$\begin{bmatrix} -\text{son} \\ -\text{cont} \end{bmatrix} \to \emptyset \ / \ \underline{\hspace{1cm}} \left(\begin{bmatrix} -\text{son} \\ -\text{cont} \end{bmatrix} \right) [+\text{WB}]_2$$

It is also possible (though not necessary) to treat two other alternations under the same heading.

(1) When the perfect active of a verb whose stem ends in a dental obstruent is formed with the suffix /ka/, the obstruent always drops. Thus the perfect of πείθω [pétʰǫ] ' persuade ' is πέπεικα [pépēka] (contrast the intransitive perfect from the same stem, πέποιθα [pépoytʰa] ' be convinced '); the perfect of δρῶ [drǫ̂] ' do ' (stem /drā/, cf. p. 9) is δέδρακα [dédrāka]. This is the only instance in which a formative ending in a dental obstruent directly precedes one beginning with a velar obstruent, so a rule can be given without reference to particular formatives:

(55) $\begin{bmatrix} -\text{son} \\ +\text{cor} \end{bmatrix} \to \emptyset \ / \ \underline{\hspace{1cm}} + \begin{bmatrix} -\text{son} \\ -\text{ant} \end{bmatrix}$

(2) A dental stop preceding /s/ is dropped. For example, the dative plural of ὄμμα ómma is ὄμμασι ómmasi, and the aorist of πείθω peíthō is ἔπεισα épeisa. This implies a third rule, deleting dental stops before /s/; this rule must naturally be later than Fricative Weakening:

(56) $\begin{bmatrix} -\text{son} \\ -\text{cont} \\ +\text{cor} \end{bmatrix} \to \emptyset \ / \ \underline{\hspace{1cm}} \begin{bmatrix} -\text{son} \\ +\text{cont} \end{bmatrix}$

Now we can combine (54–56) into a single rule:

(57) OBSTRUENT DROPPING (Second Version) [56]

$$[-\text{son}] \to \emptyset \ / \ \left\{ \begin{array}{l} \begin{bmatrix} \underline{\hspace{0.6cm}} \\ -\text{cont} \end{bmatrix} \left(\begin{bmatrix} -\text{son} \\ -\text{cont} \end{bmatrix} \right) [+\text{WB}]_2 \\[12pt] \begin{bmatrix} \underline{\hspace{0.6cm}} \\ \langle -\text{cont} \rangle \\ +\text{cor} \end{bmatrix} + \begin{bmatrix} -\text{son} \\ \left\{ \begin{array}{l} -\text{ant} \\ \langle +\text{cont} \rangle \end{array} \right\} \end{bmatrix} \end{array} \right\}$$

[55] The requirement of two word boundaries is meant to exclude proclitics such as the preposition ἐκ ek from the operation of the rule.

[56] For notational reasons, it is necessary to require the presence of a formative boundary in both subcases of the second half of (57). This is

It might be thought that (56) could instead be combined with (31), Release Retiming, to which it shows strong resemblances. But it is essential that (56) should *not* apply to clusters formed by (30), Affrication. As is fully shown on pp. 27 ff., such clusters, unless preceded by a consonant, end up as [tt], or if voiced as [zd], whereas (56) would send them to [s] or [z]. Release Retiming, on the other hand, applies *both* to underlying /nts/ clusters *and* to such clusters formed by Affrication. (56) is therefore best treated as part of Obstruent Dropping, which we see must be ordered between Fricative Weakening and Affrication.[57]

2.1.4. OTHER CONSONANT RULES

2.1.4.1. *Aspiration*

Various instances have already been given of the operation of GRASSMANN'S LAW, whereby (broadly speaking) when an aspirated sound (any of /pʰ tʰ kʰ h/) occurred in each of two successive syllables, dissimilation took place, the first of the two aspirates losing its aspiration. The productivity of Grassmann's Law in Greek is best shown by giving some forms and derivatives of such a verb as τρέφω [trepʰǭ] ' nourish ' (stem /tʰrepʰ/) – from which it will also appear that Grassmann's Law must be later than Manner Assimilation and Nasalization.

(58)

present	τρέφω	[trépʰǭ]	
future	θρέψω	[tʰrépsǭ]	
aorist	ἔθρεψα	[étʰrepsa]	
perfect	τέτροφα	[tétropʰa]	
perfect mediopassive	τέθραμμαι	[tétʰrammay]	
aorist passive	ἐτράφην	[etrápʰẹn]	
derivative nouns	τροφός	[tropʰós]	' nurse '
	θρέμμα	[tʰrémma]	' nursling '

empirically unexceptionable, as clusters of dental stop plus /s/ never occur within morphemes anyway.

[57] If Release Retiming is to be combined with another rule, it should be with Fricative Geminate Simplification. This has been done in the Summary of Rules, where the combined rule is called Coronal Cluster Simplification.

There are, however, certain restrictions on and exceptions to the working of Grassmann's Law.

(1) An aspirated consonant not immediately preceded by a vowel did not induce dissimilation. Compare ἐμεθύσθη [emet^{h}úst^{h}ę̄] ' he was drunk ' with ἐτύθη [etút^{h}ę̄] ' it was sacrificed ' (present active θύω [t^{h}ǘǭ]).

(2) Certain morphemes are partial exceptions to Grassmann's Law, chiefly verbal suffixes such as /t^{h}ē̄/ (aorist passive), /(s)t^{h}e/ (2nd person plural mediopassive), and /(s)t^{h}ay/ (infinitive mediopassive). These induce dissimilation only when the two aspirates in successive syllables are identical; so beside ἐτύθη [etút^{h}ę̄] we have ἐχύθη [ek^{h}út^{h}ę̄] ' it was poured '. We must assign to these morphemes a special feature, which we shall label [+A]. This feature is distributed to all obstruent segments of a cluster ending with a [+A] obstruent; it is this that prevents dissimilation in, for example, the alternative form of the aorist passive of τρέφω [trép^{h}ǭ], namely ἐθρέφθην [et^{h}rép^{h}t^{h}ę̄n]. This distribution of the [+A] feature is a form of assimilation, and the work can be assigned to the Manner Assimilation rule.[58]

(3) There is only one situation in which a [+A] aspirated consonant can be followed in the next syllable by another aspirated consonant: this is when the suffix /t^{h}ē̄/ is followed by the imperative ending /t^{h}i/.[59] In this case it is the imperative ending that loses its aspiration, e.g. ἐράσθητι [erást^{h}ę̄ti] ' fall in love '; the dissimilation is progressive and not, as elsewhere, regressive.

All this means that in a complicated case like the perfect passive infinitive of the verb meaning ' bury ', whose form immediately before Grassmann's Law becomes applicable is /t^{h}e+t^{h}ap^h+t^{h}ay/, and which thus contains four aspirated consonants (hence six distinct pairs of aspirated consonants), only one dissimilation takes place. Of the four aspirated

---

[58] Progressive Manner Assimilation must also have [+A] added to its output description; cf. note 50.

[59] Which is itself also [+A], as φάθι [p^{h}át^{h}i] ' say ' shows.

consonants in /$t^he + t^hap^h + t^hay$/, 1 does not dissimilate from
$\qquad\qquad$ 1 $\quad$ 2 $\;$ 3 $\quad$ 4
3 or 4, since they are not in successive syllables; 2 does not
dissimilate from 3 or 4, since 3 is [+A] and not identical with
2, and 4 does not immediately follow a vowel; and 3 does not
dissimilate from 4, since they are in the *same* syllable (or, if you
prefer to phrase it otherwise, on the same syllable boundary).
But 1 does dissimilate from 2, since (ignoring the formative
boundary as usual) 2 does immediately follow a vowel, and all
the other conditions are satisfied.

A statement of the rule follows. For the convention of
braces with identical subscripts, see McCawley (1968, 33–4).[59a]

(59)

$$
\left\{ \begin{bmatrix} -A \\ \begin{bmatrix} +\text{cons} \\ \alpha\ \text{ant} \\ \beta\ \text{cor} \end{bmatrix} \end{bmatrix} \right\}_1 \rightarrow \left\{ \begin{matrix} [-\text{hsp}] \\ \emptyset \end{matrix} \Big/ \begin{bmatrix} \underline{\qquad} \\ -\text{syll} \\ +\text{low} \end{bmatrix} \right\} \Big/ \left\{ \begin{matrix} [+A]\ V \underline{\qquad} \\ \underline{\qquad} C_0 V \begin{bmatrix} [+\text{hsp}] \\ [-A] \\ \begin{bmatrix} +\text{cons} \\ \alpha\ \text{ant} \\ \beta\ \text{cor} \end{bmatrix}_1 \end{bmatrix} \end{matrix} \right\}_1
$$

Grassmann's Law takes away aspiration: now for a rule
which adds it. Many verbs aspirate the final consonant of the
stem in the perfect active, e.g. πέμπω *pémpō* ' send ', whose
perfect is πέπομφα *pépompha*. The conditions under which this
occurs are given by Goodwin (1894, 154–5) and need not be
repeated here, except in the form of rule (60). Note that here
also we need a special feature to cover exceptions, this time
certain verbs that have an aspirated perfect active although
the stem of this tense has a long vowel in its last syllable (full
details in Goodwin). The special feature is labelled [+P].

[59a] The principle of the convention is that whereas with ordinary braces,

$$\left\{ \begin{matrix} A \\ B \end{matrix} \right\} X \left\{ \begin{matrix} C \\ D \end{matrix} \right\}$$

stands for ' AXC or AXD or BXC or BXD ', with subscripted braces

$$\left\{ \begin{matrix} A \\ B \end{matrix} \right\}_1 X {}_1\!\left\{ \begin{matrix} C \\ D \end{matrix} \right\}_1$$

stands for ' AXC or BXD ': upper alternatives must be taken with upper,
lower alternatives with lower.

(60) ASPIRATED PERFECT

$$
\begin{bmatrix} -\text{son} \\ -\text{cor} \\ +\text{Perfect} \end{bmatrix} \rightarrow \begin{bmatrix} -\text{voice} \\ +\text{hsp} \end{bmatrix} /
$$

$$
\left\{ \begin{matrix} V \\ [-\text{seg}] \end{matrix} \right\} \begin{bmatrix} C \\ -\text{hsp} \end{bmatrix}_0 \left\{ \begin{matrix} \begin{bmatrix} V \\ -\text{long} \end{bmatrix} \\ \begin{bmatrix} V \\ +P \end{bmatrix} C_0 \end{matrix} \right\} \text{——]] Stem} + V
$$

2.1.4.2. *The unvoiced liquid* [ṛ]

When initial, or when geminate, or when it follows an aspirated consonant, /r/ is realized as an unvoiced liquid. We can have no hesitation in identifying this liquid as a realization of the phonological unit /r/. It shared all the phonetic features of [r] except voice, and it was in complementary distribution with [r]. Historically, doubtless, [r] and [ṛ] were derived from quite distinct sources; [60] but there is no reasonable way of deducing this from the facts of classical Attic. We therefore postulate the following rule of R-DEVOICING.[61]

(61)

$$
\begin{bmatrix} +\text{cons} \\ +\text{son} \\ +\text{cont} \\ -\text{lat} \end{bmatrix} \rightarrow [-\text{voice}] / \left\{ \begin{matrix} \left\{ \begin{bmatrix} +\text{hsp} \\ -\text{seg} \\ -\text{FB} \end{bmatrix} \right\} \text{——} \\ r \text{——} \\ \text{——} r \end{matrix} \right\}
$$

[60] See Allen (1968, 40–1).

[61] One alleged exception to this rule is perhaps worth discussing: the name 'Ρᾶρος Ráros with its derivatives (see Allen 1968, 40). It has been suggested that the voicing of the initial /r/ in this word is due to the presence of another /r/ at the beginning of the next syllable; but this is unlikely for the following reason. There is another Greek word beginning /rVr/, namely ρωρός /rōrós/, a rare adjective preserved for us by Hesychius' lexicon (5th cent. A.D.) This word must have been known to Herodian, the grammarian who informs us about 'Ρᾶρος Ráros, since Callimachus (Hymn to Artemis 215) uses the compound ποδορρώρη podorróre; but Herodian does not mention it along with 'Ρᾶρος Ráros as having a voiced initial /r/. There is also the place-name Ραρεντός Rarentós, mentioned by Herodian (1. 222. 27 Lentz) in another connexion, in which the initial consonant is marked as voiceless with the ' rough breathing '; and ρερίφθαι reríphthai (Pindar, frag. 318) has

Furthermore, whenever [r̥] occurs, at least after a vowel, it is geminate. The aorist of ῥέω [ré̄ọ] ' flow ' is ἔρρευσα [érrewsa]; and if ' speakable ' is ῥητός [rē̆tós], ' unspeakable ' is ἄρρητος [árrē̆tos]. Even at the beginning of a word, a postvocalic voiceless liquid was pronounced long; such at least is the evidence of metre.[62] Within our grammar this phenomenon may be accounted for in two ways. We may enter each relevant form in the lexicon with initial /rr/, and have a rule simplifying this geminate after a consonant. This is objectionable because nowhere else in the language do we find an initial liquid followed by a consonant, and another solution is available. We represent the forms in question in the lexicon with initial single /r/, and then, after this has been devoiced by (61), we have a rule of R̥-DOUBLING:

(62) $\emptyset \to r̥ \ / \ V\,[-\text{seg}]_0 \text{——} r̥$

2.1.4.3. *Miscellaneous*

Glide Deletion has removed underlying intervocalic glides; but others will be introduced later. Diphthong Formation,

a rough breathing in all manuscripts of the grammarian Choeroboscus (2. 80. 24 Hilgard), who has preserved the word for us. If 'Πᾶρος Ῥάρος had a voiced initial, it can have had nothing to do with the phonological environment. More likely the ancient grammarians believed that the name was derived from the dialectal noun ῥάρος ráros (cf. Allen loc. cit.), in which the voiced initial /r/ is a dialectal feature and the accent shows that the first vowel was short. (It is suspicious, in this connexion, that the name 'Πᾶρος Ῥάρος is very often misaccented 'Πάρος Ῥάρος in manuscripts – an impossible accentuation, since the first vowel was long, as metre shows.) If such a belief existed, then the alleged voiced initial of the name could well be an invention of ancient scholarship. At any rate it cannot be taken as established that when the Homeric Hymn to Demeter was recited at Athens or Eleusis, the initial /r/ of PAPION Rárion (line 450) was voiced.

[62] At least in comedy. I have checked all the occurrences of words beginning with r in six plays of Euripides (*Alcestis*, *Bacchae*, *Electra*, *Ion*, *Iphigenia in Tauris*, *Medea*) and five of Aristophanes (*Acharnians*, *Knights*, *Clouds*, *Wasps*, *Peace*); the earliest of these eleven plays was produced in 438 B.C., the last after Euripides' death in 406. In the tragic sample, the initial voiceless liquid was necessarily double for metrical reasons in three passages, and necessarily single in five, of which three were in lyrics and four were in *Bacchae*. In the comic sample, which presumably reflects more closely the rhythm of ordinary speech, the liquid was necessarily long nine times, necessarily short only once, and that in lyrics.

discussed in the section on vowels, reduces many vowels to glides, and some of these are intervocalic. For example, the present optative of τίθημι [títhẹmi] ' put ' has a stem /thi+the+i/; Diphthong Formation reduces the last vowel to a glide, thus /ti+the+y/ (Grassmann's Law having also operated); and before endings beginning with a consonant this results, by Monophthongization (p. 32), in forms like the first person plural τιθεῖμεν [tithêmen]. When, however, the ending begins with a vowel, the glide is not merely not subject to Monophthongization, it is lengthened, and we get such forms as the first person singular τιθείην [tithéyyẹn]. Monophthongization, as formulated above, will correctly fail to apply when the segment following the diphthong is not consonantal; but we do need a rule to make the glides long.[63] This rule must be later than Diphthong Formation.

(63) GLIDE REINFORCEMENT

$$\emptyset \to y \ / \ Vy\text{----}V$$

The last rule we shall consider in this half of the chapter is an extremely marginal one. The necessity for it arises as follows. Apart from words whose final vowel is elided before the initial vowel of a following word, and some onomatopoeic words such as ὠόπ ōóp and φλαττόθρατ phlattóthrat,[64] there are only two words in Greek which ever end in a plosive, both proclitics: οὐκ ouk ' not ' and ἐκ ek ' out of '. The latter form occurs only before consonantal segments, eks being the form used before vowels and [h]; the question which of these, if either, is to be taken as basic is easily decided. If the underlying form is /eks/, then the /s/ will automatically be deleted in the required environment by the independently motivated rules of Fricative Weakening and Glide Deletion. On the other hand, no independently motivated rule inserts [s] before vowels, so that choice of /ek/ as underlying form would require an ad hoc complication of the grammar.

---

[63] For the long pronunciation of these glides, cf. Allen (1968, 79).

[64] See Aristophanes, Frogs 180, 208, 1286–96.

There remains οὐκ *ouk*, which also alternates, but in a different way, so that the same pair of rules cannot be used: its forms are οὐκ [ūk] before vowels, οὐχ [ūkʰ] (by Aspiration Shift, q.v. in section 5.2.7) before [h], otherwise οὐ [ū]. No single lexical representation can, in conjunction with independently motivated rules, account for these forms. Among conceivable lexical representations are /ow/ and /owk/. The latter cannot account for the preconsonantal form, since Obstruent Dropping applies before vowels as well as before consonants; and the former cannot account for the final velar stop of the prevocalic form. An ad hoc rule will therefore be needed somewhere.

But in which direction should it operate ? Should it add a consonant or remove one ? This question is decided by the behaviour of the other negative particle, μή *mē*. The base form of this particle clearly has no final consonant, and none appears when it precedes a *word* beginning with a vowel. But when μή *mē* is separated from a vowel only by *formative* boundary (which happens to occur only in one word), a [k] appears which is surely of the same nature as the [k] that appears after οὐ *ou*, and we find μηκέτι [mē̦-k-éti] ' no longer ' like οὐκέτι [ū-k-éti] ' id.'.[65] This shows that the rule we want is one that *inserts* a consonant in hiatus, after either negative particle when followed by a formative boundary, and after οὐ *ou* also when followed by a word boundary. Assuming that the two negative particles share all syntactic features except one, to which we shall give the descriptive label ' factual ' (οὐ *ou* being plus for this and μή *mē* minus), this K-ADDITION rule works out as follows:

$$(64) \quad \emptyset \rightarrow k \ / \begin{bmatrix} +\text{negative} \\ \langle +\text{factual} \rangle \end{bmatrix} - \left\{ \begin{matrix} + \\ \langle \#_1 \rangle \end{matrix} \right\} \ [-\text{cons}]$$

This completes our survey of rules relating to consonants in Greek.

---

[65] The last element of each of these words also appears as an independent word, ἔτι [éti] ' still '.

2.2. *RULES RELATING TO VOWELS*

2.2.1. THE MAIN VOWEL RULES [66]

2.2.1.1. *The Low Vowel Rule*

This rule has already been referred to *en passant* above (pp. 24, 27). It is the synchronic residue of the historical fronting, in early Attic, of proto-Greek /ā/ to [ẹ̄] in most environments. This fronting gives rise to numerous alternations which motivate this rule for the grammar of classical Attic.

(1) Verbs whose stems begin with /(h)a/ have augmented forms beginning with [(h)ẹ̄]; e.g. ἄγω [ágọ̄] ' lead ', imperfect ἦγον [ẹ̄gon].

(2) First-declension nouns, in the plural, show a stem vowel /a/: the plural endings are -αι [ay] -ας [ās] [67] -ῶν [-ộn] [68] -αις [ays]. In the singular, there are four different sets of endings:

(65)

	In environments where no fronting occurred		In envv. where fronting occurred	
Nom.	-ᾰ	[a] or [ā]	-ᾰ/η	[a] or [ẹ̄]
Acc.	-ᾰν	[an] or [ān]	-ᾰν/ην	[an] or [ẹ̄n]
Gen.	-ᾱς	[ās]	-ης	[ẹ̄s]
Dat.	-ᾳ	[āy]	-η	[ẹ̄y]

(3) Sometimes a stem-initial vowel is lengthened in compounds: thus ' name ' is ὄνομα [ónoma], but ' nameless ' ἀνώνυμος [an-ọ̄nümos].[69] When this lengthening is applied to a stem beginning with /a/, the resultant long vowel is [ẹ̄]: ἀκεστός [akestós] ' curable ', ἀνήκεστος [an-ẹ̄kestos] ' incurable '.

(4) Mention has already been made (p. 24) of what happens

---

[66] Two of these, ō-Raising and Monophthongization, having been discussed earlier (pp. 27, 32), will not be dealt with again here.

[67] From /ans/ by Nasal Dropping (cf. p. 27).

[68] From /áon/ by Contraction, as the accent proves (it falls on the ending even if the accent in other cases of the same noun falls on the stem).

[69] The other vowel changes in the stem are not relevant here.

to verbs such as φαίνω *phaínō* with a stem vowel /a/ when they are affected by the Resonant Aorist Rule. In non-fronting environments the aorist naturally has [ā], e.g. ἐμίανα [emíāna] from μιαίνω [miáynǭ] ' defile '.[70]

It is quite clear then that classical Attic must have a rule

(66) $\begin{bmatrix} +\text{long} \\ +\text{low} \end{bmatrix} \rightarrow [-\text{back}]$ / in certain contexts

The environments in which /ā/ fails to front are those in which it is preceded by /e i r/ (according to the usual formulation). What sort of natural class, if any, do these form ? The first two form the class of front vowels; the third forms by itself the class of non-nasal, non-lateral, sonorant consonants; and thus it appears that the class consisting of all three is an extremely complex and unnatural one.

I suggest (as already implied in tables (2–3), p. 3) that there is a natural class comprising the relevant segments and that it is

(67) $\begin{bmatrix} +\text{high} \\ -\text{back} \end{bmatrix}$

It is true that /e/ is not high; but if we order the Low Vowel Rule before Glide Deletion, we are free to assume that in νέα *néā* ' new ' (fem.) and all other words of this form, the underlying sequence is not /eā/ but /eyā/, the glide being afterwards regularly removed.[71]

More controversial is my claim that /r/ was systematically [+high] in Attic, i.e. that its articulation was palatalized. But

---

[70] There are one or two exceptions in each direction: on the one hand, ἐκέρδανα *ekérdāna* from κερδαίνω *kerdaínō* ' profit ', on the other ἐτέτρηνα *etétrēna* from τετραίνω *tetraínō* ' pierce ' (though inscriptions give τετραναι *tetrānai* for the aorist infinitive: see LSJ s.v.).

[71] This is even though νέα *néā* and some other words of this form had in early Greek a [w] at the beginning of the final syllable. They cannot have a /w/ in their underlying representations in classical Attic, since if they did, it would not be possible to account for their failing to undergo the Low Vowel Rule without unnecessarily complicating that rule. The few first-declension nouns for which there *is* reason to postulate an underlying stem ending in /wā/, such as /akowā/ ' hearing ' (cf. the verb ἀκούω [akówwǭ] ' hear ', from which it is derived), do undergo the rule (e.g. ἀκοή [akoę̄]).

a striking piece of evidence that this may be so comes from
two other branches of Indo-European.[72] IE /s/ becomes [š]—
that is, non-anterior and high—in Avestan, [ṣ] (retroflex) in
Sanskrit, and [x] in Slavonic, in the same set of environments
in each case, viz. after /k r i u/. These four segments do not at
first sight seem to form very much of a natural class. But if /r/
is taken to be [+high], these four are all and only the [+high]
segments capable of occurring before /s/.[73]   That is, this
apparently peculiar rule can be represented as basically an
assimilation rule:

$$(68) \quad \begin{bmatrix} -son \\ +cont \end{bmatrix} \rightarrow \begin{bmatrix} -ant \\ +high \end{bmatrix} / [+high] \underline{\qquad} \quad [74]$$

The fact that it is just these four segment types that are

---

[72] And we may not have to go so far afield. It may be that a palatalized
pronunciation of /r/ in Mycenaean Greek is behind the curious fact that in
its writing system, according to Lejeune (1958) and Vilborg (1960), the signs
ra_2 and ro_2, which are for the most part interchangeable with *ri-ja*, *ri-jo*,
are sometimes found to be interchangeable with *ra*, *ro*. If /r/ did have a
palatalized articulation, it would be easier to understand how the same sign
could represent both /ra/ and /ria/; also why ra_2 and ro_2 are much the
commonest of the various syllabograms that denote or have been thought
to denote syllables with palatalized consonants.

[73] This is a statement about Indo-European or a group of contiguous
dialects within it, not about Sanskrit; the latter also has retroflex obstruents
which, as F. W. Householder has pointed out to me, can sometimes occur
before /s/. Since, however, we must, I think, in view of the similarity of the
development and the conditions on it in Indo-Iranian and Slavonic, assume
that the first shift took place when these dialects were still in contact, the
matter of the retroflex consonants becomes irrelevant; for the retroflex
obstruents in Sanskrit are presumably due to contact with non-Indo-
European languages in India, which must long postdate the complete
separation of Indic and Iranian from pre-Slavonic.

[74] This section was originally written before I discovered that an explanation of the same phenomenon on essentially similar lines was proposed by
Martinet (1951). It is thus now necessary for me to comment on the criticism
of Martinet's proposal by Allen (1954). Allen is inclined, partly on the basis
of evidence he cites from Ashkun Kafiri, to hypothesize an early divergent
development of /s/ with palatalization, retroflexion and labiovelarization in
different phonological environments, after which each language generalizes
one or other of the variants to all these environments. This hypothesis,
however, does not account for the fact that in Kafiri, which is said to have

found to form a natural class seems to me overwhelming evidence that /r/ was [+high] when this rule was added to the grammar of the group of IE dialects in which its effects are found. Now we find that /i y r/ seem to constitute a natural class in Greek: this should then be explained in the same way, and we may further infer that a palatalized pronunciation of /r/ continued at least until the time when the special Attic form of the Low Vowel Rule came into existence. This rule we can now state thus:

escaped the stage of generalization and to reflect the earlier stage of environ-
mental variants, the expected (labio-)velar reflex of original /s/ after /u/
is not found; instead, according to Allen (1954, 563), the reflex in that
environment is [s] with no change at all.

An alternative historical explanation might proceed along the following
lines. In all the relevant languages, IE /s/ first developed after [+high]
segments to [š], except in two marginal areas that we know about: Kafiri,
where the change occurred only after non-back segments ([s] remaining after
/k u/), and Lithuanian, where it occurred only after /r/ (Burrow 1965, 18).
After this there was a further step of retroflexion, which occurred independently – and under different conditions – in Sanskrit and in Kafiri; in the
latter it was a further assimilation to a preceding /r/, in the former it was
part of a general shift of palato-alveolars to a retroflex articulation (cf.
Avestan[št] but Skt. [ṣṭ] from IE /kt/), and thus occurred in all environments.

The absence of any (labio-)velar reflex of IE /s/ after /u/ either in Kafiri
or in Iranian further suggests that the velar development was special to
Slavonic, and never occurred in any environment in other dialects.

The proposal in the text, originally made when I was ignorant of the
Kafiri evidence, thus seems, if anything, better able to account for it than
Allen's, although the assumed first development might be thought by some
to be lacking in phonetic plausibility.

I should mention the contention of Zwicky (1970) that /k r i u/ did not
form a natural class in Sanskrit, and that the developments of /s/ after /k/
are to be treated by a separate and distinct rule from that which accounts
for the developments after /r u i/. If Zwicky is correct, then my argument
will be considerably weakened. His argument, however, depends upon the
assumption that 'normally one can expect a lexical item to be exceptional
with respect to all applicable subrules of a rule, or to none' – an assumption
which he makes no attempt to justify, which is explicitly rejected, with
reasons, by Chomsky and Halle in a passage (1968, 175–6) to which Zwicky
refers without disputing their evidence, and which I also (see on Epenthesis
in 2.2.1.3) have found it necessary to reject. But if this assumption is not
accepted, then Zwicky's argument against the unity of the Sanskrit retroflexion process cannot be valid.

(69) $\begin{bmatrix} +\text{long} \\ +\text{low} \\ -\text{round} \end{bmatrix} \rightarrow [-\text{back}] \, / \begin{Bmatrix} [+\text{back}] \\ [-\text{high}] \end{Bmatrix}$ ——

2.2.1.2. *Contraction and related matters*

In Greek, adjacent non-high vowels often contract into a single long vowel. It would be tedious to exemplify here the alternations involved; the reader who does not know them already is invited to look at the paradigms of ' contract verbs ' in, e.g. Goodwin (1894). The basic facts are shown in the following table.

(70)

Input	Output	Written	Input	Output	Written
aa	ā	α	ea	ę̄	η
ae	ā	α	ee	ē	ει
ao	ǭ	ω	eo	ō → ū	ου
aā	ā	α	eā	?	
aę̄	ā	α	eę̄	ę̄	η
aǭ	ǭ	ω	eǭ	ǭ	ω
oa	ǭ	ω	oā	ǭ	ω
oe	ō → ū	ου	oę̄	ǭ	ω
oo	ō → ū	ου	oǭ	ǭ	ω

From (70) we can make the following generalizations regarding the contraction of two vowels (termed *input vowels*), the first of which is short, into one *output vowel* :

(71) (*a*) The output vowel is always long.
 (*b*) The output vowel is round if and only if at least one of the input vowels is round.
 (*c*) The output vowel is low if and only if at least one of the input vowels is low.
 (*d*) The output vowel is back if it is round, or if the first of the input vowels is back, and not otherwise.

This could be expressed as a rule of transformational form, like (6) or (20). So to express it, however, would result in great inelegance of presentation when other cases of contraction were brought into the picture which do not behave in quite the same way. We therefore treat contraction as a sequence of two processes. First of all, the second input vowel is modified in the direction of the first: that is, the first rule is assimilatory. Then the first input vowel is deleted. The two rules are as follows.[75]

(72) CONTRACTION I (First Version)

$$
\begin{bmatrix} V \\ -high \end{bmatrix} \rightarrow
\begin{bmatrix} +long \\ \left\langle \left\{ \begin{matrix} [\alpha\ low] \\ \begin{bmatrix} \beta\ round \\ \langle \gamma\ back \rangle \end{bmatrix} \end{matrix} \right\} \right\rangle \\ 1 \qquad\qquad 1 \end{bmatrix} /
$$

$$
\begin{bmatrix} V \\ -high \\ -long \\ \left\langle \left\{ \begin{matrix} [\alpha\ low] \\ \begin{bmatrix} \beta\ round \\ \langle \gamma\ back \rangle \end{bmatrix} \end{matrix} \right\} \right\rangle \\ 1 \qquad\qquad 1 \end{bmatrix}
\begin{bmatrix} \underline{\qquad} \\ \left\langle \left\{ \begin{matrix} [-low] \\ \begin{bmatrix} -round \\ \langle -back \rangle \end{bmatrix} \end{matrix} \right\} \right\rangle \\ 1 \qquad\qquad 1 \end{bmatrix}
$$

(73) CONTRACTION II (Truncation)

$$
\begin{bmatrix} V \\ -long \\ -high \end{bmatrix} \rightarrow \emptyset / \underline{\qquad} \begin{bmatrix} V \\ -high \end{bmatrix}
$$

[75] There are many forms which do not undergo Contraction at all, or only in certain circumstances. Thus νέος [néos] ' new ' does not undergo Contraction, but its compound νουμηνία [nūmēníā] ' new moon ' does. A fairly complex system of exceptions is required to account for all the facts, but I will not pursue the subject here.

Note that the whole of the present account of Contraction is preliminary. In the discussion of Markedness it will be shown that /e o/ are [+low] at the point where Contraction operates, and the rule will be reformulated accordingly.

The first refinement to the rules comes when we extend our consideration to cases where the second input vowel is followed by a glide. The facts in this situation are these:

(74)

Input	Output	Written
aay	āy	ᾳ
aey	āy	ᾳ
aoy	ǭy	ῳ
eay	ę̄y	ῃ
eey	ey → ē	ει
eoy	oy	οι
oay	?	
oey	oy	οι
ooy	oy	οι

Before a glide, we observe, if the output vowel is not low, it is not long either. This could be dealt with by adding a proviso to (72); but there is a more revealing alternative. If the output vowel were long, we would have, as output of Contraction, diphthongs [ōy] (whence [ūy]) and [ēy]. And as it happens, these diphthongs are not found phonetically in Greek. The proper course, then, is not to alter (72) so that it does not produce them, but to let (72) produce them and then get rid of them by a rule that says:

(75) Any mid vowel followed by a glide must be short, or formally:

(76) $\begin{bmatrix} V \\ -\text{high} \\ -\text{low} \end{bmatrix} \rightarrow [-\text{long}] / \underline{\hspace{1cm}} \begin{bmatrix} -\text{cons} \\ -\text{syll} \end{bmatrix}$

Next let us consider what happens when the first of the input vowels is long. Contraction is not so common under these circumstances and it is not so easy to get evidence of how it works as it is when the first input vowel is short. However, the following facts seem fairly clear:

E

(77) *Input*　　*Output*　　　　　　　*Evidence*

ę̄a(y)　　ę̄(y)　　　λύη [lǔę̄y] 2nd sg. pres. subjunc-
　　　　　　　　　　tive mediopassive of λύω [lǔǭ]
　　　　　　　　　　' release ': from /lu/ (stem)
　　　　　　　　　　+ /ę̄/ (mood marker) + /say/
　　　　　　　　　　(2 sg. mediopassive: cf. δύνασαι
　　　　　　　　　　dýnasai ' you are able ')

ę̄e　　　　ę̄　　　βασιλῆς [basilę̂s] nom. pl. of
　　　　　　　　　　βασιλεύς [basiléws] ' king ':
　　　　　　　　　　from /basilę̄w/ (stem – see on
　　　　　　　　　　Quantitative Metathesis) +
　　　　　　　　　　/es/ (nom. pl. ending).

ę̄o　　　　ǭ　　　ζῶμεν [zdǭmen] 1st pl. of ζῶ
　　　　　　　　　　[zdǭ] ' live ': from /zdę̄/ ← /zdā/
　　　　　　　　　　(stem: cf. 2 pl. ζῆτε [zdę̂te])
　　　　　　　　　　+ /o/ (linking vowel) + /men/
　　　　　　　　　　(1 pl.)

ǭa⎫
ǭe⎬　　ǭ　　　See Goodwin (1894, 15).
ǭo⎭

It will be seen that the output vowels follow the principles of
(71) exactly; so the only modification needed to (72) is the
removal of the requirement that the first input vowel must not
be long.

One more refinement is needed. The contracted vowel resulting from input /oę̄/ is [ǭ]: thus from the stem /dę̄lo/ ' make
plain ' plus subjunctive marker /ē/ plus 2nd person plural suffix
/te/ we get δηλῶτε [dę̄lǭte]. But the result of contracting /oę̄y/
is [oy]. The third person singular of the subjunctive of the
same verb, morphologically identical except that the person
morpheme is /i/ → /y/,[76] has the phonetic form δηλοῖ [dę̄lôy].
This phenomenon will not come under (76); by (72), as it
stands, the result of contracting this particular vowel combination should be low, and if it is low (76) will not shorten it. The

---

[76] The vowel is reduced to a glide by Diphthong Formation, to which we
shall come shortly.

output vowel must therefore be prevented from being low. The version of Contraction given now, which is for the time being [77] the final one, incorporates a proviso to this effect.

(78) CONTRACTION (Second Version)

$$
\begin{bmatrix} V \\ -high \end{bmatrix} \rightarrow \left\{ \begin{bmatrix} +long \\ \left\langle \left\{ \begin{bmatrix} [\alpha\ low] \\ [\beta\ round] \\ \langle \gamma\ back \rangle \end{bmatrix} \right\}_1 \right\rangle_1 \end{bmatrix} \begin{bmatrix} V \\ -high \\ \left\langle \left\{ \begin{bmatrix} [\alpha\ low] \\ [\beta\ round] \\ \langle \gamma\ back \rangle \end{bmatrix} \right\}_1 \right\rangle_1 \end{bmatrix} \right.
$$

$$
[-low] \quad / \quad o \begin{bmatrix} -back \\ +long \end{bmatrix} y
$$

$$
\left. \begin{bmatrix} \left\langle \left\{ \begin{bmatrix} [-low] \\ [-round] \\ \langle -back \rangle \end{bmatrix} \right\}_1 \right\rangle_1 \end{bmatrix} \right\}
$$

A process very similar to contraction, yet differing in various respects, is so-called crasis. This also involves the reduction of two vowels, in two syllables, to one vowel, in one syllable, but, unlike contraction, it occurs across word boundary. Typical examples are:

(79)

/kay épeyta/ ' and then '   → κἄπειτα   [kắpēta]
/to enantíon/ ' the opposite ' → τοὐναντίον [tūnántion]
/pro érgoo/ ' useful '   → προὔργου [prŭrgū]

For the most part the rules determining the output vowel are the same as for normal contraction, and for this reason the best way of accounting for the general phenomenon of crasis is to have a rule, earlier than Contraction, reducing the word

[77] See end of note 75.

boundaries within such phrases as those on the left hand of (79) to formative boundary so that Contraction can operate. Let us now consider the differences.

First of all, it will be seen that the presence of a /y/ between the two vowels involved in crasis is ignored (cf. the first example in (79)). This does not require a special rule: all that is needed is to order the rule reducing word boundaries to formative boundary (BOUNDARY WEAKENING) before Glide Deletion. Glide Deletion, like other rules, takes no account of the presence of a formative boundary in deciding whether its structural description is met.

The other difference is that when /a/ is the second input vowel in cases of crasis, the output vowel is always [ā], no matter what the first input vowel is.[78] This suggests a rule, preceding Contraction, which in the environment —— $+a$ sends all non-high vowels to [a]. Such a rule, however, would apply much too freely: in particular, it would apply to many cases of normal contraction. We want to restrict this kind of vowel assimilation to just the cases of crasis. The trouble is that at no stage are those vowels that are going to undergo crasis specially marked out as such. The only thing all such vowels have in common is that they provide an environment for Boundary Weakening. Can we then combine the vowel assimilation rule we want with Boundary Weakening ? The answer is that we can:

(80) CRASIS

$$
\begin{bmatrix} V \\ -\text{high} \end{bmatrix} \quad (y) \quad [-\text{seg}] \quad \begin{bmatrix} V \\ \langle +\text{back} \\ -\text{round} \rangle \end{bmatrix}
$$
$$
\quad 1 \qquad\qquad 2 \qquad\quad 3 \qquad\qquad 4
$$
$$
\begin{bmatrix} 1 \\ \langle +\text{low} \\ +\text{back} \\ -\text{round} \rangle \end{bmatrix} \quad 2 \quad \begin{bmatrix} 3 \\ +\text{FB} \end{bmatrix} \quad 4 \qquad \Rightarrow
$$

[78] For example, from /ho anḗr/ ' the man ' we have not *ὡνήρ *[hǫnḗr] but ἁνήρ [hānḗr]. The same phrase in the genitive case, underlying /too andrós/, is pronounced τἀνδρός [tāndrós].

When a high vowel precedes a non-high vowel, no contraction occurs. Some phonetic diphthongs, however, must be analysed as derived from underlying sequences of vowel plus high vowel, and I shall argue when we come to treat of accentuation that *all* [79] phonetic diphthongs should be so treated. The evidence that *some* diphthongs should be is based on cases where the same morpheme, or the same segment of the same morpheme, appears as a vowel or as a glide depending on environment. Two or three examples follow.

(1) The third declension dative singular ending is normally /i/ as in ὄμματι *ómmati*. In nouns with stems ending in /s/, however, in which, as a result of Fricative Weakening, etc., the ending comes to be directly preceded by a vowel, we find forms like γένει [génē] presumably from immediately underlying /géney/. And so in other types of third-declension nouns where the stem comes, in the course of the derivation, to end in a vowel.

(2) The adjective-forming suffix /io/ had only one syllable, and not two, when the stem to which it was added ended in a vowel; the adjective from the stem /lakedaymon/ ' Sparta ' was Λακεδαιμόνιος [lakedaymónios], but from /athēnā/ ' Athens ' it was Ἀθηναῖος [athēnâyyos].

(3) When /to himátion/ ' the cloak ' underwent Crasis, the result was θοἰμάτιον [thoymátion] with only four syllables instead of five.

The rule required to reduce these vowel sequences to diphthongs can be most easily stated if it is ordered after Glide Deletion, since with all intervocalic glides already removed it will not be necessary to specify that the vowel sequence must be followed by a non-vowel.

(81) DIPHTHONG FORMATION

$$[+\text{high}] \rightarrow [-\text{syll}] / V \text{——}$$

2.2.1.3. *Other rules*

(a) *Augmentation* – Reference has already been made (pp. 10–12) to the prefix known as ' the augment ', added to the

---

[79] Except for certain instances of [ay] and [oy].

past indicative forms of verbs. We will here recapitulate the
principal facts about this prefix. When the first segment of
the verb stem is consonantal,[80] the prefix is /e/; e.g. ἔφυγον
é-phygon ' I fled '. When the verb stem begins with a short
vowel, the augment consists in the substitution for this of a
long vowel; and the augmented forms of verbs beginning with
[a e i o ü] begin respectively with [ę̄ ȩ̄ ī ǭ ǖ], e.g.

(82)   Present   Imperfect
ἄγω   [ágǭ]   ' lead '   ἦγον   [ę̄gon]
ἐθέλω   [ethélǭ]   ' wish '   ἤθελον   [ę̄thelon]
ἱκετεύω   [hiketéwwǭ]   ' supplicate ' ἱκέτευον [hīkétewwon]
ὀρέγομαι   [orégomay]   ' reach out ' ὠρεγόμην [ǭregómę̄n]
ὑφαίνω   [hüpháynǭ]   ' weave '   ὕφαινον   [hüpháynon]

When the verb stem begins with a long vowel, this is unchanged
in the augmented tenses.

Is the augment introduced by a phonological rule, or is it a
grammatical formative already present in surface syntactic
structure, with a phonological shape of its own ?

If the augment is an independent grammatical formative, it
is necessary to inquire what its phonological shape is. If it is /e/,
then the forms exemplified in (82) are inexplicable; for underlying /ea ee ei eo eu/ would normally, by Diphthong Formation,
Contraction and Monophthongization, give, incorrectly, phonetic [ę̄ ē ē ū ew]. Evidently, the augment as such has no
inherent phonological form; rather its form depends on the
initial consonant or vowel of the verb to be augmented. If this
is so, the augment cannot be present in surface structure, since
its presence would not explain anything in phonology and it is
irrelevant to syntax; for its occurrence is fully determined by
two independently motivated syntactic sub-categories or
features, past time [81] and indicative mood, and it does not
itself predict anything in syntax.

[80] Also in some cases where, at the phonetic level, it is not; see pp. 10–12
and 18.

[81] Motivated by the rule of ' sequence of moods ' (for which see Goodwin
1894). Note that this rule cannot be made to depend on the presence of the

I therefore suggest that before any of the phonological rules have applied the underlying form of ἔφυγον [épʰügon] is /pʰug+o+n/, that of ἤθελον [étʰelon] is /etʰel+o+n/, etc., and that the augment is added by the following rule:

(83) AUGMENTATION [82]

$$\begin{cases} V \rightarrow \begin{bmatrix} +\text{long} \\ +\text{AUG} \end{bmatrix} / \begin{bmatrix} -\text{seg} \\ -\text{FB} \end{bmatrix} (h) \text{---} \\ \emptyset \rightarrow \begin{bmatrix} e \\ +\text{AUG} \end{bmatrix} / \begin{bmatrix} -\text{seg} \\ -\text{FB} \end{bmatrix} \text{---} \begin{bmatrix} -\text{syll} \\ -\text{low} \end{bmatrix} \end{cases} / \begin{bmatrix} +\text{past} \\ +\text{indic} \end{bmatrix} X]]_V$$

The diacritic feature [+AUG] is added in order to provide an environment for the next rule, which inserts the = boundary that as we have seen (note 12) always follows the augment.

(84) BOUNDARY INSERTION

$$\emptyset \rightarrow = / [+\text{AUG}] \text{---}$$

It is, incidentally, evident that unless the first part of (83) is to be split up into a number of different processes and a generalization lost, the unaugmented vowels listed on p. 62, line 7, must at the point where (83) applies differ from their augmented counterparts by one feature only, presumably length. This is strong evidence helping us to determine the underlying forms of the five long vowels in question.

(b) *Epenthesis* – The main phenomena of ablaut in Greek will be discussed in 2.2.2; here we deal with a case in which the usual rules of ablaut do not apply. One of these rules is that in the neighbourhood of liquids the vowel /e/, instead of being suppressed in the ' weak-grade ' forms, becomes [a] if it stands between two consonants; and this [a] is almost always in the

augment itself; for the verb whose pastness brings the rule into operation may be in the infinitive or participial form, and infinitives and participles do not take the augment.

[82] As syntactic features, ' past ' and ' indicative ' will by convention be distributed to every segment of the verb of which they are features (convention 2, Chomsky and Halle 1968, 173). As usual, X denotes any string of zero or more segments, with or without boundaries, and]]$_V$ indicates that the rule can only apply if the word is a verb.

same position relative to the liquid as is occupied by the [e] vowel in the ' full-grade ' forms. Thus contrasting with σπέρμα spérma ' seed ' and κρείττων kreíttōn ' stronger ' we find ἔσπαρται éspartai (perfect passive) ' it is sown ' and κράτιστος krátistos 'strongest' rather than *ἔσπραται *éspratai, *κάρτιστος *kártistos. The only exceptions among prose words [83] are the dative plurals of the small class of nouns declined like πατήρ patḗr ' father '.[84] The inflexions of a member of this very interesting class of nouns are laid out as (85).

(85)

	Sing.		Plur.	
Nom.	πατήρ	[patḗr		
Voc.	πάτερ	páter	πατέρες	[patéres
Acc.	πατέρα	patéra	πατέρας	patéras
Gen.	πατρός	patrós	πατέρων	patérōn
Dat.	πατρί	patrí]	πατράσι	patrási]

If this exception did not exist, the natural rule to account for the facts about the ' weak-grade ' forms would be one which, in appropriate morphologically defined environments, deleted /e/ before vowels [85] and lowered it [86] to [a] before or after liquids. As this rule would have no other exceptions, and as the πατήρ patḗr group of nouns are exceptional in other ways than this, it is preferable, rather than giving up the rule (which we might call VOWEL WEAKENING), to mark the πατήρ patḗr group of nouns as in some way exceptions to it.

How exactly, though, can the form πατράσι [patrási] of the dative plural be accounted for, starting from an underlying form that is presumably /pater+si/ ? If this underwent Vowel Weakening in the ordinary way, the expected surface

[83] Another exceptional form, found only in poetry, is ἔδρακον édrakon, aorist of δέρκομαι dérkomai ' look '.

[84] The other members of the group are: μήτηρ mḗtēr ' mother ', θυγάτηρ thygátēr ' daughter ', ἀνήρ anḗr ' man ' and γαστήρ gastḗr ' belly '.

[85] These vowels, as it happens, are high, and would but for this deletion have become glides by Diphthong Formation.

[86] As we shall see in the next chapter, this is really a backing rather than a lowering rule; for the vowel is already low before the rule applies, being underlying /e̬/.

form would be πατάρσι *[patársi]. The actual form could be derived if we could somehow let Vowel Weakening exceptionally delete, instead of lowering, the vowel in these dative plurals, resulting in, e.g. /patr+si/, after which a later rule would insert a vowel in a fixed place to break up these unique clusters, in all of which a resonant consonant would be imprisoned between two obstruents.

How is Vowel Weakening to incorporate the exceptional behaviour of these dative plurals ? The rule must consist of two parts, both applying to non-high vowels in certain morphologically defined environments. We shall have a look at what these environments are in the section on Ablaut, but it is of no importance just yet. The first part of the rule lowers the vowel to [a] when it is followed by two consonants, and sometimes when it is followed by one.[87] The second part deletes the vowel whenever it has not been lowered ; that is, the second part is of the form

$$(86) \quad \begin{bmatrix} V \\ -\text{high} \end{bmatrix} \rightarrow \emptyset \;/\; \begin{bmatrix} \underline{} \\ -\text{low} \end{bmatrix} \;/\; \text{in certain contexts}$$

Thus the behaviour of πατράσι patrási, etc., could be accounted for by a readjustment rule which made them exceptions to the *first part only* of Vowel Weakening.[88] Failing to undergo the first part of the rule, the relevant vowel will still be non-low when it comes to the second part, and will be deleted.

This deletion will create an environment for the vowel-insertion or EPENTHESIS rule, which may be represented thus:

$$(87) \quad \emptyset \rightarrow a \;/\; [+\text{cons}] \begin{bmatrix} +\text{cons} \\ +\text{son} \end{bmatrix} \underline{} [-\text{son}]$$

(c) *Shortening* – In various circumstances vowels which phonetically, or at some intermediate stage of derivation, are short must be regarded as underlyingly long. Among them are the following.

---

[87] As happens in the aorist passive of φθείρω *phtheírō* ' destroy ' and στέλλω *stéllō* ' send ': ἐφθάρην *ephthárēn*, ἐστάλην *estálēn*.

[88] This is a counter-example to Zwicky's assumption about exceptions; see the end of note 74. But see also pp. 78–9.

(1) Nouns of the first declension (and feminine vowel-stem adjectives) have for the most part /ā/ as the final segment of their stems: see (65), where the singular endings are shown. In the plural, however, as noted on p. 51, the stem appears to end in a short /a/. Is this variation a morphological phenomenon, or phonological? We note that in the plural the vowel in question is always followed (except in the genitive, where it undergoes contraction and might as well originally have been long as short) by either a glide or /ns/. Could there be a rule shortening vowels in these two environments? [89] An objection to such a rule might be that it does not seem to apply in the dative singular, which ends in [āy] or [ēy]. But the dative singular is only an apparent exception; I shall show when we come to consider accent that its ending, in both first and second declensions, must be regarded as contracted from /Vay/, where V is the final vowel of the stem. The dative singular is therefore not an objection to the proposed rule.

The second subrule, which we have so far assumed to apply before /ns/, may be extended to apply before nasal plus consonant generally: there are no forms in which, e.g. /nt/ is preceded by a long vowel, except those which result from contraction. The subrule must, however, be restricted so that it applies only where the nasal is preceded by a morpheme boundary; thus it does not apply to the dative plural of nouns whose stems end in /V̄n/ such as ἀγών /agǭn/ ' contest ', whose dat. pl. is underlying /agǭn+si/, phonetic ἀγῶσι [agǭsi]. [90]

We therefore now have a rule which shortens vowels (a) before glides, and (b) before /+NC/. But this is still insufficiently constrained. For one thing, the form of the nom. pl. of βασιλεύς basileús – see (77) – suggests that the /ē/ of the stem of that noun does not shorten, at any rate not before

---

[89] Such a rule would also apply in the genitive and dative dual of these nouns, which ends in [ayn].

[90] Although this form has undergone Nasal Dropping, its long vowel is not the result of the operation of that rule; Nasal Dropping lengthens /o/ to a mid (phonetically a high), not a low, vowel.

Contraction; and, as the case of vowels before /nt/ shows, the Shortening rule now under discussion must be earlier than Contraction. A consideration of the paradigm of ναῦς *naûs* ' ship ' suggests that the constraint to impose is that Shortening does not apply to a vowel followed by /wV/.

(88)   Stem: /nāw/

	Sing.		*Pl.*	
Nom.	ναῦς	[naȗ̂ws	νῆες	nẹes
Acc.	ναῦν	naȗ̂wn	ναῦς	naȗ̂ws
Gen.	νεώς	neǫ́s [91]	νεῶν	neǫ̂n [91]
Dat.	νηί	nẹ́í	ναυσί	nawsí]

Except in the genitive (regarding which, see the section on Quantitative Metathesis), the stem vowel is long where the ending begins with a vowel, and short where it begins with a consonant.

We have thus arrived at the following SHORTENING rule:

(89)
$$
V \rightarrow [-\text{long}] \, / \, \underline{\hspace{2em}} \left\{ \begin{bmatrix} -\text{cons} \\ +\text{high} \\ \langle +\text{back} \rangle \\ [+\text{nas}]\,[+\text{cons}] \end{bmatrix} \left\langle \left\{ \begin{matrix} C \\ [+\text{WB}] \end{matrix} \right\} \right\rangle \right\}
$$

This rule, of course, reflects the historical phenomenon known as ' Osthoff's Law '.

(d) *Lengthening in Irregular Comparatives* – A fair number of adjectives and adverbs form their comparatives not with one of the two usual suffixes, /tero/ and /īon/, but with a suffix /yon/ which is often disguised through fusion of the /y/ with the final consonant of the stem. Adjectives of this class always (with one exception) lengthen their stem vowels in the comparative. Examples:

(90)   *Adjective/adverb*   *Comparative*
        ταχύς [takʰús] ' swift '   θάττων [tʰáttǭn]
        μέγας [mégas] ' great '   μείζων [mézdǭn]
        μάλα [mála] ' much '   μᾶλλον [mâllon]

---

[91] By Quantitative Metathesis from /nẹos nẹǫ̂n/.

This regularity must be accounted for by a quite late rule; note
that the long vowels corresponding to [a] and [e] are [ā] and [ē]
respectively, as they are in such late rules as Nasal Dropping
and Monophthongization (contrast Augmentation). What are
the conditions that must be satisfied if the lengthening rule is
to operate ? The vowel that is lengthened is always followed
by two consonants, with a morpheme boundary between them;
for the first consonant belongs to the stem and the second to
the comparative suffix, though one of them at least, and often
both, will have been changed during the derivation by
Affrication or otherwise. The vowel that follows these two
consonants has always at this stage [92] an [o] quality, and is
always (naturally) part of the comparative suffix; so a rule
like (91) would do what is wanted:

(91)
$$V \rightarrow [+\text{long}] \, / \, \underline{\qquad} \, C_2 \begin{bmatrix} V \\ +\text{round} \\ +\text{compve} \end{bmatrix}$$

One form, as we mentioned above, exceptionally fails to
lengthen: πλείων [pléyyōn], neuter πλέον [pléon] or (by a
unique contraction) πλεῖν [plḗn][92a], ' more '. This is the only
short-form comparative in which the (originally) short stem
vowel is followed by two glides (or, in the neuter, by no
consonant at all). If we order the lengthening rule after
Lateralization and Metathesis (see pp. 31–2), so that the /y/ of
the comparative suffix will in all cases have undergone fusion
before lengthening applies, we will be able to modify it so that
glide sequences do not form an environment for it. The
modification needed is of course to replace ' C_2 ', that is ' two
non-syllabic segments ', in the environment statement by ' two
consonantal segments '. Except for the fact that it operates
only on comparatives, the conditioning of this rule can be
stated in entirely phonological terms.

(e) *High Vowel Fronting* – The reader will have noticed
that the vowel pronounced [ü] [93] is given in underlying

---

[92] If we order the lengthening rule before ō-Raising.

[92a] Only before ἤ [ē̜] ' than '.

[93] And represented in transliterations by *y*.

representations as a back vowel, /u/. This representation is required not merely by considerations of symmetry in the vowel system, but also because of the existence of alternations such as

(92) φεύγω [pʰéwgǭ] ' I flee ' : ἔφυγον [épʰügon] ' I fled '
     ζεῦγος [zdêwgos] ' team ' : ζυγόν [zdügón] ' yoke '

in which [ü] is evidently acting as the vocalic equivalent of [w]. If we wish to keep such rules as Diphthong Formation simple, we must regard [ü] in these words as being derived from /u/ by a fronting rule; and this being so, since it would be pointless to have a /u : ü/ contrast in the lexicon that had no phonetic consequences whatever, either for the actual segments concerned or for any others, it is best to derive *all* instances of [ü] from /u/ by a rule with the effect of (93).

(93) $\begin{bmatrix} +\text{syll} \\ +\text{high} \end{bmatrix} \rightarrow [-\text{back}]$

This rule, as we have just seen, must be later than Diphthong Formation; and it must be earlier than ō-Raising, otherwise the two rules, operating successively, will incorrectly send /ō/ to [ü].

(*f*) *Quantitative Metathesis* – The need for this rule arises chiefly from the vocalism and accentuation of certain third-declension genitive case forms. The genitive singular of the third declension normally ends in /os/; and one of the most basic rules of the Greek accentual system, as we shall see, is that a word whose last vowel is long must be accented on either the final or the penultimate syllable. Both these principles seem to be violated by the genitive singular of πόλις *pólis* ' city ', which is πόλεως pronounced [póleǫs]. Both principles would be fulfilled, at a slightly deeper level, if we took this vowel sequence [eǫ] to be derived from /ęo/. Compare also νεώς [neǫs] (p. 67), where the postulation of a Quantitative Metathesis rule would save the generalization there made about Shortening. It is noteworthy that phonetic [ęo] does not occur in Attic.

There are some other related irregularities that could be accounted for by extensions of the rule. The third-declension accusative singular ending, when it is not /n/, is /a/; yet βασιλεύς *basiléus* has a long-vowel ending in this case – βασιλέα [basiléā]. This could be accounted for by supposing this [eā] to be a reflex of immediately underlying /ẹa/; and once again, it is of significance that the hypothesized underlying sequence has no direct phonetic correspondent [ẹa] in Attic.

Another non-occurring vowel sequence is [ẹọ]. Quantitative Metathesis can be extended without difficulty to modify this sequence by shortening the first vowel (there is no need to lengthen the second, it being already long); so far as I know, this extension would be required only for the genitive plural of ναῦς *naûs*. It would, however, simplify Quantitative Metathesis to extend it in this way, since it would not be necessary to require that the second vowel must initially be short.

A further simplification is possible if the rule is later than High Vowel Fronting, since then no restrictions at all need be placed on the second input vowel except that it must be back. The rule:

$$(94) \quad \begin{bmatrix} \text{V} \\ -\text{back} \\ +\text{low} \\ +\text{long} \end{bmatrix} \begin{bmatrix} \text{V} \\ +\text{back} \end{bmatrix}$$

$$\qquad\qquad 1 \qquad\qquad 2 \qquad \Rightarrow$$

$$\begin{bmatrix} 1 \\ -\text{low} \\ -\text{long} \end{bmatrix} \begin{bmatrix} 2 \\ +\text{low} \\ +\text{long} \end{bmatrix}$$

2.2.2. ON VOWEL GRADATION

As is well known, vowel gradation, or ablaut, was an important feature of proto-Indo-European morphology, and continued to be so well into the prehistory of Greek – so much so that in some cases the same word is preserved with vowels of different ' grades ' in different dialects (see Buck 1955, 44–6). In classical Attic there are many sets of cognate words and forms in which vowels alternate with one another as a result of inherited gradation. Are these just survivals, or do they form a system ? We will collect together the circumstances under which the ablaut alternations are found in three key areas – in noun inflexion, in verb inflexion, and in derivational morphology – and see whether it shows signs of consistency and system, or whether, as in modern English (Chomsky and Halle 1968, 202–3), we have merely rules ' widely applicable to irregular verbs and other irregular forms ', which will require a great variety of idiosyncratic lexical marking. Then we will give the rules as they apply in Greek. Lastly we consider whether the evidence warrants us in setting up syllabic nasals in Greek underlying representations.

2.2.2.1. *Vowel gradation in nouns and adjectives* [93a]

The effect of vowel gradation on nouns and adjectives is in some ways systematic, and in others unsystematic. It is systematic in that it is possible, with only a few exceptions, to tell from the form of a noun or adjective stem whether and in what cases it will show the effect of gradation. It is unsystematic in that for the most part nothing in the synchronic phonological pattern of the language suggests why it is these forms, rather than others, that undergo gradation.

The characteristic type of gradation in nouns, scarcely found at all in verbs,[94] is VRDDHI, or lengthening. This occurs extensively in the nominative singular of third-declension nouns, mainly, but not entirely, in those in which the normal nominative singular morpheme /s/ is absent; in some of these vrddhi is found also in the vocative singular. The details are as follows:

(*a*) All nouns whose stems end in /or er on en/ – that is, in a mid vowel followed by a resonant consonant – lengthen the

[93a] In this section, since it is about noun and adjective inflexion, the word ' noun ' may be used in its ancient, broad sense, to include both nouns and adjectives (and participles). Where nouns in the narrow sense are meant, the term ' substantive ' will be used.

[94] Unless the lengthening of the thematic vowel in subjunctive forms is an example of it.

last vowel of the stem in the nominative singular. For example:

(95)　*Stem*　　　*Nom. sg.*

/rētor/	ῥήτωρ	[r̥ḗtǫr]	' orator '
/pater/	πατήρ	[patḗr]	' father '
/kʰion/	χιών	[kʰiǭn]	' snow '
/limen/	λιμήν	[limḗn]	' harbour '

Neuter adjectives and participles, however, are never subject to vṛddhi: the nom. sg. of /sōpʰron/ ' wise ' is masculine and feminine σώφρων [sǭpʰrǭn], but neuter σῶφρον [sǭpʰron]. This proviso applies to all cases in which vṛddhi is found.

(*b*) Most nouns whose stems end in /ont/ have [ǭn] in the nominative singular; e.g. λέων [léǭn], gen. λέοντος [léontos], ' lion '. Exceptions are /odont/ ' tooth ' (nom. sg. ὀδούς [odǔs] from /odont+s/) and two or three participles of irregular verbs.

(*c*) Certain forms with stems ending in /s/ also show vṛddhi in the nom. sg., in particular adjectives and proper names whose stems end in /es/, such as /aspʰales/, nom. sg. ἀσφαλής [aspʰalḗs].

(*d*) Perfect active participles, whose stems end in /ot/, have nom. sg. ending in [ǭs]; e.g. εἰκώς [ēkǭs] ' seeming, probable ', gen. sg. εἰκότος [ēkótos].

(*e*) One other noun: /alōpek/ ' fox ' has nom. sg. ἀλώπηξ [alǭpḗks].

(*f*) Nouns of types (*a*) and (*b*) normally do not have vṛddhi in the vocative singular; but those whose accent falls on the last syllable of the stem, such as ἡγεμών [hḗgemǭn] ' leader ', do, and the vocative of such nouns is therefore the same as the nominative. The only exceptions to this rule are a few nouns where the accent is shifted to the left in the vocative; in these the last vowel of the stem is short, e.g. πάτερ [páter]. That is, the length of this vowel in the vocative is settled only after the surface accentuation of that case has been assigned.

The basic principle of vṛddhi is now tolerably clear: the vowel is lengthened in all *endingless non-neuter nominative singulars*, and in the vocative singular of the same nouns if the accent is stem-final. Thus most words do not need to be marked for vṛddhi, but only for whether they take the ending /s/ in the nom. sg. If there is no ending, vṛddhi will apply; if the vowel in question is already long (as in, e.g. /lukōn/ (person's name)) it will apply vacuously. This principle will account for types (*a*), (*c*) and (*f*), and for (*b*) apart from the exceptions mentioned. It is, of course, only pushing the problem back a stage further: the question now becomes, why are these particular nominative singulars endingless ? Perfect active participles, and /alōpek/, need to be specially marked as undergoing the vṛddhi rule.

The rule of Vowel Weakening, discussed above (pp. 63–65), is of wide application among verbs, but in nouns is restricted to three groups, two of them consisting of only one noun each.

(*a*) The πατήρ *patér* group of nouns, as shown in (85), undergo weakening in the genitive and dative singular, and dative plural.

(*b*) The stem /aner/ ' man ' undergoes Vowel Weakening, followed by Excrescence (p. 38), in all cases except the nom. and voc. sg.

(*c*) The stem /kuon/ ' dog ' likewise undergoes Vowel Weakening in all cases except the nom. and voc. sg. (acc. sg. κύνα [kúna], etc.).

These nouns clearly have to be regarded as irregular. We will bear this in mind when we come to consider Vowel Weakening as it applies to verbs.

Finally we turn to the alternation of /e/ and /o/, which has its main home in derivational morphology. In noun inflexion it turns up twice.

(*a*) Neuter substantives (but not adjectives) whose stems end in /es/ have nominative-accusative singular in [os]: e.g. γένος *génos* (see pp. 8 ff.).

(*b*) Nouns of the second declension whose nominative ends in [os], and all of whose other cases imply a stem ending in /o/, have a vocative singular ending in [e]: e.g. Ἄνυτε *Ányte* from the personal name Ἄνυτος *Ánytos*.

F

These facts, while quite regular, are unrelatable to each other or to anything else in the phonology or morphology of Greek: it can but be stated as a readjustment rule [95] that nouns of these particular morphological categories are subject to *e/o* ablaut.

What we have found in this brief investigation of ablaut phenomena in nouns is that the vr̥ddhi rule seems different from the other two. Vr̥ddhi serves, for the most part, as a means of forming the nominative singular of nouns when the usual /s/ formative is not used for this purpose, and its occurrence in the vocative is phonologically conditioned. The other two rules, in nouns, are mere quirks, survivals that play no active role in the system of the language, but merely go on existing.

2.2.2.2. *Vowel gradation in verbs*

Both *e/o* ablaut and Vowel Weakening are found in the Greek system of verbal conjugation. The latter is of wide application; the former is confined to one aspect, the perfect active, where there are about 17 common verbs that show an /o/ vowel where they have an /e/ (or some vowel regularly derived therefrom) in other tenses. Typical examples are:

(96)	Present			Perfect	
	κλέπτω	[kléptǭ]	' steal '	κέκλοφα	[kéklopʰa]
	λείπω	[lḙ́pǭ]	' leave '	λέλοιπα	[léloypa]
	ῥήγνυμι	[rḙ́gnūmi]	' break '	ἔρρωγα	[érrǭga]

It is not possible to give any general rule defining the class of verbs subject to *e/o* ablaut in the perfect. Some of them, like the three exemplified above, undergo Vowel Weakening in other tenses; others, such as πέμπω [pémpǭ] ' send ', perfect πέπομφα [pépompʰa], do not. Most have a derivative noun or

---

[95] For the notion ' readjustment rule ' see Chomsky and Halle (1968). Basically, readjustment rules make minor alterations to lexical forms of morphemes, the syntactically motivated arrangement of boundaries, etc., before the phonological rules proper are applied.

adjective with an /o/ vocalism, but some do not, and many
verbs that do have such derivatives do not undergo e/o ablaut
in the perfect. This ablaut rule must be regarded, as far as
verbal conjugation is concerned, as a minor rule applying
only to those few verbs specially marked for it.

Vowel Weakening applies to far more verbs; of those used in
ordinary Attic, there are about forty or fifty which undergo it
in some tense or other. The details can be found, e.g. in
Goodwin (1894). But in no class of verbs is Vowel Weakening
the regular treatment. New verbs added to the language never
undergo it. And among these irregularities only one regularity
can be stated: that if a verb undergoes Vowel Weakening in
the perfect medio-passive it will always undergo it in the aorist
passive as well, if it has one.

In verbs, then, ablaut applies only to irregular lexical items,
with one exception to be considered directly. Rules can be
stated (just as for strong verbs in German or English) which
will give the correct form of most of these irregular tenses, but
irregular they remain, and the rules will be minor.

There is one other relic of e/o ablaut in the verb. This is
found in the so-called thematic tenses – the imperfective
(present and imperfect) and the second aorist. In these tenses
the personal endings are preceded by a linking vowel, usually
termed the thematic vowel; and this vowel is /o/ where the
ending begins with a nasal, and /e/ otherwise. For example,
the imperfect of φέρω *phérō* ' bear ' is as follows:

(87) *Singular*   *Dual*   *Plural*

1st
ἔφερον *épheron*   ἐφέρομεν *ephéromen*
2nd
ἔφερες *épheres*   ἐφέρετον *ephéreton* ἐφέρετε *ephérete*
3rd
ἔφερε(ν) *éphere(n)* ἐφερέτην *epherétēn* ἔφερον *épheron*

(Note that, in determining whether the thematic vowel is
followed by a nasal, ephelcystic nasals are ignored: that is, the
rule we are concerned with is earlier than Ephelcysis.)

This alternation is completely non-functional, and the environment in which it occurs will simply have to be added to the list of environments for e/o ablaut.

2.2.2.3. *Ablaut in derivation*

We will be considering here only one area of derivational morphology, but it is quite an important one, and it is an area in which ablaut, of the e/o variety, may well be regarded as more than just a relic.

The area is that of nouns and adjectives formed from verbs with one of the suffixes /o/ (thematic vowel) or /ā/, such as λόγος *lógos* ' speech ' from λέγω *légō* ' speak ' or ψόγος *psógos* ' blame ' from ψέγω *pségō* ' blame '. When these are formed from verbs whose stems are monosyllabic and contain the vowel /e/, they almost invariably have /o/ in its place; and most of them have a direct and obvious semantic connection with the verbs from which they are formed. It cannot be predicted whether a verb will in fact have a derivative or derivatives of this form, or, if it does, of which of the various possible types it will be;[96] but it can be predicted that any such derivative will have an /o/ vocalism. Verbs with stems of more than one syllable do not usually form derivatives of this kind, but when they do they follow the same rule; e.g. ἀλοιφή *aloiphḗ* ' ointment ' from ἀλείφω *aleíphō* ' anoint '.

What is the result of our investigation ? There are three main ablaut rules – Vṛddhi, Vowel Weakening and e/o ablaut or METAPHONY. Of these, the first is regular in certain well-defined types of nouns; the third is regular in one class of deverbal nouns, but otherwise found only in scattered morphological categories or in irregular verbs; and Vowel Weakening is confined to irregular nouns and verbs.

---

[96] The types are: masculine action noun, e.g. ψόγος *psógos*; masculine agent noun/adjective, e.g. σκοπός *skopós* ' watcher ' from /skep/ ' watch '; feminine action noun, e.g. τομή *tomḗ* ' a cutting ' from /tem/ ' cut '; feminine agent noun/adjective (rare). Many examples are listed by Vendryes (1929).

2.2.2.4. *The rules*

Vṛddhi is an early rule lengthening mid vowels;[97] its major environment has already been given (pp. 72–3). Assuming that the rule is minor, and that an earlier readjustment rule realizes the portmanteau morph {Nominative Singular} in most environments as /s/, but in some environments as a feature [+Vṛddhi] on the preceding segment, the rule will be simply this:

$$(98) \quad \begin{bmatrix} V \\ -\text{high} \\ -\text{low} \end{bmatrix} \rightarrow [+\text{long}] \, / \, \begin{bmatrix} \underline{\hspace{2cm}} \\ +\text{Vṛddhi} \end{bmatrix}$$

The vocative singular being generally, in the third declension, identical with the nominative, Vṛddhi, wherever it applies to the nominative, will have applied to the vocative also. We need therefore a rule, later than Accent Reassignment [98] (for which see Chapter V), which in the vocative singular will shorten the last vowel of the stem if it has been lengthened by Vṛddhi and is unaccented or is followed by /s/:[99]

$$(99) \quad \begin{bmatrix} V \\ +\text{Vṛddhi} \end{bmatrix} \rightarrow [-\text{long}] \, / \, \left\{ \begin{matrix} \begin{bmatrix} \underline{\hspace{1cm}} \\ -\text{sharp} \end{bmatrix} \\ \underline{\hspace{1cm}} \, s \end{matrix} \right\}$$

Metaphony, it seems, has to be made to work in both directions. In general it sends /e/ to /o/; but in second-declension nouns /o/ is plainly the base form of the stem-final vowel, /e/ appearing only in one case and hardly ever in derivatives either. We therefore state the rule thus:

---

[97] Rather, as we shall see in the next chapter, low vowels which are back and round, or non-back and non-round.

[98] For the reason for this ordering, see (*f*), p. 72.

[99] This last proviso is because, in adjectives of the type of ἀσφαλής *asphalḗs* ' safe ', shortening takes place even though these adjectives are final-accented. Shortening does *not* take place (except in names of gods) if the last vowel of the stem would have been long even without Vṛddhi, as in names like Λύκων *Lýkōn* (nom. & voc.); this suggests that a readjustment rule earlier than (98) deletes the feature [+Vṛddhi] on long vowels, so that (98) is never allowed to apply vacuously and (99) can never apply to stems whose last vowel is underlyingly long.

$$(100) \quad \begin{bmatrix} V \\ a \text{ back} \\ a \text{ round} \end{bmatrix} \rightarrow \begin{bmatrix} -a \text{ back} \\ -a \text{ round} \end{bmatrix} / \begin{array}{l} \text{in certain irregular} \\ \text{verbs, nouns \& adjs.} \\ \text{in certain contexts} \end{array}$$

The contexts have been fully described above; it would be of no interest to state them formally, since they have no points of resemblance with one another.

The effect of Vowel Weakening varies according to the phonological context. As we have seen (p. 64), it must consist of two parts, a lowering rule followed by a deletion rule. In Greek the lowering rule operates far more frequently than the other. The deletion rule operates only:

(a) In nouns (see pp. 63–5, 73).

(b) In a few reduplicated present tenses (most important being γίγνομαι *gígnomai* ' become ' from /gen/).

(c) In several forms where a long vowel is introduced between stem and ending; e.g. the perfect active, perfect medio-passive and aorist passive of /kal/ ' call ': κέκληκα *kéklēka*, κέκλημαι *kéklēmai*, ἐκλήθην *eklḗthēn*.

(d) Where the underlying vowel is followed by another (high) vowel; e.g. λείπω *leípō* ' leave ', aorist ἔλιπον *élipon*; φεύγω *pheúgō* ' flee ', aorist ἔφυγον *éphygon*.

(e) In three aorists, where the underlying vowel is between two obstruents capable of forming a cluster in Greek: ἔσχον *éskhon* ' I had ', ἐσπόμην *espómēn* ' I followed ', ἀνεπτόμην *aneptómēn* ' I flew up '.

If we treat the very few forms in classes (b) and (e) as exceptions to the lowering rule (so that, being non-low, they undergo the deletion rule), we can define an environment in which the lowering rule operates. Assume that readjustment rules have marked certain vowels, both in verbs and nouns, as [+Vowel Weakening]. Assume further that the long vowel in forms of type (c) does not constitute a formative but is an extension of the stem, so that it is not preceded by a formative boundary; this assumption is a reasonable one, since the long vowel may be any of /ē ā ō/ depending on the stem which precedes it,[100] and may be found in any tense except the aorist active and middle. Then the lowering rule can be framed so as to apply to all [+Vowel Weakening] vowels which are not of type (a), type (c) or type (d), i.e. to all such vowels which are

(101) (a) in verbs *and*
      (b) followed by a consonant which
      (c) is followed by another consonant or by a formative boundary.

To a lowering rule so restricted we add a deletion rule like (86), and we have the complete Vowel Weakening rule:

(102)

$$\begin{bmatrix} V \\ -\text{high} \\ +\text{V.W.} \end{bmatrix} \rightarrow \left\{ \begin{array}{l} \begin{bmatrix} +\text{low} \\ +\text{back} \\ -\text{round} \end{bmatrix} / \underline{\quad} C \begin{Bmatrix} C \\ + \end{Bmatrix} X \rrbracket_V \\[2ex] \emptyset \quad / \begin{bmatrix} \underline{\quad} \\ -\text{low} \end{bmatrix} \end{array} \right\}$$

2.2.2.5. *The question of syllabic nasals*

Various alternations in Greek are historical reflexes of an Indo-European positional variation between syllabic and non-syllabic nasals, the latter being represented in Greek by /n/, the former by /a/. Do these alternations give any ground for setting up underlying syllabic nasals for Greek, and if not, how, if at all, are they to be accounted for ?

The alternations in question are concerned mostly with inflexional endings. There is only one relevant alternation in a stem, that of the verb stem /ten/ ' stretch ', from which we find perfect medio-passive τέταμαι [tétamay] and aorist passive ἐτάθην [etátʰęn]. Since these forms (with those of

---

[100] With the various forms from stem /kal/ cited on p. 78 compare κέκραμαι *kékrāmai*, perfect medio-passive of κεράννυμι *keránnȳmi* ' mix ', and ἔστρωμαι *éstrōmai*, perfect medio-passive of /stor/ (aorist ἐστόρεσα *estóresa*) ' spread '. In addition to the tenses so far exemplified, presents and futures can also have long-vowel extensions of the stem: the most usual present from /stor/ is στρώνυμι *strónnȳmi*, and one form of the future of /sekʰ/ ' have ' is σχήσω *skʰḗsō*.

some nouns and adjectives derived from the same stem) stand alone, it seems best to regard them as derived by an early rule of nasal deletion (a minor rule, of course) from ordinary weak-grade forms.

More interesting are the inflexional alternations, both in nouns and verbs. In verbs the first-person singular active ending, where it is not /mi/, is sometimes /a/ and sometimes /n/, and we might think of deriving both of these from an /n/ which, when it followed a consonant, became syllabic and was realized as /a/. The difficulty with this proposal is that the form /a/ of the ending is also found after vowels; at any rate the ending [ǫ] of the 1st sg. present active is analysable as contracted from /oa/, where /o/ is the thematic vowel, and such an analysis removes two anomalies at once.[101] But if /a/ is found after vowels, then the syllabic-nasal proposal will not fully account for the alternation; we will still need to posit at least three different underlying forms for this morpheme, and we will not have simplified the grammar in any way.

In the perfect medio-passive, where the stem ends with a consonant, the usual third-person plural endings /ntay/ (present) and /nto/ (past) are not found. Usually a peri-phrastic form (participle + copula) is used for this person, but there is also found, though rarely, a pair of endings /atay ato/. These occur only and always after consonants, and, if regularly used, would be good evidence for a rule or rules with the effect

(103)   n → a / C——C

But in fact they are used so rarely that it is probably easier to regard them as borrowed from the Ionic dialects, in which they are regular.[102]

This leaves us with the /n/ : /a/ alternations in nouns. These exist in the accusative singular, where /a/ is regular after

---

[101] One anomaly would be that this ending would contain no thematic vowel; the other, that it would be yet a fourth underlying phonological form for this 1st-sg.-active morpheme.

[102] There are other such borrowings in literary Attic, e.g. Thucydides' use of the Ionic clusters σσ *ss*, ρσ *rs* rather than Attic ττ *tt*, ρρ *rr*.

consonants (including the /s/ and /w/ which are eventually deleted) and /n/ after vowels, and also in the accusative plural. In the latter case, first and second declension nouns, whose stems end in vowels, have endings derived from /ns/ (see pp. 25–6), while the ending for consonant-stem nouns is /as/. These alternations do seem to provide some justification for a rule like (103), extended to apply between consonant and major boundary as well as between consonant and consonant.

If a rule like (103) is accepted, there will, in the underlying representations of Greek words, be syllabic nasals. In the lexicon, however, there will be none; syllabicity will continue to be a redundant feature in all consonants. The sequence /CnC/ will occur in phonological representations only when the accusative morpheme /ns/ is preceded by a stem ending in a consonant.

So the answer to the question with which this section began is ' yes and no '. Yes, the underlying representations of certain Greek words contain nasals which, if these forms were pronounced, would have syllabic value. No, there is never, at any level, a syllabicity contrast in nasals, and no lexical entry fulfils either the original or the extended structural conditions of (103).

CHAPTER THREE

THE THEORY OF MARKEDNESS

3.1. *SOME MODIFICATIONS TO THE CHOMSKY-HALLE MARKING CONVENTIONS*

Up to this point, our discussion of Greek phonological processes has been conducted without taking into consideration the theory of Markedness developed by Chomsky and Halle (1968, ch. 9). This theory, as will be seen in section 3.2, has considerable advantages and few drawbacks as a partial explanation of some of these processes. The gain, however, is conditional on certain changes being made in the system of marking conventions Chomsky and Halle propose (ib. 404–7). These changes, and the reasons for making them, are as follows.

Conventions (II) and (III) [103] (ib. 404), which I reproduce here, make use of the feature of 'vocalicity', which Chomsky and Halle elsewhere (ib. 354) argue should be replaced by a feature of 'syllabicity'.

$$(104)\ (\text{II})\ [103a] \quad [\text{u cons}] \rightarrow \begin{cases} [+\text{cons}] / \begin{cases} \left\{ \begin{bmatrix} -\text{seg} \end{bmatrix} \\ \begin{bmatrix} +\text{voc} \\ -\text{cons} \end{bmatrix} \right\} \text{---} \\ \begin{bmatrix} \text{---} \\ -\text{voc} \end{bmatrix} \end{cases} \begin{matrix} (a) \\ (b) \\ (c) \end{matrix} \\ [-\text{cons}] / \begin{bmatrix} \text{---} \\ +\text{voc} \end{bmatrix} \quad (d) \end{cases}$$

[103] Unless otherwise stated, capital Roman numerals in parentheses refer to the conventions so numbered by Chomsky and Halle (1968, 404–7).

[103a] The Markedness theory holds that phonological features are not in general symmetrical: that for each feature in each environment, one of its possible values is more normal, more 'unmarked', than the other. Features are therefore supposed to be entered in the lexicon with their coefficients given, not as + or −, but as *m* (marked) or *u* (unmarked), and one of the functions of the so-called marking conventions is to interpret these *m* and *u* specifications as + and − specifications.

A marking convention is typically stated in the form

(i) $$[\text{uF}] \rightarrow [\alpha\text{F}] / X \begin{bmatrix} \text{---} \\ Z \end{bmatrix} Y$$

where F is a feature. Stating that [uF] is interpreted as [αF] implies that [mF] is interpreted as [−αF].

The other use of marking conventions is as 'linking rules' (see beginning of section 3.2). If there is a marking convention

$$(\text{III}) \quad [\text{u voc}] \rightarrow \begin{cases} [+\text{voc}] / \quad \text{C} \underline{\quad\quad} \\ \\ [-\text{voc}] / \begin{cases} \begin{bmatrix} \underline{\quad\quad} \\ +\text{cons} \end{bmatrix} \\ \begin{Bmatrix} [-\text{seg}] \\ \text{V} \end{Bmatrix} \underline{\quad\quad} \end{cases} \end{cases} \begin{matrix} (a) \\ \\ (b) \\ (c) \\ (d) \end{matrix}$$

These conventions were intended to define relative marked-ness among the four major classes of segments. If consonantality and vocalicity are regarded as the 'major class features', these four classes are vowels, glides, liquids, and so-called true consonants. If, however, syllabicity is used rather than vocalicity, then the four major classes are vowels, glides, ordinary consonants, and syllabic consonants.[104] The conventions of (104) naturally have consequences for the relative markedness, in various environments, of the four classes of segments they define. For initial, postvocalic and post-consonantal position these consequences are:

$$(105)^{\,105} \qquad \begin{bmatrix} \text{u cons} \\ \text{u voc} \end{bmatrix} \quad \begin{bmatrix} \text{u cons} \\ \text{m voc} \end{bmatrix} \quad \begin{bmatrix} \text{m cons} \\ \text{u voc} \end{bmatrix} \quad \begin{bmatrix} \text{m cons} \\ \text{m voc} \end{bmatrix}$$

$[-\text{seg}]$ —	true cons.	liquid	glide	vowel
C ——	vowel	true cons.	liquid	glide
V ——	true cons.	liquid	glide	vowel

[note 103a continued]

(ii) $\qquad\qquad [\text{uF}] \rightarrow [a\text{F}] / \text{X} \begin{bmatrix} \underline{\quad\quad} \\ \overset{\cdots}{\beta\text{G}} \\ \cdots \end{bmatrix} \text{Y}$

(where G is a feature distinct from F), and if some phonological rule gives feature G the value β in an environment such that the other conditions of (ii) are satisfied, then that rule is said to *link* to (ii), and feature F in the segment in question automatically takes the value a unless the phonological rule explicitly says (at a cost of one extra unit of complexity) that it shall not. As we shall see in section 3.2, linking rules allow many rules of the phonology to be simplified.

Later on we shall be putting linking rules to another use in phonology; a formal definition of the effect of linking rules for this purpose will be found on p. 168.

[104] The division between the last two classes cuts across that between 'true' consonants and liquids.

[105] The symbols V and C in this book normally stand for 'syllabic' and 'non-syllabic' respectively; but in a system, such as that implied by (105), which does not use the syllabicity feature, V refers to all segments which are vocalic and non-consonantal, i.e. vowels, and C to all other segments.

There is nothing obviously wrong with (105);[106] but once the feature ' syllabic ' is recognized, it demands the principal place in what is, after all, supposed to be an account of ' the universal constraints on syllable structure ' (Chomsky and Halle 1968, 408); for, unlike all other features, it is actually defined in terms of syllable structure.[107]

I therefore propose that the marking conventions should first specify the value of the feature ' syllabic ' and then use this to predict the value of the feature ' consonantal '. The most obvious proposal is that the unmarked value of ' syllabic ' should be minus initially or after a vowel, and plus after a consonant; this is to claim that an alternation of syllabics and non-syllabics is more normal than sequences of two or more of either.

As for the feature ' consonantal ', in (105) ' true ' consonants are always more unmarked than glides, and this will likewise be true as between our classes of non-syllabic consonants and

[106] It might seem that the Semitic languages constitute a standing reproach both to (105) and to (106) and (107) below; for on the usual analysis, as Cairns (1969, 883) points out, virtually all stem morphemes in these languages are highly marked with respect to the feature ' vocalic ' (or ' syllabic ', as the case may be), since they consist entirely of consonants. There must, however, be some doubt about the validity of this analysis. It requires not merely lexical morphemes of an unusual form, but also an unusual type of readjustment rule to get the lexical and grammatical morphemes combined – and the output of all this is a set of representations which are quite normal from the point of view of general phonology ! Is is not possible that Semitic stems should be analysed as containing, in their underlying forms, unspecified or unmarked vowels, which readjustment rules then specify, alter or delete, according to grammatical category ? Nor are all the vowels, even in verbs, predictable by rule; in Biblical Hebrew, for example (see, e.g. Weingreen 1959, 97), if a verb is stative, it may have any one of three stem vowels (e.g. zāqēn ' was old ', qāṭōn ' was small ', gādal ' was great '). The most natural way for the necessary lexical information to be given is for the stem vowel itself to be indicated in the lexical entries for these verbs; but this is impossible if the lexical matrices for verb stem morphemes are assumed not to contain any vowels.

[107] See Chomsky and Halle's characterization of it (1968, 354) as ' constituting a syllabic peak '—although they do not define the term ' syllabic peak '.

glides. Among syllabics, there can be no doubt that vowels are unmarked as against syllabic consonants: some languages have been said to lack vowel contrasts, but they are very few, and the interpretation of the facts has been disputed,[108] whereas it is certain that many languages have no syllabicity contrast in consonants.

These proposals can be summarized in the pair of conventions (106), which are together considerably simpler and less repetitive than (104). Like (104), they are intended to apply in the order given between Chomsky-Halle conventions (I) and (IV).

$$(106) \quad [u \text{ syll}] \rightarrow \begin{Bmatrix} [-\text{syll}] / \begin{Bmatrix} [-\text{seg}] \\ [+\text{syll}] \end{Bmatrix} \underline{\quad} \\ [+\text{syll}] / \quad [-\text{syll} \underline{\quad} \end{Bmatrix}$$

$$[u \text{ cons}] \rightarrow [\alpha \text{ cons}] / \begin{bmatrix} \underline{\quad} \\ -\alpha \text{ syll} \end{bmatrix}$$

These conventions result in the following pattern of relative markedness:

(107)

	$\begin{bmatrix} u \text{ syll} \\ u \text{ cons} \end{bmatrix}$	$\begin{bmatrix} u \text{ syll} \\ m \text{ cons} \end{bmatrix}$	$\begin{bmatrix} m \text{ syll} \\ u \text{ cons} \end{bmatrix}$	$\begin{bmatrix} m \text{ syll} \\ m \text{ cons} \end{bmatrix}$
$[-\text{seg}]$ —	consonant	glide	vowel	syllabic cons.
C ———	vowel	syllabic cons.	consonant	glide
V ———	consonant	glide	vowel	syllabic cons.

In languages where vowels are traditionally distinguished as long and short, generative phonological analysts have often interpreted the distinction as one of tenseness. This is so, for

---

[108] The languages in question are Abaza (Allen, 1965), Kabardian (Kuipers, 1960; 1969), and Wishram (Hockett 1955, 84). The analyses suggested by these scholars, and similar analyses proposed for pre- or proto-Indo-European, are challenged by Szemerényi (1964; 1967) and Halle (1970).

example, in Chomsky and Halle's (1968) analysis of the English vowel system. Can what is usually termed the length distinction in Greek be interpreted in the same way ?

If it were, it would clash with another claim made by Chomsky and Halle which seems to have some empirical justification. In their convention (XII) Chomsky and Halle (1968, 405) claim that tense vowels are unmarked as against lax ones; and more recently Lass (1969) has supported this claim with a new interpretation of the restructuring of the Latin vowel system between Classical Latin and Proto-Romance. The claim would be very curious from the point of view of Greek, if Greek were to be analysed as having a tenseness contrast in vowels. For short vowels far outnumber long ones in non-alternating lexical forms; and in forms which alternate, the vowel is always long in some one specific category [109] and short in all other contexts, so that the natural treatment is to leave it short in the lexicon and lengthen it (by the Vṛddhi rule) in the appropriate environments.[110]

This is hard to reconcile with the fairly well motivated convention (XII) – so long, that is, as we assume that the contrast in Greek was basically one of tenseness. But it is also possible that, as the Greek grammarians themselves thought,[111] the relevant feature for the contrast in Greek was length. This hypothesis is more than merely a way of reconciling convention (XII) with the facts of Greek; for it simultaneously accounts for another phenomenon, one distinguishing Greek from English, German and Latin, languages where the contrast is (or, in the case of Latin, is presumed to be) primarily one of

---

[109] See pp. 71–73, on Vṛddhi, for examples.

[110] Even at the most superficial level the preponderance of short vowels is evident. Counting *eu*, *au*, *oi*, and *yi* as sequences of short vowel plus glide, but *ei* and *ou* as long vowels (in accordance with their pronunciation), there are 23 long vowels among the first 100 vowels in Thucydides, book 1; 41 among the first 100 in Plato, *Phaedo*; and 37 among the first 100 in Demosthenes, *On the Crown*.

[111] They regularly speak of the distinction as one of ' time ', using, e.g. the term δίχρονα *dikhrona* ' two-timed ' for the letters α ι υ, which can stand for either a long or a short vowel (Allen 1968, 85).

tenseness. This is that there is not in Greek, as there is in these languages, evidence that the short vowels were pronounced in a less extreme (more mid and more central) position than the corresponding long vowels. Such a difference is frequently found where there is a tenseness contrast,[112] but would not be expected to accompany a length contrast apart from tenseness.

I therefore suggest that the main feature, other than features of tongue and lip position, distinguishing vowels in Greek is not tenseness [113] but length, and that where length is distinctive its unmarked value is minus.[114] The question now arises how the marking conventions should be modified to incorporate this proposal. We might simply add a new convention

(108) [u long] → [−long]

But the mere juxtaposition of this and Chomsky-Halle convention (XII) is somewhat unsatisfactory. What we really want to say is that where length is distinctive and tenseness redundant, the unmarked vowel is short; where tenseness is distinctive and length redundant, the unmarked vowel is tense (and incidentally long). This is a problem already noted in connection with voicing by Postal (1968, 184–5), that the unmarked value of the same feature in the same environment may be different according as the feature is distinctive or redundant in that environment. A solution can be found by allowing some marking conventions to apply only when the feature they control is distinctive. More precisely, I propose that phonological theory should allow conventions of the form

(109) [mF) → [aF] / X —— Y

The interpretation of (109) is defined to be the same as that of

(110) [uF] → [−aF] / X —— Y

[112] See Chomsky and Halle (1968, 324–5).

[113] If tenseness was non-distinctive, then, according to convention (XII), all vowels should have been tense. Some support for the view that this may have been so may perhaps be found in the fact that though Greek has had a stress accent for about 1,600 years, unstressed vowels have firmly resisted reduction to schwa.

[114] In consonants, of course, as well as vowels.

except that (109) only applies *just in case the lexicon contains some segments specified as* [mF] *in the context* X —— Y. This will make it possible to state the following three conventions, in the order given, for length and tenseness:

(111) (a) [m long] → [+long]

(b) [u tense] → [+ tense]

(c) [u long] → [α long] / $\left[\overline{}_{\alpha \text{ tense}} \right]$

Convention (111a) will operate only if there is a length contrast; after it has applied, (111b), assuming no tenseness contrast, will make all vowels tense (cf. note 113), and (111c) will have no segments to apply to, since all will have been marked plus or minus for length by (111a). If, on the other hand, there is only a tenseness contrast and no length contrast, (111a) will not apply, and after (111b) has defined [+tense] as the normal value, (111c) will make length agree with tenseness.

Whether (111a) really has universal validity is a question whose resolution requires evidence from present-day languages in which there is a length contrast without, or independently of, a tenseness contrast in vowels.[115]

Chomsky-Halle conventions (XIII) and (XIV) are based on a feature system including vocalicity as a major feature. If syllabicity is used instead, the class of ' true ' consonants comes to include liquids as well as nasals, so that at first sight it seems that nasality ceases to be a suitable feature for dividing this class into two major subclasses, and that it would be preferable to use sonorancy for this purpose. If this is done, however, one of the two major subclasses will consist of nasals

[115] It is possible that Finnish is such a language; at any rate it is stated that ' one can observe no qualitative difference between short and long vowels in educated speech ' (Hakulinen 1961, 11; cf. Aaltio 1964, 15). And short vowels appear to be far commoner than long vowels in Finnish text; counting *uo, ie* and *yö* as long vowels, and ignoring diphthongs entirely, of the first 100 vowels in the two longest paragraphs of the ' Suomen historiaa vuosilukuina ' given by Aaltio (1964, 275–7), 15 and 17, respectively, are long vowels. Thus if Finnish is admitted as a witness, it tends to confirm (111a).

and liquids, and it is far from clear which of these two types of consonant is unmarked as against the other. This difficulty could be avoided by not having a marking convention for nasality at all; it can also, however, be avoided, and the number of features that have to be given a value other than ' unmarked ' in the lexicon considerably reduced,[116] by giving priority, with Chomsky and Halle, to nasality over sonorancy in the feature hierarchy. Our conventions for these two features will then be (112a, b), of which the first is identical with Chomsky-Halle convention (XIII).

(112) (a) [u nas] → [−nas]

(b) [u son] → [α son] / $\begin{bmatrix} \underline{} \\ \alpha \text{ nas} \end{bmatrix}$ [117]

This decision has empirical consequences. It results in the claim being made that a rule changing the value of nasality will (unless specially stated otherwise) change the value of sonorancy as well; i.e. that it is more normal for a nasal to change (whether by a rule of a grammar, or in the course of linguistic history) to an obstruent non-nasal stop than to a sonorant non-nasal stop (which is obviously correct since sonorant non-nasal stops are impossible by definition); and also that it is more normal for a plosive to change to a sonorant nasal than to an obstruent nasal − which is also correct,

[116] If the first division of the class of ' true ' consonants is into obstruents and sonorants, it should surely be provided that the unmarked consonant is an obstruent. (Sample checks suggest that about 60% of consonants in running Greek text are obstruents; the proportion in French and in English (pronounced ' r-fully ') is almost exactly the same, and in Finnish, Hebrew and Swahili text obstruents averaged 60%, 56% and 54% respectively.) Thus on this hypothesis all liquids and nasals will be marked for sonorancy, and, if there is no marking convention for nasality, they will further be marked plus or minus for that feature. Under conventions (112a, b), on the other hand, nasals will be marked for nasality and unmarked for sonorancy, while liquids will be unmarked for nasality and marked for sonorancy. Thus the saving in the number of marked features in the lexicon will be equal to the whole number of nasals and liquids in all lexical matrices. On both hypotheses, obstruents would be unmarked for both features.

[117] For the possible existence of obstruent nasals cf. Chomsky and Halle (1968, 317, note 20).

G

obstruent nasals, if they exist at all, not being found in very many languages, whereas sonorant nasals occur in almost all.

Although from the available evidence a good deal can safely be inferred about the pronunciation of the Greek plosives, it is hardly possible to say now by exactly what production feature the ' plain voiceless ' stops /p t k/ were distinguished from the ' voiced ' stops /b d g/. The distinguishing feature may well have been tenseness, as, according to Chomsky and Halle (1968, 328), it is in Spanish; but there can be no certainty that this was so, and to avoid confusion I will call the distinguishing feature voicing, without thereby intending to claim that it was in fact the feature which Chomsky and Halle (ibid.) so designate. I assume that, as in English and Hindi (ibid.), the aspirated stops were [+heightened subglottal pressure] – or, as we usually abbreviate it, [+hsp].

The only convention in the Chomsky-Halle set dealing with this group of features is (XXI). Another is needed for the feature ' hsp '. It is fairly clear that the unmarked value for this feature is minus; there is perhaps no language with only aspirated stops, whereas French, Spanish and many other languages have no aspirated consonants at all.[118]

Chomsky-Halle convention (XXIVa) claims that the unmarked obstruent in initial position before a consonant is a fricative. No evidence is given to justify this claim, and I do not see how it can be upheld as far as position before sonorants is concerned. In Greek, indeed, the one fricative, /s/, cannot even occur in initial position before a sonorant consonant other than /m/, whereas initial stop-sonorant clusters are common.

The claim that *is* supported by the facts of Greek is that the unmarked obstruent in initial position before a *plosive* is a fricative; for, although Greek has initial clusters /pt kt pʰtʰ

---

[118] Furthermore, in languages where there is an aspiration contrast, the unaspirated consonants have almost always been found to be in a majority where studies of text frequency have been made. See, for instance, Zipf (1932, 5) (Chinese) and Greenberg (1966, 64–66) (Chiricahua). For Greek, checks of voiceless stops at the beginning of the three works mentioned in note 110 showed that on average 15% of voiceless labial stops were aspirated, 15% of dentals, and 20% of velars.

kᴴtᴴ bd/, they are rare compared with /st stᴴ sd/, and before non-dental stops an initial obstruent can only be /s/. In revised convention (XXIV′) below I do not go beyond this claim.

I now summarize the conventions discussed since p. 85, where they differ from the Chomsky-Halle conventions. A Roman numeral followed by a prime indicates that the convention in question is intended to *replace* the Chomsky-Halle convention of the same number. A Roman numeral followed by a lower case letter indicates that the convention is intended to apply immediately *after* the Chomsky-Halle convention designated by the Roman numeral.

(113) [m long] → [+long]   (XII′ i)

[u tense] → [+tense]   (XII′ ii)

$$[\text{u long}] \rightarrow [\alpha \text{ long}] / \left[\begin{array}{c} \overline{} \\ \alpha \text{ tense} \end{array} \right] \quad \text{(XII′ iii)}$$

$$[\text{u son}] \rightarrow [\alpha \text{ son}] / \left[\begin{array}{c} \overline{} \\ \alpha \text{ nas} \end{array} \right] \quad \text{(XIV′)}$$

[u hsp] → [−hsp]   (XXIb)

$$[\text{u cont}] \rightarrow \left\{ \begin{array}{l} [+\text{cont}] / [-\text{seg}] \underline{} \left[\begin{array}{c} -\text{son} \\ -\text{cont} \end{array} \right] \\ [-\text{cont}] \end{array} \right\}$$
(XXIV′)

3.2. *THE EFFECT OF THE THEORY ON SOME PHONOLOGICAL RULES*

The object of this section is to determine whether the effect of the theory of Markedness and linking rules on the system of phonological rules for Greek is a simplifying or a complicating effect. What a linking rule does is specify a segment for a feature or features for which the segment was not specified by the phonological rule which directly or indirectly brought the linking rule into operation. The use of linking rules *simplifies* a grammar to the extent that linking rules correctly predict feature specifications which would otherwise have had to be specially mentioned in phonological rules. If this happens, not only is the grammar made shorter, but certain phenomena, which would otherwise have had to be stated ad hoc in the particular grammar (possibly several times), are shown to be a function of universal constraints. On the other hand, a given set of linking rules *complicates* grammars to the extent that extra specifications have to be added to phonological rules to prevent linking rules from operating.

For instance,[119] the ' First Velar Palatalization ' of Slavonic being the kind of change it was, the theory of linking rules, so far as this rule is concerned, simplifies the grammars of Slavonic languages; if, however, Slavonic /k g x/ in the relevant environment had developed not (as they did) to palato-alveolars [č ǰ š] but to true palatals [k_1 g_1 ç], the theory would have had a complicating effect. For if that had been the development, then in a theory *not* making use of Markedness the simplest rule to state it would have been (114):

$$(114) \quad [-\text{ant}] \rightarrow [-\text{back}] \, / \, \underline{\quad\quad} \begin{bmatrix} -\text{cons} \\ -\text{back} \end{bmatrix}$$

but if linking rules were used, it would have been necessary to add to the structural change of (114) at least the feature [−coronal], in order to block convention (XXIIIb). In this case the theory of Markedness implies that the actual and not the hypothetical Slavonic situation is the more typical of what happens in languages generally.

Let us now investigate the effect of the theory on the phonological rules of Greek, beginning with some that can be simplified with its help.

1. *Epenthesis* (see pp. 63–5) This rule was previously stated in the form

$$(115) \quad \emptyset \rightarrow a \, / \, [+\text{cons}] \begin{bmatrix} +\text{cons} \\ +\text{son} \end{bmatrix} \underline{\quad\quad} [-\text{son}]$$

---

[119] This example is taken from Chomsky and Halle (1968, 423).

which seems a simple enough rule until it is remembered that
the symbol ' a ' is in fact an abbreviation for

(116)

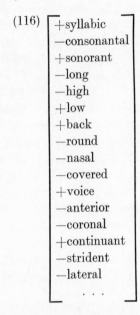

+syllabic
—consonantal
+sonorant
—long
—high
+low
+back
—round
—nasal
—covered
+voice
—anterior
—coronal
+continuant
—strident
—lateral
. . .

and, in a non-Markedness theory, would have to be assigned the
degree of complexity corresponding to the specification of all
these features plus the other features covered by the etcetera
sign in (116).

The theory of linking rules enables us to reduce (116) to

(117) [+syllabic]

– all the other features being given by universal conventions.
That is, according to the theory, if an epenthesis rule inserts a
vowel, that vowel will automatically be [a] unless otherwise
stated.

Note that under the pre-Markedness theory, in any given
environment, an epenthesis rule could insert any vowel or
consonant whatever, with no variation in the cost to the
complexity of the grammar. Thus, if in the environment of
(115) a labial implosive consonant had been inserted instead of

[a], the rule would not have been any more ' expensive '. This was a serious inadequacy in the old theory.[120,121]

2. *Augmentation* (see pp. 61–63) As with the rule just discussed, the [e] introduced by the second part of rule (83) would, under the pre-Markedness theory, have had to be specified for twenty or more features. Under the Markedness theory, it seems that three ought to be sufficient – [+syll, −back, −high].

But there is a difficulty. According to the theory of linking rules (Chomsky and Halle 1968, 420), a linking rule comes into operation only when a feature specification *which is part of its environment* is introduced by a phonological rule. The only one of the eight conventions for vowels in the Chomsky-Halle set which thus links to the proposed version of the Augmentation rule is (XIa); so that the existing theory of linking rules would supply the added vowel with only one of the many feature specifications it needs to become fully specified. The fact is that the theory was not designed to be used in connection with rules which introduce segments, and so, if it is to be so used, a new account of such rules is needed.

The natural, and I think correct, proposal is that in all rules of the form

$$(118) \quad \emptyset \to U_1, \ldots, U_n \, / \, Y \underline{\quad\quad} Z$$
$$(n \geqslant 1)$$

(where each U_i is a unit, i.e. a single column of specified features) each U_i must be fully specified *with m and u markings*, which are then interpreted by the marking conventions as

---

[120] There is more to the matter of epenthesis rules than this: see the next subsection.

[121] This statement does not depend on the acceptance of a feature-counting simplicity metric. P. H. Matthews, in a seminar at Cambridge, has criticized the assumption that such a metric is the appropriate evaluation measure for grammars. Nevertheless, whatever evaluation measure is used, it must be such as to rank epenthesis of [a] in the environment of (115) above epenthesis of [6]; and a theory that requires [a] in such a rule to be represented as (116) is in effect claiming that it is quite accidental that the introduced segment is [a] rather than anything else; whereas, as we have said, according to the Markedness theory [a] is the segment type whose introduction was most to be expected.

+ and — specifications. Thus for rules which introduce units, the marking conventions will not function as linking rules, but rather in the same way in which they operate on lexical matrices. If we further agree that in each U_1 in a rule of the form (118), every feature not mentioned is understood to be marked as u, we can arrange for the [e] of the ' syllabic ' augment to be introduced as

(119) $\begin{bmatrix} \text{m syll} \\ \text{m high} \\ -\text{back} \end{bmatrix}$

which the conventions will interpret as [e].[122]

3. *Fricative Weakening* (pp. 8–14) Rule (8) makes the changes involved seem remarkable for their complexity. There are two different changes, in which /s/ is represented as changing seven and five features respectively. If this were really how the rule ought to be stated, one would expect the probability of such changes as these to be vanishingly small, and it would be almost incredible that the more apparently complex of the two, the seven-feature change, should also have taken place (though in different environments) in Sanskrit and in certain American Spanish dialects.[123]

With the help of the theory of linking rules we can replace the seven-feature output description of the first half of (8) by

(120) $\begin{bmatrix} -\text{cons} \\ +\text{low} \end{bmatrix}$

The first part of (120) specifies that the output is a glide; [124]

---

[122] The vowel is [m syll] because of the major boundary which always immediately precedes the augment. In general, throughout the marking conventions, it must be assumed that what is true when part of the environment is a formative boundary remains true for word boundary, and the intermediate boundary =, also. This is a notable distinction between these conventions and ordinary phonological rules; in the latter, formative and word boundaries typically have quite different effects.

[123] See Gonda (1966, 12); Hockett (1958, 433–4).

[124] A glide, not a vowel; recall that in the feature system we are using, syllabicity is the highest feature in the hierarchy, and consequently no rule can ever alter its value unless syllabicity is explicitly mentioned in the rule.

this ensures, by Chomsky-Halle convention (XXXV), that it is sonorant, non-anterior and non-coronal.[125] The second part of (120) is in effect an instruction not to operate convention (XXXVI); but it itself triggers the convention stated twice by Chomsky and Halle as (IX) and (XVII).[126]

As for the output description of the second, nasalizing part of (8), this can be reduced to simply [+nas], thus turning this part of Fricative Weakening into a simple assimilation rule. The rule links to our convention (XIV') (p. 91), specifying the nasal as sonorant, and to Chomsky-Halle convention (XV), specifying it in addition as non-continuant and non-strident. The Chomsky-Halle conventions do not provide for the specification of voicing in nasals; all that is needed, however, is the following generalization of their convention (XXI) for consonants:

$$(121) \quad [\text{u voice}] \rightarrow [\alpha \text{ voice}] / \left[\begin{array}{c} \underline{} \\ \alpha \text{ son} \end{array} \right]$$

4. *K-Addition* (see pp. 49–50) This is another epenthesis rule, this time introducing [k]. We seem to meet a difficulty in prescribing an appropriate output description for it in a system making use of Markedness; for on our assumption that epenthesis rules should be made to introduce segments specified *m* or *u* for all features for which *m* and *u* specifications are possible, we find that with the otherwise motivated lexical representations for the two negatives, /ow/ and /mē/, we cannot specify the introduced segment correctly for syllabicity: whether we made it [m syll] or [u syll], it would be realized as a vowel after one of the two negatives and a consonant after the other. There are, however, ways of obviating this difficulty: one is to assume /ou/ as the lexical representation of the

---

[125] And no doubt, by an extension of this convention, non-strident also.

[126] It will also trigger convention (XXXVIII), which will ensure that the glide is back. This convention itself, though, is hardly consistent with the table given by Chomsky and Halle (1968, 176–7) showing English /h/ as non-back, nor indeed with their definition of the feature ' back ' (ib. 305) as ' produced with a retraction of the body of the tongue '. Most probably it is convention (XXXVIII) that is wrong, and so I have ignored it in the text.

negative *ou*, and to order K-Addition before Diphthong Formation. Then the only specification needed for the introduced segment, apart from [m seg], will be [m ant]. For the unmarked segment after a vowel is non-syllabic, consonantal, non-nasal, non-sonorant, non-continuant, unvoiced and unaspirated; and once we know that it is [m ant], which for consonants means non-anterior, we can add that the unmarked non-anterior obstruent is also non-coronal.

5. *Fricativization* (see pp. 15–16) As it stands, rule (9) changes three features. Using Chomsky-Halle conventions (XXV) and (XXVIIc), it can be formulated as a rule changing just one feature, continuancy.

6. *Nasalization* (see pp. 21–23) The output description of rule (18) contains four features. Suppose we reduce it to simply [+nas]. Then the assimilated segments will become sonorant by convention (XIV′) and voiced by our convention (121); moreover, Chomsky-Halle convention (XV) admits of a natural extension to make nasals redundantly [−hsp]. The feature of nasality also links to Chomsky-Halle convention (XXIIIc), which states, among other things, that /n/ is the unmarked nasal, and, if applied, would convert the [m] which is one possible output of (18) to [n], which is incorrect. Here, however, we see a confirmation of the principle (Chomsky and Halle, 1968, 431) that ' a linking rule applies either to all or to none of the segments formed by a given rule '; for another output of (18) is [ŋ], and [ŋ] does not meet the structural description of convention (XXIIIc); therefore, because of the principle mentioned, the convention is in this case barred from applying even to those segments which do meet its structural description, so that the [m] which is the output of (18) remains unaltered.[127]

[127] I have ignored the claim made by Chomsky and Halle (1968, 413) that convention (XXIIIc) is so formulated that it cannot in any case function as a linking rule. This claim rests on some kind of confusion. If convention (XXIIIc) cannot function as a linking rule, this can only be because part of its environment includes a feature specified as *m*. But ' convention (XXIIIc) ' is in fact an abbreviation for two conventions:

[*continued on next page*]

There are a number of other cases in Greek where rules are simplified by the theory of linking rules. These, however, do

(i) $[u \text{ cor}] \rightarrow [+\text{cor}] / \begin{bmatrix} +\text{ant} \\ +\text{nas} \end{bmatrix}$

(ii) $[u \text{ cor}] \rightarrow [+\text{cor}] / \begin{bmatrix} +\text{ant} \\ m \text{ cont} \end{bmatrix}$

And while (ii) clearly cannot function as a linking rule, (i) should be able to. Chomsky and Halle claim that this is not so. Presumably the position they hold must be one of the following three:

(iii) In the fully expanded form of the marking conventions, any convention whose environment includes features specified as u or m is incapable of functioning as a linking rule.

(iv) In the fully reduced form of the conventions, any convention forming part of a schema in which some environment description includes features specified as u or m is incapable of functioning as a linking rule.

(v) In the form of the conventions (neither fully expanded nor fully reduced) given on pp. 404–7 of *The Sound Pattern of English*, any convention forming part of a schema marked with a single reference letter such that some environment description in the schema includes features specified as u or m is incapable of functioning as a linking rule.

Chomsky and Halle cannot be intending to claim (iii) since they assert that ' convention ' (XXIIIc) – that is, (i) and (ii) taken together – cannot be a linking rule. Nor can they be intending to claim (iv), since convention (XXIIIc) is part of a larger schema, namely convention (XXIII), and part of the latter schema – (XXIIIb) – plays an essential role as a linking rule in Chomsky and Halle's account (1968, 422–4, etc.) of the Slavonic palatalizations. It thus seems that they wish to uphold position (v); if so, a statement of the criteria determining the allocation of reference letters would be valuable. If position (v) is regarded, as surely it must be, as incoherent, then the only position remaining, consistent with all the facts mentioned by Chomsky and Halle, is (iii). If (iii) is accepted, it will follow that (i) – though not (ii) – will be capable of functioning as a linking rule. This, together with the restriction on the applicability of linking rules mentioned on p. 97, amounts to a hypothesis that when a rule applying only to [+anterior] segments makes them nasal, it is more to be expected that they will all become dental than that the previously labial segments will remain labial. If, in languages where such rules exist, the predicted consequence is not in general found, then something is wrong either with (i), or with the theory of linking rules, or both. Perhaps this is so. It cannot be evaded by pretending that some kind of intermediate position between (iii) and (iv) is tenable without ever stating what that position is. Perhaps, on the other hand, the evidence does support the hypothesis mentioned. In that case the implied acceptance of position (v) by Chomsky and Halle is not only incoherent but also unnecessary.

not illustrate any further points of principle, and I shall now pass to consider those rules which the theory, in appearance or reality, complicates.

7. *Diphthong Formation* (see p. 61) can in a non-Markedness theory be expressed very simply as (81). If we are not careful, when this is exposed to the theory of linking rules, the results will be catastrophic. For (81) links to the second half of (106), p. 85, which, if allowed to apply, will specify the output of (81) as a consonant rather than a glide, and then will in turn link to all the conventions for consonants; so that the theory appears to be making the absurd claim that when vowels become non-syllabic, it is most normal for them to go further and become obstruents ! The only way I can see to avoid this result is to establish the metaconvention (122), which in effect predicts that when a vowel becomes a glide, or a consonant syllabic, or vice versa, this change will not normally affect any other features of the segments concerned:

(122) The system of linking rules does not apply to the feature ' syllabic ': that is, a convention whose environment description includes some specification for this feature is not triggered merely by the fact that some phonological rule switches the value of syllabicity.

This will not affect our previous discussion of epenthesis rules; in connection with these the marking conventions do not function as linking rules, but as blank-filling rules.

Do any other features have exemptions of this kind ? I have not found any evidence suggesting that any do; and indeed we have already seen evidence that consonantality, the feature next in the hierarchy after syllabicity, does not; for in (8), as modified by (120), we have used a switch in consonantality to trigger switches in several other features, and we have seen (p. 95) that rules like the first part of (8) are not unknown in other languages. Thus (122) appears to be unique. It will be observed that not only cannot a change in syllabicity ever automatically trigger a change in any other feature, but, since syllabicity is the highest feature in the hierarchy, neither can a change in another feature ever automatically trigger a change in syllabicity. In other words, syllabicity specifications can be altered only if a phonological rule explicitly directs their alteration, and such a rule has of itself no further phonological consequences.

This is a very great difference between syllabicity and all other segmental features; and metaconvention (122) has been criticized on this ground. But this difference is not unreasonable. In an important respect syllabicity does differ from most other features and is similar to the feature ' segment '.[128] Both these features control the number of units of a certain kind into which a phonological string is exhaustively divided – in the one case segments, in the other, syllables. No other feature (except the two universal boundary features) has this property. It is not surprising that syllabicity, like the other three features mentioned, should stand somewhat apart from ordinary phonological processes, and in particular should be exempted from the operation of the theory of linking rules.

8. *Low and mid vowels* Up to now I have been assuming throughout that Greek [ę] and [ǫ] (written η and ω) are derived from underlying /ē ō/, that is, from mid rather than low vowels. The main evidence for this is that they participate in alternations with the short vowels [e o], and that these alternations include some (such as the ' temporal ' augment – see p. 62) which with other vowels appear as alternations of length only. If the two long vowels are underlyingly mid, a rule is needed to lower them, the effect of which must be:

$$(123) \quad \begin{bmatrix} -\text{cons} \\ +\text{long} \\ -\text{high} \end{bmatrix} \rightarrow [+\text{low}]$$

But a rule of this form will link to Chomsky-Halle conventions (X) and (XIb); these conventions will make the low vowels

---

[128] The feature ' segment ' is subject to restrictions far tighter than those of (122); in particular, no phonological rule can ever change its specification, i.e. change a segment into a boundary or vice versa (cf. p. 5).

which are the output of (123) back and non-round, i.e. [ā] –
which is incorrect. This time the principle mentioned on p. 97
will not help us; for both convention (X) and convention (XI)
apply to all vowels, hence to all segments formed by (123).
Thus it seems that the theory of linking rules makes it necessary
to state (123) in the considerably more complex form:

$$(124) \quad \begin{bmatrix} -\text{cons} \\ +\text{long} \\ -\text{high} \\ \alpha \text{ back} \\ \alpha \text{ round} \end{bmatrix} \rightarrow \begin{bmatrix} +\text{low} \\ \alpha \text{ back} \\ \alpha \text{ round} \end{bmatrix}$$

This seems a most unwelcome consequence of the theory.
There is, however, a preferable alternative. All that it is
necessary to assume is that both the short mid vowels [e o]
and the long lower-mid vowels [ę ǭ] are derived from underlying low vowels. On this assumption (124) is unnecessary,
and in its place there must be a rule to raise the short vowels:

$$(125) \quad \begin{bmatrix} +\text{syll} \\ -\text{long} \\ \alpha \text{ back} \\ \alpha \text{ round} \end{bmatrix} \rightarrow [-\text{low}]$$

This rule does not have to state specially that it does not affect
the features ' back ' and ' round ', since it does not trigger any
linking rule; it is therefore preferable.

Thus we are now postulating that the underlying vowel
system for Greek (both for short and for long vowels) is

$$(126) \quad \begin{matrix} i & & u \\ & \\ ę & a & ǫ \end{matrix}$$

At no stage in derivations previous to the application of (125)
are there any mid vowels.[129]

This decision will not have great effects on the rest of the
phonology (except for Contraction, which we will discuss

---

[129] This is, of course, directly contrary to Chomsky and Halle's theory of
' optimal n-vowel systems '. See below, on High Vowel Fronting.

directly), though it will alter the phonological shape of many
lexical items; for there was not in any case any contrast
between low and mid vowels except where this was accompanied by a backness or rounding contrast. It will, however,
alter the way we specify the vowel of the syllabic augment (see
p. 95). This will now be introduced as low instead of a mid
vowel, hence as

$$(127) \quad \begin{bmatrix} \text{m syll} \\ \text{m low} \\ \text{m back} \end{bmatrix};$$

thus its degree of complexity will be the same as before.

9. *Contraction* (see pp. 55–60). In the statement of the
Contraction rule, which we left in the form (78), a problem
arises very similar to that discussed in the previous subsection.
It is soluble in a very similar way, and in fact the two solutions
turn out to be one.

One of the subcases of (78) is the following rule of lowness
assimilation:

$$(128) \quad \begin{bmatrix} V \\ -\text{high} \end{bmatrix} \rightarrow [a \text{ low}] / \begin{bmatrix} V \\ a \text{ low} \\ -\text{high} \end{bmatrix} \begin{bmatrix} \underline{\quad\quad} \\ -\text{low} \end{bmatrix}$$

This is an abbreviation for two rules, one of which always
applies vacuously and the other non-vacuously; the latter is:

$$(129) \quad \begin{bmatrix} V \\ -\text{high} \end{bmatrix} \rightarrow [+\text{low}] / \begin{bmatrix} V \\ +\text{low} \end{bmatrix} \begin{bmatrix} \underline{\quad\quad} \\ -\text{low} \end{bmatrix}$$

This rule, just like (123), should link to conventions (X) and
(XIb), and so all low contracted vowels might be expected to
merge to [ā]—which, as we have already seen, they do not.
Just as in the last subsection, the best solution seems to be to
account for the facts by means not of a lowering but of a
raising rule. This can be done as follows. There is nothing to
prevent (125) from being so placed in the ordering as to apply
just at the point where (128) would otherwise have to apply;
then, if (125) is restricted to the environment complementary

to that of (128), (128) becomes unnecessary. In other words, both (125) and (128), which together cost [129a] eight features, can be replaced by (130), which also costs eight [130] and does not have any unwanted consequences.

$$(130)\ ^{131}\ \begin{bmatrix} V \\ -\text{high} \\ -\text{long} \\ a\ \text{back} \\ a\ \text{round} \end{bmatrix} \rightarrow [-\text{low}]\ /\ \begin{cases} \begin{bmatrix} \begin{bmatrix} -\text{seg} \\ -\text{FB} \end{bmatrix} \end{bmatrix} & (a) \\ [-\text{syll}] \\ [-\text{low}] \end{cases}\ - \begin{matrix} (a) \\ (b) \\ (c) \end{matrix}$$

There is still one problem with (130), namely how it will apply to three-vowel sequences such as /ǫęǫ/ where all three

[129a] The ' cost ' of a rule is simply the number of features required to state it.

[130] Both (128) and (130) are intended to form part of the larger rule schema of Contraction; I have therefore in each case adjusted their ' cost ' to take account of this. The whole Contraction schema applies to non-high vowels, and the two features in question have therefore been ignored in the cost statements of both (128) and (130); in addition, the same two features have been ignored where they occur in the environment description of (128), since they are required in any case for the environment description of other subcases of Contraction.

[131] Like several other rules in this phonology, this rule would be simplified, and the relevant generalization more clearly expressed, if the proposal of Lass (1971) were accepted that major boundaries should be regarded as voiceless obstruents; for this would make environment (a) of (130) a special case of environment (b).

Halle (1971b) has criticized Lass's suggestion on the ground that ' there are attested cases in languages where word boundary functions on a par with a vowel '. Halle's two examples, however, from Southern Paiute and Latvian, are not such cases; in both of them, word boundary functions on a par, not with a vowel, but with a morpheme boundary followed by a vowel; they thus tell neither for nor against Lass's proposal. And Halle's own ' much simpler answer to the whole question ', which is that ' initial word boundary functions on a par with any environment that must be located to the left of the segment subject to the rule, ... final word boundary ... with any environment located to the right ', is no answer at all, since not all rules with left-hand environments can apply word-initially, nor all rules with right-hand environments word-finally, and the distribution of those that can, as Lass has observed, is not haphazard. Further, Halle's proposed solution is rejected by his own simplicity metric; this metric will prefer Halle's rules (2) and (3) to his (5a) and (5b) respectively. I consider therefore that Halle has failed either to substantiate his criticism of Lass or to suggest an acceptable alternative.

vowels meet its input description. The rule consists of three cases, (*a*) (*b*) (*c*),[132] conjunctively ordered; an underlying sequence /o̧ȩo̧/ would emerge from case (*b*) as [oȩo̧] and from case (*c*) as [oeo̧], which by the working of the other contraction rules, including Truncation, would ultimately yield [o̧]. Now such sequences do occur; an example is the first person plural, present, of the verb meaning 'not know', whose underlying form is /a+gno̧+ȩ+o̧+mȩn/. Applying to this the three cases of (130) results in [a+gno+e+o̧+men]. As it happens, in this verb the first of the three adjacent vowels is not deleted; allowing for this, we would expect the pronunciation to have been *[agno̧o̧men], whereas it was in fact [agnoûmen] (ἀγνοοῦμεν).

Thus it is essential to make (130) operate in such a way that it raises *every* vowel in such a sequence, no matter how long the sequence. This can only be done by allowing the rule to reapply to its own output. This is not unique – it will also be necessary for Truncation. It may be that being 'iterable' is an option available to rules generally; most do not reapply to their own output, but some, specially marked, can do so.

I now give a revised version of the Contraction rule, incorporating (130).

(131) CONTRACTION (FINAL VERSION) (Iterable)

$$
\begin{bmatrix} V \\ -high \end{bmatrix} \rightarrow
\left\{
\begin{array}{ll}
[-low] \,/ \left\{ \begin{array}{l} \left\{ \begin{bmatrix} -seg \\ -FB \end{bmatrix} \\ \begin{bmatrix} -syll \\ -low \end{bmatrix} \end{array} \right\} \begin{bmatrix} \underline{\quad} \\ -long \\ \alpha\ back \\ \alpha\ round \end{bmatrix} \\[3mm] o \begin{bmatrix} \underline{\quad} \\ -back \\ +long \end{bmatrix} y \end{array} & (a) \\[8mm]
 & (b) \\[4mm]
\left[\begin{bmatrix} +long \\ \langle \beta\ round \rangle \\ \langle \gamma\ back \rangle \end{bmatrix} \right] \,/ \begin{bmatrix} V \\ -high \\ \langle \beta\ round \rangle \\ \langle \gamma\ back \rangle \end{bmatrix} \begin{bmatrix} \underline{\quad} \\ \langle -round \rangle \\ \langle -back \rangle \end{bmatrix} & (c)
\end{array}
\right\}
$$

---

[132] Or, if the suggestion in the previous note is adopted, of two cases; it makes no difference to the problem under discussion.

10. *High Vowel Fronting* (see pp. 68–9) So far, the apparent problems presented by Markedness for certain rules have been found to be either non-problems or due to defects in the rules themselves. With the last one, to which we now come, it may prove otherwise; it may be that in this case Greek actually had a less than optimal rule. It would of course be hardly surprising if this should prove to be so for one rule in the language.

High Vowel Fronting was previously stated in the simple form (93). In that form, however, it will link to convention (XIa) and incorrectly make the vowel non-round, i.e. send it to [i]. If this is to be avoided, it will not be sufficient merely to add [+round] to the output description of (93), since this would wrongly round underlying /i/ to [ü]; rather the choice must be between (132) and (133):

$$(132) \quad \begin{bmatrix} +\text{syll} \\ +\text{high} \\ +\text{back} \end{bmatrix} \rightarrow \begin{bmatrix} -\text{back} \\ +\text{round} \end{bmatrix}$$

$$(133) \quad \begin{bmatrix} +\text{syll} \\ +\text{high} \\ \alpha \text{ round} \end{bmatrix} \rightarrow \begin{bmatrix} -\text{back} \\ \alpha \text{ round} \end{bmatrix}$$

(93) is, in fact, the rule mentioned by Chomsky and Halle (1968), 433) as less favoured by the theory than a rule that both fronted and unrounded /u/, or a rule that fronted (but did not unround) *all* back vowels. It is, nevertheless, what Greek offers us.

It might be suggested that the complication would be avoided if we were to take /ü/ as the underlying form for the vowel, and /ẅ/ as the underlying form for the glide. No objection could be brought to this on the ground of alternations, since the vowel and glide alternate only with each other. The glide could be altered to [w] by the context-free rule

$$(134) \quad \begin{bmatrix} -\text{cons} \\ -\text{syll} \\ +\text{round} \end{bmatrix} \rightarrow [+\text{back}]$$

This solution accounts for all the relevant facts, and does so at the cost of one feature less than the solution making use of (132) or (133); but its whole cost has not yet been counted. For Markedness principles will necessarily select the simplest vowel and glide systems for use in the lexicon, and these systems will certainly not include /ü/ or /ẅ/. Thus, in order for /ü/ and /ẅ/ to appear in the input to the phonological rules, it would be necessary to have a readjustment rule with precisely the effect of (133) (extended to cover glides as well as vowels); so that the proposed solution requires all the machinery the other analysis requires, and more.

Here we must take up again the question of the theory of ' optimal *n*-vowel systems ' as promised in note 129. For it may be asked: if a special readjustment rule is necessary for an underlying vowel system /i e a o ü/ as suggested in the last paragraph, will one not be equally necessary for the vowel system (126) (p. 101) ? Will we not need a special rule to lower the vowels there represented as /ę ǫ/ before (131a) raises them again ? This will only be so if the theory necessarily selects

(135)   i   u
      e   o
         a

as *the* optimal five-vowel system. The question that is begged is whether the theory ought to do this. Chomsky and Halle (1968, 409) say that it should, but they do not say why, nor indeed why for each value of *n* there should be just one optimal *n*-vowel system. Moreover, the claim (ib. 410, (9)) [133] that ' no vowel segment can be marked for the feature " round " unless some vowel segment in the system is marked for the feature " high " ' ' is a claim that no vowel system can have a rounding contrast unless it also has an underlying three-way height contrast, i.e. that the vowel system of Turkish does not exist.[134] And it is on condition 9 that the further claim is

[133] This claim is hereinafter referred to as ' condition 9 '.
[134] I base this statement on the analysis of the eight-vowel system of Turkish made by Lees (1961, 5). He uses the features ' compact ', ' flat ' and

based that the theory selects (135) as optimal among five-vowel systems.

It is admittedly true that Chomsky and Halle's condition 10 (cf. note 134) favours system (135) over (126). There is, however, something suspicious about the representation of (135) in Markedness terms:

(136)

	a	i	u	e	o
low	u	u	u	u	u
high	u	u	u	m	m
back	u	—	+	—	+
round	u	u	u	u	u

In (136), five vowels are being kept apart by two features, and in particular three (/a i u/) are being distinguished by the single

' grave ', which for vowels correspond to ' low ', ' round ' and ' back ' in Chomsky and Halle's system; his analysis, if translated into Markedness terms, would most naturally appear as

	i	ɨ	ü	u	e	a	ö	o
low	u	u	u	u	m	u	m	m
high	u	u	u	u	u	u	u	u
back	—	+	—	+	m	u	m	u
round	u	m	m	u	u	u	m	m

But this system violates condition 9. That condition could only be satisfied by making highness distinctive, e.g. by treating some one non-high vowel as systematically non-low. It would, of course, be a purely arbitrary choice which this vowel should be; let us suppose that /o/ was chosen. Then the system would be the same as above except for the last column, which would read

	o
low	u
high	m
back	+
round	u

This system is exactly as complex in terms of number of non-unmarked features (thirteen) as the former system, and more complex in terms of Chomsky and Halle's condition 10 (1968, 410), which favours maximization of the number of features that are non-distinctive (i.e. are unmarked in all segments). Nor would any phonologist want to say that Turkish has a three-way height contrast. Yet since roundness is unquestionably distinctive in Turkish, condition 9 requires a three-way height contrast to appear in the system. We may well conclude that condition 9 is a hasty, speculative and thoroughly bad generalization.

feature of backness, which is thus being used as if it were ternary.

One way to avoid this might be to specify backness in non-low as well as in low vowels by a marking convention; but how this could be done is not easy to see.[135] Another way would be to abandon (in spite of subsection 1) the assertion that /a/ is the single most unmarked vowel, i.e. to drop Chomsky-Halle convention (VIa),[136] making the unmarked value of the feature ' low ' minus for all vowels. This would make the representation of system (135):

(137)	a	i	u	e	o
low	m	u	u	u	u
high	u	u	u	m	m
back	u	—	+	—	+
round	u	u	u	u	u

complexity $\quad 1 + 1 + 1 + 2 + 2 = 7$
(= no. of marked features)

and that of system (126):

(138)	a	i	u	ẹ	ọ
low	m	u	u	m	m
high	u	u	u	u	u
back	u	—	+	m	u
round	u	u	u	u	m

complexity $\quad 1 + 1 + 1 + 2 + 2 = 7$

Now Chomsky-Halle condition 10 no longer distinguishes the

[135] The only attempt to do this known to me has been made by Sanford Schane, whose proposal I know from a 1971 Cambridge seminar. It suffers from the drawback that the conventions proposed make back, unrounded vowels maximally unmarked, despite their frequent total absence from vowel systems at all tongue heights except the lowest.

[136] It is remarkable that, in spite of this convention, Chomsky and Halle (1968, 236) are able to propose an underlying system for English of six lax vowels among which /a/ is not included. Nowhere, not even in the discussion of optimal n-vowel systems, do they go back on this proposal, although conditions 9 and 10 would appear to point to a system containing /i e a o u/ plus one of /æ ü ɨ/ as optimal, rather than Chomsky and Halle's system /i e æ ɔ o u/.

two systems; and we have seen that condition 9 cannot be part of an adequate linguistic theory, since it would make a descriptively adequate analysis of the Turkish vowel system impossible.

Consequently, since (126) happens to give the simpler grammar for Greek, we can assume that (126) is the vowel system, both for short and for long vowels, in the lexical representations of Greek. Other languages, of course, may perfectly well have system (135) in their lexical representations.

On the other hand, the vowel system /a i ü ẹ ọ/ rejected on p. 106 would be represented:

(139)	a	i	ü	ẹ	ọ
low	m	u	u	m	m
high	u	u	u	u	u
back	u	—	—	m	u
round	u	u	m	u	m
complexity	$1 + 1 + 2 + 2 + 2 = 8$

which is more complex than either (137) or (138).

Thus we have found that the proposed grammar incorporating rule (134) is wasteful in a way in which the proposed grammar incorporating rule (130) is not. This means that we must accept the underlying vowel system (126) and a rule like (132) or (133), despite the fact that these rules are not optimal as high-vowel-fronting rules.

Except in this one case, use of the ideas of the theory of Markedness has everywhere either simplified the grammar of Greek (in the sense that certain parts of rules have been found not to need stating in the grammar because they are deducible from statements of universal grammar) or suggested rule revisions that do away with apparent complications introduced by the theory. The theory (in the somewhat modified form we have given it) is thus strongly confirmed.

In the next chapter I turn to an aspect of phonological theory where the Markedness hypothesis has up to now had a retrogressive effect.

Chapter Four

ON MORPHEME STRUCTURE RULES

4.1. *THE THEORETICAL PROBLEM* [137]

This is quite simple. An adequate description of a language requires morpheme structure rules or their equivalent, and the current version of the theory of Markedness does not provide them. More fully put, the point is this.

The theory, as presented by Chomsky and Halle (1968), suffers from the grave defect that it implicitly claims that it is unnecessary to characterize the notion ' possible morpheme in language L '. In previous versions of generative phonology, morpheme structure rules, which were needed in any case to fill in feature specifications that were omitted as redundant in lexical representations, defined this notion for each language. Since under the theory of Markedness no feature specifications are omitted in the lexicon or anywhere else, morpheme structure rules are abandoned, [138] with the result that there is no way of accounting within the grammar for the fact that an English speaker knows that /blik/ is a possible English morpheme in a sense in which /bnik/ is not. Yet such knowledge is surely part of his linguistic competence: he has it precisely because he is an English speaker, and a purported grammar of English that fails to account for it fails to that extent to distinguish English from other actual or possible human languages. [139]

[137] Lakoff (1971b, 154–5) notes the problem we are about to discuss, and proposes his own solution. I do not fully understand it, but it seems to be based on the assumption that MS rules must at all costs somehow or other be given a role in the generation of grammatical sentences. It is surely more natural to regard them as conditions on the phonological shape of lexical terms.

[138] Except for a few rules of low generality: see the discussion by Chomsky and Halle (1968, 416).

[139] This failing is also noticed by Cairns (1969, 874): ' There must be some formal way of assuring that a language allowing only +CV . . . stem-initial clusters can NOT have a morpheme whose second segment is marked for consonantality or vocalicity, [if] the first segment is a consonant.' To account for such facts he proposes a universal set of ' neutralization rules ';

Chomsky and Halle (1968, 416) seem to regard this loss of adequacy as some kind of gain; for they assert that ' a real solution to the problem of " admissibility " will not simply define a tripartite categorization of occurring, accidental gap, and inadmissible ', and go on to propose a measure of degree of admissibility.

What makes this proposal unacceptable is that under it there is no form not actually in the lexicon which is *completely* admissible. For every form not in the lexicon some rule can be found to ' distinguish ' it from the lexicon in the sense of Chomsky and Halle (1968, 417), so that its ' distance ' from the lexicon will be greater than zero. Such an approach makes it impossible to account for the kind of linguistic knowledge described on p. 110. What is needed is a way of showing that there is a significant difference in degree of admissibility between /bnik/ and /bnzk/ without having to claim that /blik/ is inadmissible to any degree at all. This can only be done by having, independently of any admissibility measure, a set of rules or conditions for each language defining for that language the notion ' possible morpheme '.

We may regard morpheme structure (MS) rules as generalizations extracted by the language learner from the lexicon and subsequently used to test potential new lexical items [140] for phonological admissibility. They are of one of the three forms posited by Stanley (1967): if-then conditions, positive conditions and negative conditions.[140a]   Features in MS

such rules, or their equivalent, if statable, are necessary (on the principle that if some generalization can be shown to be universal, it should not be stated in particular grammars) but cannot of course be sufficient to state all the restrictions on possible morphemes in individual languages. The present treatment ignores the question whether any of the rules discussed are universals.

[140] The typical case of a potential new lexical item is simply a word heard for the first time, whose phonological representation has to be reconstructed on the basis of an imperfect auditory impression of an articulatory implementation of its phonetic representation.

[140a] An ' if-then ' condition is of the form

(i) X   A   Y

↓

B   [continued on next page]

conditions are specified plus or minus, not *m* or *u*; the procedure for determining whether a potential new lexical item is phonologically admissible is as follows:

> (140) Use the universal marking conventions to convert
>   the *m* and *u* markings in the candidate matrix to
>   plus and minus specifications. Submit the result
>   (called the *interpreted candidate matrix* or ICM) to
>   the MS conditions. If it meets all positive conditions
>   and no negative conditions, and if there is no if-then
>   condition of which it meets the ' if ' description
>   without meeting the ' then ' description, then the
>   ICM is phonologically acceptable. Otherwise, use
>   the Chomsky-Halle distance measure to determine
>   its degree of inadmissibility.

A question that has become traditional in connection with MS rules and conditions is: which of the indefinite number of possible sets of such rules for any one language is the optimal set ? Which MS rules express significant generalizations ? The criterion formerly used, which was based on the saving of feature specifications in lexical matrices (see, e.g. Chomsky and Halle's account, 1968, 381), is unworkable under the Markedness theory. Another evaluation measure is proposed by Stanley (1967, 434–5), but it does not adequately tackle the problem of the effect of exceptions.[141] In an earlier version of

and is interpreted ' If in any morpheme in the lexicon a segment with the feature(s) A occurs in the environment X—Y, it must also have the feature(s) B '. XAY is called the *if description* of the condition, and B the *then description*.

Positive and negative MS conditions are stated as strings of feature complexes. A positive condition is one that must be matched by every morpheme in the lexicon; a negative condition is one that may not be matched by any morpheme in the lexicon.

[141] Indeed, Stanley's whole attitude to exceptions is unsatisfactory. He discusses them (1967, 431), but apparently without realizing that he has so formulated and interpreted his ' true generalization condition ' (ib. 421) that under it MS rules or conditions would not be allowed to have exceptions. Since, however, it is quite clear (as Stanley elsewhere admits) that exceptions to MS rules or conditions *must* be allowed, it follows that the true generalization condition cannot be a correct constraint to impose on MS components. Its

this work (Sommerstein 1971) I suggested a modification of Stanley's measure, incorporating a penalty to be added to the cost of an MS rule for each violation of it in the lexicon; a proposed MS rule would then be included in the grammar just in case its cost, including any penalties, was less than its ' generality index' (see Stanley, loc. cit.). Detailed work on Greek morpheme structure, however, shows that this proposal too is unworkable, and I now think it is not possible to determine by means of an evaluation measure whether a grammar does or does not contain a particular MS rule. For the application of such a measure requires knowledge of the total contents of the lexicon; this raises a number of questions, for example: can most speakers be presumed to have such knowledge ? is the content of a speaker's lexicon that of his active or of his passive vocabulary ? etc.

If not an evaluation measure, though, what criterion *do* we have for deciding which rules to include in an MS component and which not to ? The same, surely, as we use in syntax: acceptability to a native speaker of test-generated structures. It follows from this that with a dead language, complete certainty about the MS component is unattainable.

Nevertheless, I shall now investigate part of the MS component of Greek, to illustrate something of the form and effect of MS conditions viewed as constraints on the lexicon.

4.2. *SOME MS RULES FOR GREEK*

The rules I shall be concerned with are those dealing with the permitted shapes of morpheme-initial consonant clusters. Some of them, of course, may be of wider application.

1. *Consonantality* The place of glides in lexical representations in Greek is somewhat marginal, except for /h/, which can

abandonment does not lay the grammar open to ' specious simplifications '. The other constraints imposed by Stanley, that MS rules or conditions must be unordered and that they must be regarded only as defining and restricting the class of possible lexical matrices in the language, and not as filling in the cells left blank in such matrices, are sufficient to prevent this; neither of these constraints is incompatible with the existence of exceptions.

occur by itself as an initial cluster.[142] Otherwise there are a few verbs (discussed on p. 18) which might be analysed as having an underlying initial high glide; but, for the reasons stated in note 23, they are perhaps best treated as having an initial vowel underlyingly, as they do phonetically.

There are also the words that phonetically begin with [zd]. In medial position this combination must often be taken as derived from /dy/ or /gy/;[143] should this also be done in initial position ? Probably not; for there is another possible underlying representation for [zd], namely /sd/; and whereas there are many other initial clusters of /s/ plus a stop, viz. /sp st sk sp^h st^h sk^h sb/, so that /sd/ fits into a well-established pattern, there would be no parallels for a set of lexical items beginning with a consonant plus a glide, with one exception.

The exception is the name of the god Zeus. This has, in the nominative, the form Ζεύς [zdéws], but the oblique cases appear to be based on a stem /diw/, e.g. the genitive is Διός [diós]. These two divergent sets of forms can both be derived from an underlying stem /dyęw/: in the oblique cases this is subject to Vowel Weakening, resulting in a derived stem /dyw/, which then undergoes the following GLIDE VOCALIZATION rule:

(141) $[-\text{cons}] \rightarrow [+\text{syll}] \, / \, [-\text{syll}] \mathop{\text{------}} [-\text{syll}]$

Thus the derivation of Διός [diós] is:

(142) /dyęw+ǫs/ → (Vowel Weakening)
　　　　dyw+ǫs → (Glide Vocalization)
　　　　diw+ǫs → (Glide Deletion)
　　　　di+ǫs → (Contraction (a))
　　　　[dios]

With this one exception, it is possible to say that morpheme-initial consonants are not followed by glides; that is:

---

[142] Not all instances of initial [h] are derivable from underlying /s/; verbs beginning with [h], for example, fall into two classes with respect to the augment, the behaviour of one class implying that the underlying initial segment is consonantal, that of the other class that it is not. See p. 10.

[143] See pp. 27–31.

(143) Negative Condition:

$$* \, [-\text{seg}] \, [-\text{syll}] \begin{bmatrix} -\text{cons} \\ -\text{syll} \end{bmatrix}$$

2. *Lowness* Lowness is distinctive in Greek only in vowels and glides; that is, there is a general rule that consonants are non-low:

(144) If [+cons], then [−low].

Further, if we adopt the suggestion of note 23, no lexical morpheme can begin with a high glide:

$$(145) \, [-\text{seg}] \begin{bmatrix} -\text{cons} \\ -\text{syll} \end{bmatrix}$$
$$\downarrow$$
$$[+\text{low}]$$

This last rule raises something of a problem. By Chomsky-Halle conventions (XXXVI) and (XXXVII), the unmarked glide is high; but in (145) we have a rule directing that in a particular environment in a particular language, any glide must be low. This will have the effect that in the lexicon, a feature which in the given environment is non-distinctive will always be marked *m*. There are two possible ways of excluding MS rules that have this effect. One is to allow the universal marking conventions to be partly reversed in the lexica of particular languages: for example we might say that although the universal convention is that [u low] for glides means [−low], nevertheless in initial position in Greek [u low] for glides means [+low]. But to take this course is to deprive the term ' universal ' of any empirical content: in what sense is a marking convention universal, if a language can contradict it ? The better solution, then, is to concede that not all features in all contexts are covered by universal marking conventions; rather, there are some universal conventions and other cases in which different languages can assign markedness in different ways.[144]   Rule (145) then is evidence that conventions

[144] There might be yet another suggestion for handling the situation that gives rise to rule (145). This would be to say that the 100 or so morphemes

(XXXVI) and (XXXVII) are not universal but subject to variation across languages.[145]

3. *Backness*   This feature also is distinctive only in vowels and glides, and among the latter only in high glides; all other segments are unmarked for this feature.   The MS rules for backness in initial clusters will therefore be essentially the same as the universal marking conventions governing backness.

4. *Nasality*   On pp. 22–3, we decided that phonetic [mn] ought not to be regarded as derived from underlying /bn/. Had we taken the opposite decision, we would have posited an MS rule that if an initial cluster consisted of consonant plus nasal, its first segment had to be an obstruent.   As it is, we find that the initial consonants after which a nasal is allowed are:

(146) /p^h t^h k^h p t k d g s m/

This implies the following MS condition:

(147) [−seg]   [−syll]   [+nas]

$$\downarrow$$

$$\begin{bmatrix} +\text{cons} \\ \left\{ \begin{matrix} -\text{cont} \\ +\text{strid} \end{matrix} \right\} \\ \alpha \text{ voice} \\ \beta \text{ nas} \\ \gamma \text{ ant} \\ \delta \text{ cor} \end{bmatrix}$$

where, if $\alpha = +$ and $\gamma = +$, then $\beta = -\delta$.

that obey that rule did in fact have a high glide in their lexical representations and were subject to an early phonological rule lowering the glide to [h]. Such a rule would be entirely ad hoc, and would be posited solely for the purpose of bolstering the assumption that there are universal phonological norms for lowness in glides and that a language can never, at the lexical level, go against these norms. This and similar devices, indeed, would render that assumption impervious to empirical disconfirmation.

[145] The variation is not of course unrestricted.   Presumably, if the unmarked glide is [−high], it must be [+low], and if it is [−low], it must be +high].   We would want it to be impossible for the unmarked glide in any language to be mid. Indeed, pace Chomsky and Halle, we would probably want it to be impossible for mid glides to exist at all.

There are a couple of other rules that can be stated in the MS component about nasality. After *two* initial consonants a nasal may not occur: [146]

(148) Negative Condition: $*$ [$-$seg] C_2 [$+$nas].

On the other hand, after initial /s/ a sonorant *must* be nasal:

$$(149) \quad [-\text{seg}]\,[+\text{strid}] \begin{bmatrix} +\text{cons} \\ +\text{son} \end{bmatrix}$$
$$\downarrow$$
$$[+\text{nas}]$$

5. *Sonorancy* Logically there are four possible distinct types of two-consonant initial cluster with respect to this feature and eight types of three-consonant cluster. Three of the four two-consonant types are actually found in Greek (there are no initial sonorant + obstruent clusters), but only one of the eight three-consonant types (viz. obstruent + obstruent + sonorant, e.g. /str/). These facts may be summarized by the following two rules:

$$(150) \quad [-\text{seg}]\,[+\text{cons}]\,[+\text{cons}]\,[+\text{cons}]$$
$$\qquad\quad \downarrow \qquad\quad \downarrow \qquad\quad \downarrow$$
$$\qquad [-\text{son}]\,[-\text{son}]\,[+\text{son}]$$

(151) Negative Condition: $*\,[-\text{seg}] \begin{bmatrix} +\text{cons} \\ +\text{son} \end{bmatrix}[-\text{son}]$

6. *Anteriority and Coronality* Among MS rules that might be suggested to predict values of these features, we may note the following four.

(i) ' A stop preceding an obstruent may not be dental.' This rules out morphemes beginning with $*$/ts tk dg . . ./.

$$(152) \quad [-\text{seg}]\,[-\text{cont}]\,[-\text{son}]$$
$$\downarrow$$
$$[-\text{cor}]$$

---

[146] There is one doubtful exception. There is an insect called σκνίψ *sknips* by Aristotle; but it is called κνίψ *knips* both by Aristophanes (*Birds* 590) before him and by Theophrastus (*Historia Plantarum* 2. 8. 3 and 4. 14. 10) after him.

(ii) ' A stop immediately following a stop must be dental.'
This allows /pt bd kʰtʰ .../ while excluding */pk gb kʰpʰ .../.
The rule applies in all positions within morphemes, not merely
initial position; its form can be:

$$(153) \quad \begin{bmatrix} -\text{son} \\ -\text{cont} \end{bmatrix} \begin{bmatrix} -\text{son} \\ -\text{cont} \end{bmatrix}$$
$$\downarrow$$
$$\begin{bmatrix} +\text{ant} \\ +\text{cor} \end{bmatrix}$$

(iii) ' An obstruent preceding /m/ may not be labial.'
Clusters such as /p+m/ are found across morpheme boundaries,
where Nasalization reduces them to [mm]; within morphemes
there is nothing that might lead one to postulate any such
clusters.

$$(154) \quad \text{Negative Condition:} \quad {}^{*}\begin{bmatrix} -\text{son} \\ +\text{ant} \\ -\text{cor} \end{bmatrix} \begin{bmatrix} +\text{nas} \\ -\text{cor} \end{bmatrix}$$

(iv) ' A nasal following an initial dental obstruent must be
labial.' This rule is restricted to initial position. Among
counter-examples in other positions are ἔθνος *éthnos* ' nation '
and ἔτνος *étnos* ' soup '. But no morpheme can begin with any
of the clusters /tn tʰn dn sn/.[147]

$$(155) \quad \text{Negative Condition:} \quad {}^{*}[-\text{seg}]\,[+\text{cor}] \begin{bmatrix} +\text{nas} \\ +\text{cor} \end{bmatrix}$$

7. *Continuancy* in Greek is distinctive only in obstruents.
The constraints on these in initial clusters are partly given by
rules already noted; for example, (152)[148] ensures that a
coronal obstruent preceding another obstruent will always be
/s/, and (149) that /s/ cannot occur initially before a liquid.

---

[147] Θνῄσκω *thnḗiskō* ' die ' is not a counter-example; the underlying form
of its stem is /tʰan/, as in its aorist ἔθανον *éthanon* and its derivative θάνατος
thánatos ' death '.

[148] Which could alternatively be expressed as a negative condition
excluding initial clusters of dental stop plus obstruent.

The only remaining constraint relating to continuancy has to do with three-consonant clusters. In these the *first* consonant is always /s/, and the *second* always a plosive.

(156) [−seg] [+cons] [+cons] [+cons]
$$\downarrow \qquad \downarrow$$
[+cont] [−cont]

8. *Voicing* Since Regressive Manner Assimilation ensures that all obstruents in obstruent clusters agree with the last member of the cluster in their specifications for voice and h.s.p., obstruents preceding obstruents can remain unmarked for these features in the lexicon. The MS rule for this, in plus-minus form, will be

(157) [−son] [−son]
$$\downarrow$$
$$\begin{bmatrix} -\text{voice} \\ -\text{hsp} \end{bmatrix}$$

There are also other environments where these features are partly predictable. I will deal with voicing first.

(i) ' An obstruent preceded by an initial velar must be voiceless '; that is, no morpheme may begin with */gd/.

(158) Negative Condition: $* + \begin{pmatrix} +\text{cons} \\ -\text{ant} \end{pmatrix} \begin{pmatrix} -\text{son} \\ +\text{voice} \end{pmatrix}$

(ii) ' Fricatives are voiceless before vowels '. More than that, there is nowhere in Greek a voicing contrast in fricatives.[149] They are voiceless in all environments except before voiced consonants; in the last-named environment voicing must be supplied by a phonological rule, since fricatives are voiced in this environment even though they may not, in the lexicon, have been fricatives at all (e.g. fricatives derived from stops via Fricativization). Thus in the lexicon voicing can be left

---

[149] A possible exception might be the name 'Αριοβαρζάνης *Ariobarzānēs*, but it is not known precisely how the ρζ *rz* was intended to be pronounced in Greek. If PW are correct, it represents a Persian [rz], since they give, as the original of the name, an unattested **ariyavarzāna*.

unmarked for fricatives in all environments, as it can also for liquids and vowels:

(159) If $\begin{pmatrix} +\text{cont} \\ \alpha\ \text{son} \end{pmatrix}$, then [$\alpha$ voice],

as it would be put in plus-minus terms.

(iii) ' A labial or velar obstruent preceded by an initial fricative must be voiceless ': that is, there can be no initial clusters */sb sg/.

(160) Negative Condition: * [−seg] [+strid] $\begin{bmatrix} -\text{son} \\ +\text{voice} \\ -\text{cor} \end{bmatrix}$

There is one exception to this principle, namely /sbẹs/, the stem of the verb σβέννυμι [zbénnŭmi] ' extinguish ', but it is quite isolated.

(iv) ' The cluster /dl/ is excluded in all positions '. (All the other logically possible stop-lateral clusters are found in at least some position).

(161) Negative Condition: * $\begin{bmatrix} -\text{cont} \\ +\text{cor} \\ +\text{voice} \end{bmatrix}$ [+lat]

(v) ' The clusters /dl tl tʰl/ are excluded in initial position '. This partially overlaps (iv), and may be combined with it as follows:

(162) Negative Condition:

* [α seg] $\begin{bmatrix} -\text{cont} \\ +\text{cor} \\ \beta\ \text{voice} \end{bmatrix}$ [+lat] where, if $\alpha = +$, then $\beta = +$

That is, clusters of dental stop plus /l/ are excluded if either the cluster is morpheme-initial or the dental stop is voiced.

Condition (162), however, has three exceptions, more than any other MS condition we have considered so far. They are the stems of the verbs θλῶ thlô ' crush ' and θλίβω thlíbō ' chafe ' and the adjective τλήμων tlémōn ' wretched '. Is it possible to determine whether (162) was part of the MS component of Greek ? As I have pointed out, certainty is impossible, but there is evidence we can use. If (162) was a MS condition of Greek, we would expect to find that Greek was as resistant to non-Greek proper names beginning with /tl tʰl/ as it was to those beginning with /dl/. And this is indeed the case. According to Pape (1911), the only foreign proper name beginning with one of these clusters traceable before 300 B.C. is *Τλῆτες Tlêtes*, the name of a people, quoted from the historian Theopompus. Even this may not be a genuine exception: the name may have been analysed by Greeks as containing the stem of *τλήμων tlḗmōn* and of *τέτληκα té-tlēka* ' I have endured ', which is also found in such indigenous proper names as *Τληπόλεμος Tlē-pólemos* (literally 'he who endures war '); *Τλῆτες Tlētes* would stand to this stem as *ἀσπιδαποβλής aspid-apo-blḗs* ' one who throws away his shield ' does to the stem of *βέβληκα bé-blēka* ' I have thrown '. The evidence, being negative, is not conclusive, but it is at any rate not inconsistent with the hypothesis that /tl tʰl/ were inadmissible as initial clusters in Greek.

9. *The feature ' heightened subglottal pressure '* I find only one regularity involving this feature in initial clusters, namely that all stops are unaspirated in the environment /+s——l/. This may be represented by the following negative condition:

(163) * [+strid] [+hsp] [+lat]

10. *Conclusion* The facts discussed in this section are not earth-shaking, but they are facts, and an adequate generative grammar of Greek will have to state them somewhere. I hope to have shown that it is possible to make the grammar do so.

CHAPTER FIVE

THE ACCENTUAL SYSTEM OF GREEK [150]

5.1. *PRELIMINARIES*

We can really only be sure of two things about the phonetic realization of the Greek accent: that on vowels which in writing are marked with an accent (other than grave) there was high pitch, and that on the vowel following an acute-accented vowel, as also on the latter part of a circumflex-accented vowel, there was a falling glide.[151] Almost everything else, including the pitch of vowels marked traditionally with the grave sign,[152] is uncertain. But the two things we are sure of tell us already that an adequate account of accent will require the use of at least two binary features.

It might be thought that a single feature would be sufficient if we were to analyse all long vowels as sequences of two short vowels; and Kiparsky (1967) does just that. But the saving just is not made. It is still necessary to distinguish vowels with svarita from accented and from unaccented vowels, and to do this before the end of the phonological rules. This may be proved in the following way.

The rule governing the svarita glide may be stated thus:

(164) Assign falling glide to the mora [153] next following an accented mora, and also to the succeeding mora, if in the same syllable.

Now there is a rule of Greek phonology called the RULE OF ENCLISIS, which will be more fully discussed below in the section on Enclitics. If we assume, with Halle (1971a), that ' " dynamic " tones such as " rising ", " falling " or " fall-rise " ' are never needed in a phonological description but are

---

[150] Kiparsky (1967) offers a very different analysis to that here presented. I will make some comments on his rules and their ordering during the course of the ensuing discussion.

[151] Hereinafter often referred to as *svarita*; see Allen (1968).

[152] See the section on Enclitics below.

[153] A ' mora ' is a unit of which a long vowel contains two and a short vowel one. A word thus contains as many morae as, on Kiparsky's analysis, it contains vowels.

only ' phonetic phenomena of a superficial sort ', then svarita, or falling glide, must be assigned after the end of the phonological rules. Therefore, at the stage when the Rule of Enclisis applies, there are only two categories of vowels with respect to accent, accented and unaccented.[154] The Rule of Enclisis will then have to be stated thus:

(165) Accent the last mora of a word when an enclitic follows, provided that neither that mora nor any other mora in the same syllable is the immediate successor of an accented mora.

But if the Rule of Enclisis is ordered after the svarita rule, it can be stated far more simply:

(166) Accent the last mora of the word when an enclitic follows, provided that that mora does not have a falling glide on it.

By all the usual principles by which phonologists determine the ordering of rules, it follows that svarita must be assigned before the Rule of Enclisis operates, and that at that stage vowels which have the svarita glide must be distinct in feature composition from both accented and unaccented vowels. But three distinct kinds of vowel cannot be distinguished by one feature. Therefore, unless some loophole is found, Greek must have two accentual features, one of which must be ' falling '.

Kiparsky's way out of the problem is to treat all post-tonic vowels (not just svarita vowels, but all vowels at any distance to the right of the accent in a word) as accented. This makes an elegant statement of some accentual phenomena possible, but it also makes it completely impossible to account for the Rule of Enclisis. If post-tonic vowels with svarita are not distinct from those without, how can the environment for the Rule of Enclisis be stated ?

An alternative would be to treat svarita vowels as accented,

---

[154] It is not possible to regard the Rule of Enclisis as a phonetic detail rule; the rule does not merely assign degrees of accent, it shifts a vowel from the category ' unaccented ' to the category ' accented '. No version of generative phonology I know of permits category changes in phonetic detail rules.

and other post-tonic vowels as unaccented. If this was done, a reasonable statement of the Rule of Enclisis would be possible:

> (167) Accent the last mora of the word when an enclitic follows, provided that that mora is not accented already.

Indeed, the rule can be made even simpler than that, since the proviso is unnecessary: when the mora in question is already accented, the rule can be allowed to apply vacuously. However, this apparent gain is bought at the price of two clumsy, unmotivated and otherwise unnecessary extra phonetic detail rules:

> (168) (*a*) Assign falling glide to the second of two successive accented morae.
>
> (*b*) Where there are three successive accented morae, if the second and third are in the same syllable, assign falling glide to both; otherwise, only to the second of the three.

Such are the results of attempts to describe the Greek accentual system with only a single feature. It will also be observed that such an analysis would do away with the one-one relationship between vowels and syllables, but it would not do away with the necessity for rules like (168*b*) to refer to syllables or to syllable boundaries. On a single-feature analysis, under which each underlying vowel filled one mora, it would thus be necessary to mark syllable boundaries: on a more traditional analysis, with two accentual features and long vowels treated as single segments, it is unnecessary.

In general, therefore, we reject analyses of Greek which treat long vowels as underlying vowel sequences, and we also reject Halle's (1971a) hypothesis about ' dynamic ' tones.

In one limited case, however, a vowel-sequence analysis would be useful to our understanding of the Greek accentual system. Not only long vowels but also diphthongs count as long nuclei for accentual purposes, with the exception of certain instances of word-final [ay] and [oy].[155] Now since we

---

[155] These count as long nuclei when they constitute the ending of the optative mood (third person singular), or of a locative adverb such as *oîκοι oikoi* ' at home '; otherwise they count as short nuclei.

have in any case in the grammar the rule of Diphthong Formation, which collapses sequences of vowel plus high vowel into diphthongs, we can simplify the grammar by regarding *all* diphthongs, with the exceptions mentioned, as derived by this rule from vowel sequences. This will do away with the distinction between the notions of 'long nucleus' and 'long vowel'; the class of nuclei which are long for accentual purposes will be identical with the class of long vowels. Diphthongs will be analysed and accented as sequences of two vowels, except for [ay] and [oy] where these are accented as short nuclei; the latter will be analysed as vowel-glide sequences, the vowel, of course, being short, and hence accented like any other short vowel.[156] The rule of Diphthong Formation will be so formulated that a sequence of unaccented vowel plus accented high vowel becomes an accented diphthong without svarita, while a sequence of accented vowel plus high vowel with svarita becomes an accented diphthong with svarita.[157]

---

[156] I cannot understand the statement of Kuryłowicz (1958, 112) that [-ay] and [-oy] are regarded as short for accentual purposes just in case they do not contain an internal morphological boundary. What independent justification is there for the assumption, which this necessitates, that there is such a boundary in οἴκοι *oíkoi* 'at home', where the final diphthong is accentually long, but not in οἶκοι *oȋkoi* 'houses' (nominative plural), where it is accentually short ?

[157] Most contraction rules, though, have essentially the same effect on accent, if any of the contracted vowels happens to be accented, and it would not be desirable to state these accentual consequences over and over again for each rule. I therefore propose that there should be a global derivational constraint (see next paragraph but one) to the following effect:

' When a rule deletes, or reduces to a glide, one of two adjacent vowels (not separated by a major boundary) with opposite values for accentual feature F, then the remaining vowel must simultaneously be made [+F] '. In other words, when any form of contraction occurs, the output vowel is accented if either input vowel was accented, and has a svarita glide if either input vowel had a svarita glide.

For global derivational constraints see Lakoff (1970; 1971a) and Kisseberth (1969; 1970). I have given reasons (Sommerstein 1972b) for considering such constraints unnecessary in syntax, but they do seem to be needed in phonology.

Henceforward, in the statement of phonological rules, it will be assumed

The only case in which this analysis appears at first sight to give incorrect results is that of words of the shape of ἕτοιμος [hetoymos] ' ready ', which is barytone [158] and whose underlying representation, according to the proposal now being made, will be /hętǫimǫ+s/. The rule of limitation [159] will ensure that the accent comes no earlier than the antepenultimate, yielding /hętǫimǫ+s/, from which we should expect to derive * ἕτοῖμος *[hetoȳmos].[160] How can we account for the actual accentuation ἕτοιμος [hétoymos] ?

The answer is: by an independently needed rule, namely ' VENDRYES' LAW ' (Vendryes 1929, 263). This rule, which must operate after Diphthong Formation but before Contraction,[161] moves the accent one syllable to the left in words which but for the rule would be properispomena,[162] and which have a rhythmically light antepenultimate syllable.[163,164] Words with diphthongs in the penultimate which do not meet the conditions for Vendryes' law, such as ἀλλοῖος alloîos ' of another kind ', are in fact generally properispomenon, as would be expected from the operation of the Rule of Limitation on an

that this constraint operates, and the accentual consequences of contraction rules will therefore not be stated as part of the rules themselves.

Note that the constraint does not apply to Elision (q.v. in section 5.2), since it is only before a major boundary that a vowel can be deleted by Elision.

[158] This term is here used to refer to words whose accent is placed as early as the Rule of Limitation allows.

[159] Discussed at the beginning of section 5.2.

[160] Which was, in fact, the accentuation of the word in older Attic.

[161] If later than Contraction, it would incorrectly apply to contracted verb forms, giving, e.g. *φίλουμεν [pʰílūmen] from φιλοῦμεν [pʰilûmen] ' we love '.

[162] As I shall be making frequent use of the traditional terms for words accented in various ways, I shall give them here. Words accented *acute* on the final, penultimate and antepenultimate syllables are termed oxytones, paroxytones and proparoxytones respectively; those accented *circumflex* on the final and penultimate syllables are respectively termed perispomena and properispomena.

[163] A syllable is *rhythmically light* if it contains a short vowel followed by no more than one consonant before the next vowel; otherwise it is *rhythmically heavy*.

[164] The last-mentioned restriction does not apply in the case of verbs. See in Summary of Rules.

underlying form in which the second element of the diphthong was a vowel in a syllable of its own.[165]

Since, however, as we have seen, a similar analysis of long vowels is not possible without otherwise unnecessary complications being introduced, two features are needed to describe the accentual system of Greek. Wang's (1967) system of tonal features, though primarily intended for the description of languages with distinctive tone on each syllable, can also be used for Greek. His features ' high ' (which, to avoid confusion with the segmental feature ' high ', I will call ' sharp ') and ' falling ' will define four classes of vowels:

(169) (a) $\begin{bmatrix} +\text{sharp} \\ +\text{falling} \end{bmatrix}$ circumflex

    (b) $\begin{bmatrix} +\text{sharp} \\ -\text{falling} \end{bmatrix}$ acute

    (c) $\begin{bmatrix} -\text{sharp} \\ +\text{falling} \end{bmatrix}$ post-acute

    (d) $\begin{bmatrix} -\text{sharp} \\ -\text{falling} \end{bmatrix}$ all other

In Wang's system these feature combinations are interpreted as a high-falling, a high-level, a low-falling, and a low-level tone respectively. The distinction between (a) and (c) may not be justified on phonetic grounds in Greek,[166] but it is abundantly justified on structural grounds: if (a) and (c) were not distinguished there would be no definable class of accented or of unaccented vowels. If it is the case that vowels of class (c) were phonetically high-falling rather than low-falling, all that is needed to give this result is a late rule

(170) SVARITA ADJUSTMENT

   $[+\text{falling}] \rightarrow [+\text{sharp}]$

[165] That the accent of such words as ἀλλοῖος *alloîos* was a perfectly regular barytone accent, disguised by the reduction of two syllables to one, was pointed out by Bally (1945, 112 and 123).

[166] ' The compound (= circumflex: AHS) tone was probably identical with the falling glide which occurred on a long vowel or diphthong in the syllable following a high tone ' (Allen 1968, 112).

I must now mention certain rules of general application. These are not constrained to any particular stage in the order of phonological rules; rather, they may be regarded as becoming applicable after each application of one of the ordinary phonological rules. If, with Postal (1968), we regard the rules of the phonology as not linearly but partially ordered, we may alternatively say that these particular rules are ordered among themselves but not with respect to the other rules.[167] If rules of this type were not permitted, many of the ordinary rules would have to be made more complex and repetitive.

I call these rules *special linking rules* – ' linking rules ' in a sense similar to that of Chomsky and Halle (1968); ' special ' because they are not intended to be universal. The conditions of applicability of linking rules are assumed to be as follows: a linking rule of either the form (171) or the form (172)

$$(171) \quad [\alpha F] \rightarrow \begin{bmatrix} \beta_1 G_1 \\ \cdots \\ \beta_n G_n \end{bmatrix} / X \begin{bmatrix} \underline{\quad} \\ Z \end{bmatrix} Y$$

$$(172) \quad Z \rightarrow \begin{bmatrix} \beta_1 G_1 \\ \cdots \\ \beta_n G_n \end{bmatrix} / X [\alpha F] Y$$

Notes: In both (171) and (172), F and $G_1, \ldots, G_n$ are features; Greek letters, as usual, are variables ranging over the values + and —; other symbols are variables over feature matrices, which may be null.

The variables X and Y may denote matrices with any number of columns, the variable Z a matrix with no more than one column.

In (172), either X or Y must have an environment bar in place of one of its columns.

---

[167] Except that (i) two applications of the same special linking rule must be separated by at least one application of some main-sequence rule and (ii) as will hereafter be seen, some special linking rules cease to operate after a certain stage in derivations.

LINKS to any rule, whether a main-sequence rule or another linking rule, of the form

$$(173) \quad W \rightarrow \begin{bmatrix} \cdots \\ \alpha F \\ \cdots \end{bmatrix} / P \longrightarrow Q$$

where W, P and Q are arbitrary matrices (possibly null) except that W has no more than one column.

A linking rule is applied immediately after each rule to which it links, provided its structural description is met, and subject to the general constraints of note 167.

In the lexicon, only the feature ' sharp ' of the tonal features will ever take any value other than ' unmarked ', and that only for one vowel in the word; and the Rule of Limitation and other main sequence accent rules likewise simply specify some one vowel as [+sharp]. In traditional terms, these rules state only the position of the accent, and not whether it is acute or circumflex, nor what becomes of the other syllables. We begin the task of accounting for these other facts by wiping the slate clean so far as the feature ' falling ' is concerned by means of the following linking rule:

$$(174) \quad [\alpha \text{ sharp}] \rightarrow [-\text{falling}]$$

This rule ensures that whenever any rule accents or de-accents a vowel, that vowel loses any svarita glide it may previously have possessed. Like rules (176) and (178) below, it has a cut-off point; that is, after a certain late stage in the phonology it ceases to be operative. This is because these rules must not be allowed to apply after the Rule of Enclisis. For, as far as we can tell, the Rule of Enclisis, unlike other accentuation rules, had no effect on syllables other than the one to which it gave an accent, except possibly to introduce svarita on the succeeding syllable. It did not disturb svarita glides already present, and any accent it introduced was in addition to, and not in place of, any accent already present as a result of other rules.

We must now specify when accented vowels are circumflex. The assignment of circumflex accent in the final syllable of words is dealt with by main-sequence rules; on the penultimate syllable, however, it is always predictable whether an accented vowel will be circumflex.[168] The following rule states that it will be circumflex in the case known as ' the law of the trochee ', i.e. in long accented penultimate nuclei, including diphthongs, when the nucleus of the final syllable is short.[169]

(175)
$$[+\text{sharp}] \rightarrow [+\text{falling}] \Big/ \left\{ \begin{matrix} \begin{bmatrix} \underline{} \\ +\text{long} \end{bmatrix} \\ \underline{} \begin{bmatrix} -\text{cons} \\ -\text{syll} \end{bmatrix} \end{matrix} \right\} C_0 \begin{bmatrix} V \\ -\text{long} \end{bmatrix} C_0 [+\text{WB}]$$

After (175), three further rules complete the assignment of tonal features. The first and third, as already stated, cut off before the Rule of Enclisis is reached; there is no evidence on whether the second, (177), cuts off or not.

(176) $V \rightarrow [-\text{sharp}] /$ ## X [+sharp] Y —— Z ##

Conditions: 1. This is a mirror-image rule.[170]

2. X, Y, Z contain no occurrence of ##.

The effect of (176) is that there can be only one accent in each word, where ' word ' refers to a unit comprising an accentable word plus any attached proclitics and enclitics.

The next rule, (177), puts the svarita glide on post-acute syllables, after which (178) removes any other svarita glides in the word.

(177)
$$\begin{bmatrix} V \\ -\text{sharp} \end{bmatrix} \rightarrow \left\{ \begin{matrix} [-\text{falling}] \\ [+\text{falling}] \Big/ \begin{bmatrix} +\text{sharp} \\ -\text{falling} \end{bmatrix} C_0 ([-\text{seg}]) C_0 \underline{} \end{matrix} \right\}$$

(178) $V \rightarrow [-\text{falling}] /$ ## X [+falling] Y —— Z ##
Conditions: same as for (176).

In all subsequent discussion (174–178) will be assumed.

[168] Subject to a few exceptions, discussed later on.

[169] The circumflex on certain vowels which have undergone Contraction, Diphthong Formation, etc., is taken care of by the global constraint of note 157.

[170] For mirror-image rules see note 52.

5.2. *RULES FOR GREEK WORD ACCENT* [171]

First, the Rule of Limitation. This precedes all other rules of the phonology, except those having to do with vowel gradation,[172] with the augment, and the Initial Accent Rule (for which see 5.2.1). It specifies how far from the end of the word the accent can come, and with the help of linking rule (176) shifts any accent that would otherwise come too early in the word.[173]

(179)

$$V \rightarrow [+\text{sharp}]/[+\text{sharp}] \; X \text{——} C_0 \, (=)C_0 V C_0 \left(\begin{bmatrix} V \\ -\text{long} \end{bmatrix} C_0 \right) \#$$

where X contains no occurrence of $\#$.

By the usual notational conventions, (179) abbreviates two subrules, disjunctively ordered. By the first, a word whose final syllable has a short nucleus, and whose accent is on the fourth syllable from the end or earlier, shifts its accent to the antepenultimate. Words that do not meet this condition pass to the second subrule, and if accented on the antepenultimate or earlier, shift their accent to the penultimate.[174] If a word

---

[171] The facts on which the discussion in this section is based are derived from Vendryes (1929) and Koster (1962); this applies to all statements about accentuation which are factual rather than analytical, and assumed rather than argued for. I hope I have made explicit below points on which I disagree with Vendryes.

[172] If vowel gradation was at one time conditioned by accent, this relationship has been almost completely obscured in Greek.

[173] I disagree, therefore, with the statement of Kiparsky (1967) that there are no rules in Greek which shift the accent to the right. His proposed accentual universal, that no rule can de-accent a vowel, is also violated by one of my proposed rules, the Acute-Grave Rule (discussed in the section on Enclitics). This universal, however, is highly suspicious. Of McCawley's (1968, 180–182) seven accentual rules for Japanese, one (C-5) is a rule to remove accents, and another (C-7) he calls an ' accent reduction rule ', but disguises as a rule assigning primary accent to a syllable that already has it. Chomsky and Halle (1968) also have two de-accenting rules, one of them avowed (' Auxiliary Reduction I ', op. cit. 240), the other disguised (' Compound, Nuclear Stress, Stress Adjustment ', ibid.). I therefore see no justification for Kiparsky's proposed universal.

[174] The rules for ' recessive ' accent given by Kiparsky (1967) and Warburton (1970), though different from (179) in form, have in essentials the

contains a = boundary – that is, if it contains an augment or a prepositional prefix – the accent may not be more than one syllable to the left of the boundary.[175,176]

5.2.1. VERB FORMS

The vast majority of verb forms are barytone (see note 158); and the easiest way of accounting for this is to assign them, at some stage before the Rule of Limitation, accent on the *first* syllable, and then allow the Rule of Limitation to shift the accent to the right if necessary.

At what stage, though, should this initial accent be assigned ? Not by a lexical redundancy rule before the phonological rules begin. If we did that, we would have to reassign accent after

---

same effect. Both, however, put this rule very late, after all other accentuation rules, and give it the function of assigning an accent to words that have not received one in any other way. The result is, as Kiparsky expressly states, that the rule must be later than Vendryes' Law (which he subsumes under a more general rule of ' iambic retraction '). But if this is so, we are deprived of Bally's insight (see note 165); we are no longer able to regard the pre-Vendryes' Law accentuation */hẹtọimọs/, */họmọ́iọs/, etc., as a regular barytone accent, in the way we did on pp. 164–5 above. In fact, we will have a situation where most nouns and adjectives, other than those which take a stem-final accent, can have their accent assigned by the recessive-accent rule, but the accent of those which happen to undergo Vendryes' Law must be given in the lexicon. It is the height of implausibility that whether a form has to have its accent given in the lexicon should depend on whether or not its phonological shape is such that it undergoes some quite general phonological rule; yet this is the inevitable consequence of the late ordering of the rule assigning accent to barytone words.

[175] See note 12. There are certain other morphological junctures which also have the property that the accent cannot precede them by more than one syllable, and possibly these too should be regarded as = boundaries. Such are the internal boundaries of ἠπειρόθεν, ēpeiró-then ' from the mainland ' and ποικιλό-θριξ poikiló-thriks ' with spotted hair '. Cf. Kuryłowicz (1958, 138–9). There are also some other cases of apparently exceptional behaviour of morphologically complex words under various rules that might be accounted for in the same way – for example, the apparent violation of Grassmann's Law in Κορινθό-θεν Korinthó-then ' from Corinth '.

[176] There are two separate sets of parentheses in (179), neither enclosed within the other, and in theory the question could arise which of them should be expanded first. The two possibilities, however, do not, in this case at least, differ in their empirical consequences.

Augmentation, since the augment may bear the accent.[177] The INITIAL ACCENT RULE must itself be a phonological rule, later than Augmentation.

We can make use of the Initial Accent Rule to give formal expression to what is clearly the fact, that the ' unmarked ' accentuation in Greek was barytone. Not only most verb forms and most classes of derived nouns, but also most proper names and loan words were accented in this way. Let us suppose that barytone words are completely unspecified for accent in the lexicon, i.e. that every segment of them is [u sharp]. Then it will be just these words that undergo the Initial Accent Rule, and just the words some segment of which is [m sharp] that fail to undergo it. The feature ' exception to the Initial Accent Rule ', then, will not appear on any segment of any lexical matrix; it will be added by a readjustment rule:

(180) [m sharp] → [−Initial Accent Rule]

Then all words unmarked for accent will undergo the Initial Accent Rule:

(181) $V \rightarrow [+\text{sharp}] / [+\text{WB}] \, C_0$ ——

There are of course a number of real or apparent exceptions to the principle that verb forms are barytone; these are detailed by Koster (1962, 33). Many of these are evidently the result of contraction, and can be derived without difficulty on the assumption that the Rule of Limitation operates before contraction takes place. These contracted forms will not concern us further. I will now consider the remainder.

(a) Five verbs are said to be oxytone in the aorist imperative; all are disyllabic, e.g. λαβέ [labé] ' take ', and all are oxytone only when not preceded by a prepositional prefix. There is also an isolated imperative ἰδού [idú] ' look ' which is oxytone. We may postulate a readjustment rule, applying before (180), which makes these forms oxytone when a word

---

[177] As may the reduplicative syllable of perfect tense forms.

boundary (and not a = boundary) immediately precedes them.
It is also possible, however, that they should be regarded not as
oxytone but as unaccented; for the high tone on their final
syllable would only be heard before an enclitic or a pause,
where it could be otherwise explained than as due to an
inherent accent; see on Enclitics. If these forms, together with
those discussed in the next paragraph, are treated as
unaccented, it becomes possible to make the generalization that
no verb form is *ever* oxytone. If we treat the six exceptional
imperative forms in this way, the readjustment rule applicable
to them, instead of assigning them an oxytone accent, would
make them [—accentable].

(b) *Φής phés* ' you (sg.) say ' has two peculiarities: it is
oxytone; and unlike the other forms of the present indicative
of *φημί phēmí* ' say ', it is never enclitic. Observe that other
verb forms which are normally enclitic, such as *εἰμί eimí* ' I
am ', *ἐσμέν esmén* ' we are ', and *φημί phēmí*, are all, except for
ἔστι ésti ' is ', oxytone when not enclitic. This fact requires,
independently of *φής phés*, a rule with the effect

$$(182) \quad \begin{bmatrix} V \\ +\text{enclitic} \\ +\text{verb} \end{bmatrix} \rightarrow \begin{bmatrix} -\text{enclitic} \\ +\text{sharp} \end{bmatrix} / \text{——} C_0 [+\text{WB}] \text{ [178]}$$

in certain contexts.

And this rule can be used to account for the behaviour of *φής
phés* by the supposition that it applies to *φής phés* not merely in
some, but in all contexts. This treatment in effect reduces the
two peculiarities of *φής phés* to one.[179] It is true that *εἶ eî*
' you (sg.) are ' is not enclitic and yet is not oxytone, though
the rest of the present indicative of *εἰμί eimí* is normally

---

[178] It is assumed that all syntactic, morphological, diacritic, etc., features
which are assigned by a rule to any segment of a word are by convention
distributed to every segment of the word. Thus (182) means that enclitic
verbs under certain circumstances cease to be enclitic and receive an accent
on their final syllable.

[179] For an alternative account of these phenomena, compare the previous
paragraph.

enclitic. But εἶ *eî* is a different kind of exception: it is an exception to the rule that makes the present indicative of εἰμί *eimí* and φημί *phēmí* enclitic in the first place. Not being enclitic at any stage of derivation, εἶ *eî* is not subject to (182), and so never becomes oxytone and retains its original recessive accent.

(c) Χρή *khrḗ* ' it is necessary ' is no exception to the general principles of verbal accentuation, since it is a noun. I do not mean by this that it was historically derived from a noun (though no doubt it was) but that in classical Attic it was synchronically a noun. Its future form, χρῆσται *khrêstai* (found, e.g. at Sophocles, *Oedipus at Colonus* 504), is sufficient proof of this. All normal third person future middle forms have a vowel before the ending -ται *-tai*. The only exception is ἔσται *éstai* ' he/she/it will be '. Χρῆσται *khrêstai*, therefore, must be analysed as a contraction of χρὴ ἔσται *khrḕ éstai*, literally ' there will be need '. If χρή *khrḗ* had been a verb, its future could only have been *χρήσεται *khrḗsetai*.

(d) Koster (1962) treats as exceptional the fact that optatives whose first person singular ends in -ην [ẹ̄n] rather than the usual -μι [mi] are always accented on the penultimate syllable. Now this syllable is always either [oy], [ay], [ey] or [ē] – a diphthong or a long vowel derived from a diphthong. Will the analysis of diphthongs that we have adopted be able to account for this phenomenon ? Consider the first person plural of the present optative of τίθημι *títhēmi* ' put '. Its underlying form, after the Rule of Limitation, is /tʰi+tʰẹ́+i+mẹn/. This would result in the actual phonetic form τιθεῖμεν [titʰêmen] *but for Vendryes' Law*. Those optatives, therefore, that have in the singular the endings /ẹ̄n ẹ̄s ẹ̄] must be marked as exceptions to Vendryes' Law, or Vendryes' Law must be so formulated as to exclude them. The former is more probable, since the exceptional behaviour is not found in any other optatives, and hence its statement as part of Vendryes' Law would require an ad hoc feature to be inserted in the SD of that rule.

(e) In infinitives and participles, the accent must fall on the stem, never on a prepositional prefix. Thus the aorist infinitive of ἀποπλέω *apo-pléō* ' sail away ' is ἀποπλεῦσαι *apopleûsai* not *ἀπόπλευσαι **apópleusai*. The rule to account for this must be stated in terms of the (of course, independently needed in the grammar) syntactic features ' infinitive ' and ' participle ', thus:

(183) RULE OF LIMITATION, PART II

$$V \rightarrow [+\text{sharp}] \,/\, [+\text{sharp}] \; X = C_0 \left[\overline{\left\{ \begin{array}{l} +\text{infin} \\ +\text{partic} \end{array} \right\}} \right]$$

where X contains no word boundary.

In conjunction with linking rule (176), this rule takes an accent lying in a prepositional prefix to an infinitive or participle and moves it to the first syllable of the verbal part of the compound.

5.2.2. THE ARTICLE

Vendryes (1929, 76) holds that the definite article in Greek was never proclitic. He does not give any evidence in support of this. I have sought evidence from metre.

The iambic trimeter, which is the chief metre of dialogue in Greek drama, is governed in tragedy by, among other constraints, a rule known as Porson's Law, which may be stated thus:

(184) In the last of the three *metra* of which the line is composed, which has the rhythmic form

˘̄   ˘ ˘   ˘   ˘̄

1   2   3   4,

if position 1 [180] is occupied by the last syllable of a word, this syllable must be rhythmically light.

Thus (185a) is a violation of Porson's Law, while (185b) (which has been proposed as an emendation of it) conforms to the constraint:

---

[180] Position 1 is hereinafter referred to as ' Porson position '.

(185) (a) Ἄτλας ὁ χαλ | κέοισι νώ | τοις οὐρανὸν
      Átlās ho khal | kéoisi nṓ | tois ouranòn
                         1   2 3 4

      (Euripides, *Ion* 1, mss.)

    (b) Ἄτλας ὁ νώ | τοις χαλκέοι | σιν οὐρανὸν
      Átlās ho nṓ | tois khalkéoi | sin ouranòn.
             1   2 3 4

Now certain apparent violations of Porson's Law are permitted in tragedy, notably in the case of certain monosyllables which are regarded as cohering with the word which follows them. These monosyllables, when they are not forms of the article, are overwhelmingly either proclitic or elided. I have checked through the 32 tragedies which have survived more or less complete, and I have found 606 apparent violations of this kind. In 344 of these the monosyllable in ' Porson position ' is a word admitted by Vendryes to be proclitic; in 42 an elided word; in 189 the article; and 31 lines come under none of these heads.

This evidence is, of course, hard to interpret unless we have a control group, so to speak, to compare it with. In this case the control can be provided by the iambics of comedy, where Porson's Law is not observed. In the eleven extant plays of Aristophanes, the number of iambic trimeters where a heavy monosyllable occurs in Porson position is 1,011; the monosyllable is 363 times an admitted proclitic, 411 times the article, 59 times an elided word, leaving 178 other cases, of which 130 involve ' non-lexical ' monosyllables [181] (compared with 24 out of 31 in tragedy).

The most significant of these figures, from the point of view of the status of the article, are summarized in (186).

(186)	Comedy	Tragedy
Non-lexical proclitics	363	344
Non-lexical non-proclitics	130	24
Article	411	189

[181] A word is classed as non-lexical if it is not a noun, a verb, an adjective or an adverb.

Prima facie, this evidence seems to point to no conclusion. For if, in Porson position, the article were as much avoided in tragedy as were non-lexical non-proclitic monosyllables, we should expect to find it there only about 75 times rather than 189; while if it were used as freely as an undoubted proclitic, the expected frequency would be 390.

We have, however, overlooked a very important factor that biases the figures. The article is much less used in tragedy than in comedy regardless of metrical position. In a sample of 1,100 Aristophanic iambic lines [182] I found the article to occur 600 times; in 1,100 lines of tragic iambics [183] only 251 times. The number of occurrences of undoubted proclitics was 807 in the comic sample, 813 in the tragic. Thus, relative to undoubted proclitics, the article is only $\frac{251}{600} \cdot \frac{807}{813} = 0 \cdot 414$ times as frequent in tragedy as in comedy; so that a more reasonable feature for its expected frequency in tragedy, if it were used as freely as an undoubted proclitic, would be not 390 but $0 \cdot 414$ of 390 = approximately 161; the actual frequency, as shown in (186), is 189.

We thus find that in tragedy the article occurs as freely as a proclitic in Porson position – more freely, if anything. The inference seems highly probable that the article was itself proclitic.

One loophole for objection remains. It might be suggested that the key factor in determining admissibility in Porson position in tragedy was not procliticness but lexicality. It would follow from this suggestion that we should find that non-lexical non-proclitic monosyllables were not specially

---

[182] Those which occur between the following points (inclusive): *Acharnians* 1–100, *Knights* 101–205, *Clouds* 206–637, *Wasps* 760–859, *Peace* 868–1053, *Birds* 1054–1221, *Lysistrata* 1–68, 1222–end, *Thesmophoriazusae* 69–197, *Frogs* 198–499, *Ecclesiazusae* 504–748, *Plutus* 749–848.

[183] Those which occur between the following points (inclusive): Aeschylus, *Seven* 181–385, *Choephori* 479–528, *Eumenides* 1–100; Sophocles, *Ajax* 719–819, *Antigone* 531–580, *Oedipus Tyrannus* 581–715; Euripides, *Rhesus* 481–618, *Alcestis* 820–1038, *Medea* 337–480, *Heracleidae* 1–116, *Ion* 237–336, *Electra* 1039–1143.

avoided in Porson position in tragedy, i.e. that the more than five-to-one ratio between their frequencies in that position in comedy and tragedy, shown in (186), is simply a consequence of their relative frequency in all positions. Using the same 1,100-line samples as before, we find 422 relevant monosyllables [184] in all positions in our comic sample, and 346 in our tragic sample; so that taking non-lexical proclitics as a standard, non-lexical non-proclitic monosyllables are $\frac{346}{422} \cdot \frac{807}{813} = 0 \cdot 814$ times as frequent in tragedy as in comedy, in all positions. The crude figure for the expected frequency of such monosyllables in Porson position in tragedy, derived from (186), assuming them to have been used as freely as proclitics, is $130 \times \frac{344}{363} =$ about 123. Multiplying by $0 \cdot 814$, we get a better estimate for the expected frequency of 100 – the actual frequency is 24.

The situation is thus that proclitic monosyllables, other than the article, are used relatively freely in Porson position in tragedy; non-proclitic monosyllables, even non-lexical ones, are not; the article is used with as great or greater freedom than the proclitics. Is it, then, likely that the article had an accent of its own ? Note especially that most of the appearances of the article in Porson position are of the genitive and dative cases, which are traditionally regarded as perispomenon and would therefore, if Vendryes is right, have had as full an accent phonetically as a monosyllabic noun like παις paîs ' child '.

I conclude, therefore, that the article did not have an accent.

Here, however, we seem to face a difficulty on syntactic grounds. For the article is syntactically a *pronoun*, not in some of its occurrences but in all; as such, it is an NP and a major category in the sense of Chomsky and Halle (1968, 366), and, by their conventions (loc. cit.), would be expected to be an

---

[184] Excluding (*a*) enclitics, which cannot in any case occur in Porson position in tragedy; (*b*) words ending in a short vowel, which cannot normally form a heavy syllable and so would only obscure the situation; and (*c*) elided words, which were above treated as a special class.

independent word.   I will now explain these assertions –
beginning with the claim that the article is syntactically a
pronoun; for this is not generally recognized as far as classical
Attic is concerned.[185]

The Greek definite article had at least one construction not
found in most other European languages having a definite
article. This was the construction exemplified by

(187) τὰ περὶ τῆς δίκης
       tà perì tês díkēs
       the about the trial
       (N.PL)
       ' the circumstances relating to the trial '

and by

(188) οἱ νῦν
       hoi nŷn
       the now
       (M.PL)
       ' the men of today '

in which the article, preposed to a prepositional phrase or to
certain kinds of adverb, constitutes a noun phrase capable of
functioning (according to the case of the article) as the subject
of a sentence, the object of a preposition, or anything else that
an ordinary noun phrase may be.

In a transformational-generative grammar of Greek, noun
phrases with an article but no head noun could be either directly
generated in the base or introduced by a transformation.[185a]

---

[185] In Sommerstein (1972a), I give reasons for considering the English
definite article to be likewise a remote-structire pronoun.

[185a] This is not the place for a detailed account of transformational
syntax. Suffice it to say that in most versions of the theory the ' base ' is
regarded as specifying, by a series of expansion rules whose initial input is
the symbol S (Sentence), the underlying (' deep ') structures of sentences,
while the ' transformational component ' converts these into ' surface
structures ', i.e. the syntactic structures of the sentences as actually spoken.
Syntactic structures, deep, surface or intermediate, are usually represented
on paper either as constituent-structure trees such as (190) or as strings with
labelled bracketing such as (196), which corresponds exactly to the tree (194)

(i) There could be base rules of, say, the form

(189) (a) NP → (ART) NP'

(b)
$$NP' \rightarrow \left\{ \begin{array}{l} N \\ ADJ \\ ADV \\ PP \end{array} \right\}$$

But such a set of rules could never explain a very significant restriction on which adverbs and PPs can be expansions of NP'. These adverbs and PPs are precisely those that can be predicates, i.e. can be ' complements ', in traditional terminology, of copulative verbs, so that all manner adverbs, for example, are excluded: there cannot be a sentence *οὗτοί εἰσι βραδέως *hoûtoí eisi bradéōs ' *these people are slowly ', and equally there cannot be a noun phrase *οἱ βραδέως *hoi bradéōs ' *those who are slowly '.[186]

This sort of identity between the classes of constituents that can occur in apparently disparate syntactic environments is usually evidence of a transformational relationship. This leads us to the second possibility mentioned above.

(ii) NPs consisting of the article plus an adjective, adverb, participle or prepositional phrase may be formed by a transformation from an underlying structure in which the

except for the addition of word boundary symbols. Labelled brackets in (191), which is the input description of a transformation, are interpreted in the same way as in (196).

Further information on transformational syntax is provided by Katz and Postal (1964), Koutsoudas (1966), Lees (1960), and in various works by Noam Chomsky, notably *Aspects of the Theory of Syntax* (MIT Press, Cambridge, Mass., 1965).

The following abbreviations are used in this section:

ADJ(ective)	P(repositional) P(hrase)
ADV(erb)	PRED(icate)
ART(icle)	PRO(nominal)
COP(ula)	REL(ative)
N(oun)	S(entence)
N(oun) P(hrase)	V(erb) P(hrase)
P(reposition)	V(erb)

[186] Except, irrelevantly, by ellipsis from such phrases as οἱ βραδέως καταβάντες hoi bradéōs katabántes ' those who came down slowly '.

adjectives, adverbs, etc., *are* predicates. What structure can this be?

A structure is available that meets the conditions required and also the condition (Katz and Postal 1964, 71) that transformations must not affect meaning. It is that of restrictive relative clauses. For example, (187) could be derived from an intermediate-level structure

(190)

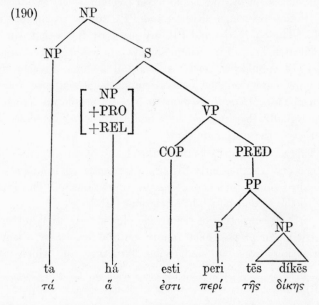

Moreover, there is a rule, which must be in the grammar in any case and independently of any consideration of the article, that will carry out the required structural change. This is Relative Clause Reduction, a rule operative in many languages, which is used in the formation of many NPs containing attributive adjectives;[187] its structural description is

---

[187] Cf. Lees's rule (1960, 94) numbered T58 with his comment (ib. 91): 'In fact, it seems that Relative + *be* should be deletable before anything at all which can occur after *be*.' Although Bolinger (1967) is severely critical of Lees's account of the derivation of noun phrases containing attributive adjectives, he still (p. 21) wishes to derive some such NPs (his example is *a drowsy policeman*) from structures containing restrictive relative clauses.

(191)

$$X \underset{NP}{} [NP \begin{bmatrix} NP \\ +PRO \\ +REL \end{bmatrix} \quad COP \quad PRED] \quad Y$$

$$\begin{matrix} 1 & 2 & 3 & 4 & 5 & 6 \end{matrix}$$

and its effect is to delete items 3 and 4. (190) meets the structural description (191); the result of applying the rule is

(192) [188]

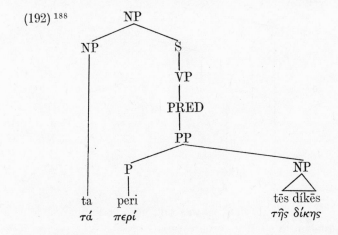

This analysis implies that in phrases of this type the article is still, synchronically, in classical Attic, a pronoun. A similar analysis is necessary for those few phrases such as τὰ καὶ τά tà kaì tá ' this, that, and the other ' and ὁ δέ ho dé ' and he ' in which it is universally agreed to be a pronoun.

If we go no further than this, we will be saying that the article is an underlying pronoun in some of its occurrences and an underlying article in others. There is, however, no need for this split. The occurrences of the article we have not so far considered are those in which it precedes a noun or an infinitive; and just like the other constituent types we have been considering, nouns and infinitives too occur as predicates. If we

---

[188] The Ross (1969) tree-pruning convention will delete the S node in (192); it is possible that one or both of the nodes VP and PRED should also be deleted.

analyse them as remote-structure [189] predicates, rather in the manner of Bach (1968), the category ' article ' can be banished from the base and indeed from the entire grammar, and just as we gave (190) as a remote structure of τὰ περὶ τῆς δίκης *tà perì tês díkēs* so we can give (193) as a remote structure of ὁ ἀνήρ *ho anér* ' the man ':

(193)

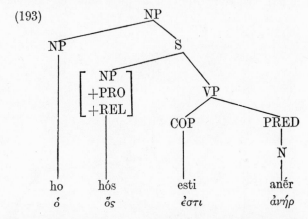

ho   hós   esti   anér
ὁ   ὅς   ἐστι   ἀνήρ

The article is thus, as was said on p. 139, analysable as a pronoun in *all* of its occurrences.

Note now that while Relative Clause Reduction and tree-pruning operations will reduce (193) to (194), which is the syntactically motivated surface structure, the relevant NP when the article stands alone as a pronoun will have only the structure of (195). In both cases the article belongs to the syntactic category NP and to no other.

(194)   (195)

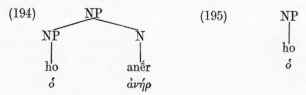

ho   anér   ho
ὁ   ἀνήρ   ὁ

---

[189] This convenient term was introduced and defined by Postal (1970, 101); basically, a remote structure is any tree in a derivation which has still to go through one or more transformations to emerge as a surface structure.

This analysis, which has very strong syntactic motivation, raises the question how the grammar is going to ensure that the article will be proclitic. For without some further rule or convention it leads to results very different from those at which we have arrived on other grounds. In Chomsky-Halle terminology, NP and N are both major categories. By the conventions for introducing word boundaries proposed by Chomsky and Halle (1968), the terminal string of (194) should have the following configuration of word boundaries and category brackets:

(196) $[_{NP} \# [_{NP} \# ho \#] [_N \# anér \#]\#]$

And this configuration, given Chomsky and Halle's convention about 'word termini' (1968, 367–8), incorrectly predicts that in ὁ ἀνήρ *ho anér*, the article will be an independent word.[190] The phonology requires only a single word boundary between article and noun, just as in preposition-noun phrases like ἐκ προνοίας *ek pronoíās* 'intentionally'. The latter phrase, if prepositions are not a major category,[191] may have a surface structure

(197)

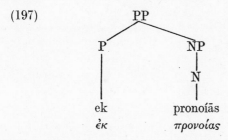

[190] The difficulty still remains even under the attractive proposal of Comrie (1970) to define 'word termini' solely in terms of category brackets and labels, without reference to ⧺ boundaries.

[191] It has often been proposed (see, e.g., the trees given by Lakoff 1971, 102 and 168) that prepositions should be treated as dominated by V. In that case presumably they would be a major category, and there would be an extra pair of ⧺ boundaries in (198). It would then be necessary to extend (199) so that it pruned any non-branching node whatever, except one that directly dominated a lexical item. (The extended convention would always prune NP where this node did not branch, since NP can never directly dominate a lexical item).

for which the Chomsky-Halle word boundary conventions would place the boundaries thus:

(198) $[_{PP} \# [_{P}ek] [_{NP} \# [_{N} \# \text{pronoíās} \#] \#] \#]$

Thus this kind of problem is not special to the article, and some general new convention seems to be necessary. Various suggestions might be made, but it is noticeable that correct results would be got from both (194) and (197) if we adopted the following convention:

(199) Prune any NP node which does not branch.[192]

By applying (199), we change configurations (196) and (198) respectively to:

(200) $[_{NP} \# \text{ho} [_{N} \# \text{anér} \#]\#]$

(201) $[_{PP} \#[_{P}ek] [_{N} \# \text{pronoíās} \#]\#]$

What, in general, is the effect of convention (199) ? NP nodes which do not branch dominate [192a] either N, or S, or a terminal element directly. If they dominate N or S, the constituent in question will still be a major category after pruning and will be a word or words (perhaps a clause), or at least (like *pronoíās* in (201)) the nucleus of a word. If they do not dominate one of these categories, the substring they do dominate will become some kind of clitic; this will chiefly apply to pronouns, when these are not accompanied by an emphasis morpheme in the manner described in note 192.

The proposed convention has nothing to do with Ross's (1969) S-pruning convention. That convention is meant to

---

[192] Given this convention, the fact that in many languages pronouns which are 'emphasized', in some sense, are treated for accentual and other purposes as independent words can be explained by treating an emphasis morpheme as a daughter node of NP coordinate with the pronoun itself.

[192a] A node ' dominates ' the node(s) to which, in a tree representation, lines run downwards from it; the relation is transitive, so that a high-level node can be said to dominate a terminal element, and S dominates every node in the tree. A node ' directly dominates ' the node(s) *immediately* below it in the tree; direct domination is an intransitive relation.

apply at all stages of a derivation, whereas (199) applies only
at one stage – probably just before the convention inserting
word boundaries.

5.2.3. VARIATION OF ACCENT IN NOUN AND ADJECTIVE DECLENSION

The basic principle usually enunciated, e.g. by Koster
(1962, 2), is that ' the accent remains as far as possible on the
syllable that bears it in the nominative singular '. This may
be captured in our framework, for the most part, without very
much difficulty. For non-barytone nouns, we simply accent
the syllable in question in the lexical entry (whether directly
or by a redundancy rule). Barytone nouns, as we have already
arranged, will receive their accent by the Initial Accent Rule
and the Rule of Limitation; in general the case forms are such
that the accent in cases other than the nominative singular will
sometimes fall to the right of its position in the nominative
singular, but never to the left. The following are some of the
problems which arise.

(a) Barytone adjectives of the first and second declension,
such as δίκαιος díkaios ' just ', accent the antepenultimate in
the nominative plural feminine, e.g. δίκαιαι díkaiai; this is
what the Rule of Limitation would lead one to expect. One
would expect also that first-declension nouns which were
barytone (or which, at least, were accented in the nom. sg.
in the same way in which they would be accented if they were
barytone) would likewise be accented on the antepenultimate
in the nominative plural. But this is not so; the accent in
the nom. pl. of these nouns falls on the same syllable as
in the nom. sg. The nom. pl. of τράπεζα trápeza ' table ' is
τράπεζαι trápezai, but the nom. pl. of ἐκκλησία ekklēsíā
' assembly ' is ἐκκλησίαι ekklēsíai. I do not know of a really
satisfactory solution to this problem within the framework of
generative phonology. That framework does not allow us to
make a statement like Koster's above. Solutions that work,
however, are available; one, which I adopt without a great
deal of enthusiasm, is to regard words like ἐκκλησία ekklēsíā as

having, before the Rule of Limitation operates, an underlying penultimate rather than initial accent.

(b) The genitive and dative, all numbers, of first- and second-declension nouns and adjectives are perispomenon, if accented. This is most easily explained if their forms are all regarded as due to contraction of the final vowel of the stem with a vocalic ending. I show in (202) and (203) how this could come about by application of only the ordinary rules of contraction. Note that the dative singular ending must be /ay/, with a final glide; if it were, say, /ai/ or /ei/ – an underlying disyllable – the accent would never be able to fall further back than the final vowel of the stem, so that we would have not only (as we do) ζυγῷ *zygôi* from ζυγόν *zygón* ' yoke ' but also (as we do not) *τεκνῷ *teknôi* from τέκνον *téknon* ' child '. And, for rather similar reasons, the second-declension genitive plural ending must be taken to be /an/; if it were /on/ the contracted form would be [ūn], and if it were /ōn/ the contracted form would *always* be perispomenon (*τεκνῶν *teknôn* as well as ζυγῶν *zygôn*), as it is in the first declension.

(202) Forms of ὀργή [orgḗ] ' anger '

Gen. sg. /orgá̯+es/ → /orgḗ̯+es/   → [orgḗs]   ὀργῆς

Dat. sg. /orgá̯+ay/ → /orgḗ̯+ay/   → [orgéȳ]   ὀργῇ

G.D. du. /orgá̯+in/ → /orgá̯+in/[193] → [orgaȳn] ὀργαῖν

Gen. pl. /orgá̯+ōn/ → /orgḗ̯+ōn/   → [orgǭn]   ὀργῶν

Dat. pl. /orgá̯+is/ → /orgá̯+is/[193] → [orgaȳs] ὀργαῖς

(203) Forms of ζυγόν [zdügón] ' yoke '

Gen. sg. /sdugó̯+o/   → [zdügû]   ζυγοῦ

Dat. sg. /sdugó̯+ay/ → [zdügǭy]   ζυγῷ

G.D. du. /sdugó̯+in/ → [zdügoȳn] ζυγοῖν

Gen. pl. /sdugó̯+an/ → [zdügǭn]   ζυγῶν

Dat. pl. /sdugó̯+is/ → [zdügoȳs] ζυγοῖς

(c) How, on the other hand, do we account for the fact that the nominative-vocative-accusative dual is always oxytone if

---

[193] The final vowel of the stem has undergone Shortening and so has not been affected by the Low Vowel Rule.

accented, e.g. ζυγώ *zygó* ? No other rule, except the quite different third-declension ' rule of monosyllables ' (see paragraph (*h*)), accents a case ending. And since the peculiarity occurs in contracted forms like χρυσώ *khrūsó* ' golden ' (from /+ę̄+ǭ/) and in uncontracted forms like ζυγώ *zygó* in exactly the same way, it must result from a rule which, unlike the ' rule of monosyllables ', is ordered after Contraction. Such a rule could take the form:

(204) AUXILIARY REASSIGNMENT [194]

$$\begin{bmatrix} V \\ +\text{back} \\ +\text{sharp} \\ 2 \text{ Number} \end{bmatrix} \rightarrow [-\text{falling}] / \text{——} [+\text{WB}]$$

(*d*) Some vocative forms, such as δέσποτα *déspota* ' master ', πάτερ *páter* ' father ', ἄδελφε *ádelphe* ' brother ', are accented like barytones even though the basic accent of these nouns is on the final or penultimate syllable – cf. nom sg. πατήρ *patḗr* and ἀδελφός *adelphós* and nom. pl. δεσπόται *despótai*. These vocatives must be marked as irregular in that they undergo the ACCENT REASSIGNMENT RULE, which is of the form

(205)

$$\begin{bmatrix} V \\ +\text{A.R.R.} \end{bmatrix} \rightarrow [+\text{sharp}] / \text{——} C_0(VC_0(\begin{bmatrix} V \\ -\text{long} \end{bmatrix} C_0)) [+\text{WB}]$$

Accent Reassignment (whose effect, it will be seen, is very similar to that of the Rule of Limitation [195]) is a minor rule.

---

[194] The environment statement ensures that the accent will not be changed in the genitive and dative, where the vowel is not word-final. Since gender, case, number and person features are peripheral to phonology, I have arbitrarily chosen to regard them as multi-valued. Their values are integers from 1 upwards, their ascending order being: (gender) masc., fem., neut.; (case) nom., voc., acc., gen., dat.; (number) sg., du., pl.; (person) first, second, third.

[195] To this extent the analysis is undesirably repetitive. It may be preferable to extract the common core from (179) and (205) and treat this core as a linking rule of ' recessive accent ' triggered by a rule feature [+RA]. In that case (179) and (205) would be replaced by rules assigning this feature – the former assigning it just in case the accent is on the antepenultimate or earlier; the latter, just in case the word has the feature [+A.R.R.]. Note that it is not necessary to invoke Accent Reassignment to account

If we require every minor rule R_i to include in its structural description the specification $[+R_i]$, the result will be that a minor rule, simply by being minor, is more complex than an otherwise identical major rule; this suggestion is at once intuitively satisfactory and a solution of the problem of how to indicate that minor rules are minor.[196]

The application of (205) to a form like *[despóta] produces the correct phonetic form [déspota], δέσποτα.

(e) And in the same way, Accent Reassignment applies to ἔκπλους *ékplous* ' a sailing out ' and to compounds of ῥοῦς *rhoûs* ' flow, stream '. These are declined like contracted nouns whose stems end in /ǫǫ/; they are manifestly derived from the verbs πλέω *pléō* ' sail ' and ῥέω *rhéō* ' flow ', whose stems must be /plęw/ and /ręw/,[197] so that the expected forms for action nouns would be /plǫw+ǫ+s/ and /rǫw+ǫ+s/; the nouns have no semantic specialization; yet they are accented like uncontracted barytones, ἔκπλου *ékplou*, ἔκπλοις *ékplois*, etc., not *ekploû, *ekploîs. All this can be not perhaps explained, but at least accounted for, if these words are marked [+A.R.R.] and undergo Accent Reassignment.[198]

for the accentuation of adjectival neuters like εὔδαιμον *eúdaimon*, neuter of εὐδαίμων *eudaímōn* ' happy '. If all adjectives of this type are assumed to be barytone (that is, subject to the Initial Accent Rule), the Rule of Limitation will automatically give the masculine its correct accent, and the neuter will get its accent by an extension of Vendryes' Law – a similar extension being required in any case (see note 164 and Summary of Rules) because of certain verb forms.

[196] We do not always give rules in the most theoretically correct form, and below we shall often simply label minor rules as such and omit the specification [+R_i]. Note that it will be necessary to modify a convention proposed by Chomsky and Halle (1968, 173, convention 1) to read:

Every segment of a lexical matrix is automatically marked [+n] for every major rule *n* and [−m] for every minor rule *m*.

As in the case of the original convention, it is assumed that the markings prescribed by this convention can be altered by readjustment rules or by lexical specifications for particular formatives.

[197] The evidence for this, in the case of ῥέω *rhéō*, is given on p. 17; the forms and derivatives of πλέω *pléō*, though not so numerous, are exactly parallel.

[198] If this is done, Accent Reassignment must be placed later than Contraction, since otherwise its application to forms of these nouns will be vacuous.

(f) The contrary situation is found in nouns and adjectives
of the so-called Attic declension, like λεώς *leṓs* ' people ',
which are oxytone in all cases, even the genitive and dative.
This might seem to suggest the desirability of a second Accent
Reassignment Rule, shifting the accent to the last syllable of
the word. Since, however, there is no other phenomenon for
which such a rule would be of any use,[199] its introduction
would be a fifth wheel in the machinery, and it will be simpler
to assign accent directly to the final vowel of these words on
the basis of their declensional class, rather than saying that
they have a rule feature which triggers the supposed second
Accent Reassignment Rule.

(g) Another apparent problem is the feminine genitive
plural of second-declension adjectives; this is perispomenon
or paroxytone according as the adjective itself is oxytone or
not, whereas first-declension nouns and the feminines of other
adjectives are always perispomenon in this case. The genitive
plural of ἐκκλησία *ekklēsíā* is ἐκκλησιῶν *ekklēsiôn* (from
/ęk+klęsiá+ǫn/); the gen. pl. of the feminine of the third-
declension adjective ἡδύς *hēdýs* ' sweet ' is ἡδειῶν *hēdeiôn*;
but in the feminine of ἄξιος *áksios* ' worthy ' it is ἀξίων
aksíōn, not *ἀξιῶν *aksiôn*. This form can only be accounted
for by supposing it to be the masculine form taken over by the
feminine. Some second-declension adjectives never have a
feminine form distinct from the masculine; the gen. pl. may
perhaps be regarded in a special environment in which *no*
second-declension adjective has a distinct feminine form.

(h) Third-declension nouns are subject to a so-called ' rule of
monosyllables ', under which, to over-simplify a little, nouns
with monosyllabic stems are accented on the final syllable in
the genitive and dative (all numbers). It might be thought
that this could be regarded as a special case of the second
Accent Reassignment Rule rejected in paragraph (f). This,
however, is not possible. The nouns discussed in paragraph (f)

---

[199] It is not of any use with respect to the third-declension ' rule of
monosyllables '; see paragraph (h).

are accented *acute* on the final syllable in all cases, whereas
third-declension nouns with monosyllabic stems are accented
circumflex on the final syllable where this has a long nucleus.
Contrast λεών *león*, genitive plural (as well as accusative
singular) of λεώς *leós*, with ἀνδρῶν *andrôn*, genitive plural of
ἀνήρ *anér* ' man '.

There are several apparent exceptions to the Rule of Monosyllables; most of these, such as κῆρ *kêr* ' heart ' and πρών
prón ' headland ', can be eliminated if the rule is ordered before
Contraction, since their stems can be regarded as still disyllabic
at the point at which the rule applies.

The following is one form in which the rule could be stated:

(206) RULE OF MONOSYLLABLES (First Version)

$$
\begin{bmatrix} V \\ +\text{accentable} \end{bmatrix} \rightarrow
\left\{ \begin{array}{l} [+\text{sharp}] \\[2ex] [+\text{falling}] \Big/ \left\{ \begin{bmatrix} \underline{} \\ +\text{long} \end{bmatrix} \\ \underline{} \begin{bmatrix} -\text{cns} \\ -\text{syl} \end{bmatrix} \right\} \end{array} \right\}
$$

$$
\Big/ \# \, C_0 V C_0 \begin{bmatrix} \underline{} \\ -\text{partic} \\ a \ \text{case} \\ 3 \ \text{Decl} \end{bmatrix} C_0 \#
$$

where $a = 4$ or 5.

This form of the rule accounts indeed for all the facts, apart
from the exceptions (which we will consider later); but it is not
explanatory. We are left with no idea why, when the case
ending contains a long nucleus, it should be accented circumflex. Is there any way in which we can explain this ?

Normally, except in the case governed by linking rule (175),
a circumflex-accented vowel is the result of the contraction of
two vowels, the first of which is accented. Could we treat the
circumflex in forms like ἀνδρῶν *andrôn* as due to contraction ?
We could indeed; the immediately underlying form would be
/andróan/. And to assume /oan/ as the third-declension genitive
plural ending would have the added advantage that this

ending would be similar to that of the same case in second-declension nouns (see p. 148). It would, however, require (206) to be reformulated. The Rule of Monosyllables can no longer be treated as accenting the final syllable of a word; it will have to be regarded (following an unpublished suggestion of Kiparsky's, communicated to me by Andrew Carstairs) as accenting *the syllable following the stem*. The following version of the rule will do this:

(207) RULE OF MONOSYLLABLES (Second Version)

$$\begin{bmatrix} V \\ +\text{accentable} \end{bmatrix} \rightarrow \ [+\text{sharp}]$$

$$/\,[+\text{WB}]\ C_0VC_0 + \begin{bmatrix} \rule{1cm}{0.4pt} \\ -\text{partic} \\ a\ \text{case} \\ 3\ \text{Decl} \end{bmatrix} (V)C_0\,[+\text{WB}]$$

where $a = 4$ or 5.

We have not yet accounted for the other case in which an accent assigned by the Rule of Monosyllables is circumflex: the genitive-dative dual, e.g. ἀνδροῖν *androîn*. This can be accounted for by (207) if we order the rule before Diphthong Formation; at that stage the ending, underlying /ǫin/, is disyllabic; (207) will accent its first syllable, and Diphthong Formation, collapsing the two syllables into one, will make the accent circumflex. It seems impossible, however, for the Rule of Monosyllables to be ordered before Diphthong Formation. For consider a word like κλής [klę̄ys] ' key ': this is subject to the Rule of Monosyllables (its genitive is κληδός [klę̄ydós]), but its stem contains a diphthong, and therefore, before Diphthong Formation, was not monosyllabic. It follows that if we modify the Rule of Monosyllables to (207), we will be able to account in a principled way for the form of the genitive plural, but for the genitive-dative dual the rule will incorrectly predict forms like *[andróyn].

We would not wish, however, to give up the gain in simplicity and explanation achieved by (207) over (206). I therefore

L

suggest that the Rule of Monosyllables should be allowed to produce these incorrectly accented genitive-dative duals, and that their accent should be corrected by an extension of the Auxiliary Reassignment Rule (204), which already applies to other dual forms. The revised Auxiliary Reassignment Rule would be something like this:

$$(208) \quad \begin{bmatrix} V \\ +\text{back} \\ +\text{sharp} \\ 2 \text{ Number} \end{bmatrix} \rightarrow [\alpha \text{ falling}] \,/ + \underline{\quad\quad} [\alpha \text{ seg}] \,^{200}$$

Rule (208) makes *all* genitive-dative dual forms circumflex if accented – which, with the exception mentioned in note 200, is correct.

I now wish to turn to the apparent exceptions to the Rule of Monosyllables. The rule itself, as I have framed it, excludes participles from its operation, and its position in the ordering will exclude contracted words. Once these are left out of consideration, there is little regularity to be found in the exceptions, and they will simply have to be marked as exceptions (full or partial) in the lexicon.[201] One apparent reverse exception, however, is of interest, namely γυνή *gyné* ' woman '. This noun is subject to the Rule of Monosyllables (e.g. its genitive singular is γυναικός *gynaikós* not *γυναῖκος *gynaîkos*)

---

[200] Genitive-dative duals of the ' Attic declension ' are oxytone; this rule will therefore have to precede the rule which makes all forms of nouns of that declensional class oxytone. All nominative-accusative dual forms end in a vowel; all genitive-dative dual forms in [yn].

[201] Kuryłowicz (1958, 124) points out that many of the partial exceptions only violate the rule when the final syllable of the word has a long nucleus. Kiparsky (1967) seeks to explain this via his ' iambic retraction ' rule. This is an extension of Vendryes' Law to include an alleged similar retraction of accent in polysyllables with iambic endings. As he points out, however, ' iambic retraction ' would have far more exceptions than Vendryes' Law; and his proposal also requires the use of a notational device not known to be otherwise needed in phonology to denote the disjunction ' XYZ or XY or YZ '.

even though its stem is not monosyllabic. There seem to be two possible ways of bringing γυνή *gyné* within the compass of (207). One is to recognize, in this morpheme only,[202] a new systematic phoneme /gᵂ/, thereby introducing a new contrast (roundness) into the consonant system; the other is to regard the stem as /gnaik/, /g/ being identical in its feature composition to /g/ except that it has the property of being subject to a minor rule, later than (207), inserting [u]. There seems little to choose between these solutions; however, considerations brought forward by Hyman (1970) might lead one to prefer the former.[203]

(i) The small group of nouns represented by πατήρ *patér* ‘ father ’ and ἀνήρ *anér* ‘ man ’ show some remarkable features, discussed above (pp. 63 ff., 73 ff.), but in the matter of accent they do not require any rules peculiar to themselves. The basic accent of all of them is on the last syllable of the stem. The genitive and dative are subject to (207), but only, of course, where the stem is monosyllabic—not, therefore, in the gen.-dat. dual or genitive plural, with the exception of ἀνδρῶν *andrôn* and ἀνδροῖν *andrôin*. This leaves two major points as yet unexplained. One is the behaviour of θυγάτηρ *thygátēr* ‘ daughter ’, which acts with respect to (207) as if its stem were monosyllabic; in this it must be regarded as a pure exception. Secondly, most nouns of this class have recessive accent in the vocative, and μήτηρ *mḗtēr* ‘ mother ’ and θυγάτηρ *thygátēr* in the nominative; this can be handled by Accent Reassignment.

(209) shows the derivations of all the singular and plural forms of πατήρ *patér*.

---

[202] Scattered and unproductive alternations such as present πέττω *péttō* ‘ cook, bake ’: future πέψω *pépsō*, πού *poû* ‘ where ’: τίς *tís* ‘ who ’, etc., though resulting from various developments of early Greek labialized velars, are hardly adequate evidence for postulating other occurrences of labialized velars in lexical representations in classical Attic.

[203] The Markedness theory ensures that this proposal will not make it necessary to specify every other /g/ in the lexicon as non-round.

(209)

Underlying form after ablaut rules	*Epenthesis*	*Rule of Mono-syllables*	*Accent Reassign-ment*	
patẹ̄r				πατήρ
patẹ̄r			páter	πάτερ
patẹ̄r+a				πατέρα
pátr+ọs [204]		patrọ́s		πατρός
pátr+i [204]		patrí		πατρί
patẹ̄r+ẹs				πατέρες
patẹ̄r+as				πατέρας
patẹ̄r+ọan		(Contraction)	patérọn	πατέρων
pátr+si [204]	pátr+asi	patrási		πατράσι

(*j*) Why are the vocatives of nouns ending in [éws] (e.g. βασιλεῦ *basileû* ' O king ') always perispomenon ? I think there is lurking here a generalization of some interest: *word-final* [aw] *and* [ew] *are always perispomenon if accented*; and as this fully explains the accent of these vocatives without the need to invoke any special irregularities, I am led to propose a late rule:

$$(210) \quad [+\text{sharp}] \rightarrow [+\text{falling}] / \left[\overline{ -\text{round} } \right] \text{w} [+\text{WB}]$$

This rule also accounts for the accent of εὖ *eû* ' well ', of which Vendryes (1929) says: ' Apollonius Dyscole était déjà fort embarrassé par l'accent de l'adverbe εὖ. Nous ne sommes pas plus avancés que lui '. Kretschmer and Locker (1963) give only one form which is an exception to (210), viz. βαύ *baú* ' bow-wow ', *frag. com. adesp.* 1304 Kock.

5.2.4. PREPOSITIONS

Vendryes (1929, 67 ff.) makes out a convincing case that prepositions in Greek had no accent when preposed to noun

[204] In these forms the stem-final vowel has been deleted by Vowel Weakening, and the accent with it; the accent shown on the first syllable is assigned automatically to accentless words by the Initial Accent Rule.

phrases; but the question what their underlying accent is, if any, and whether they undergo an accent deletion or an accent insertion rule, do not really arise within his frame of reference. In ours, on the other hand, they are important. We can best approach them by asking when and how prepositions were accented when *postposed* to noun phrases.

The traditional rule is that postposed prepositions are accented on the first syllable, except for ἀμφί *amphí* ' around ' and ἀντί *antí* ' instead of '. Is this rule recoverable from the way postposed prepositions were actually used in classical Attic ? And if not, what rule (if any) is ?

In prose, only disyllabic prepositions are postposed, and ἀμφί *amphí* and ἀντί *antí* are not among those so treated. We are thus forced to turn for evidence to postposing in verse – in particular, in tragic iambics.

Postposed prepositions at the end of the line tell us nothing new, since in that position ἀμφί *amphí* and ἀντί *antí* are metrically impossible. In mid-line ἀμφί *amphí* is not found postposed, and ἀντί *antí* only once (Aeschylus, *Agamemnon* 1277), where it is elided.

But what is interesting is that we are told by an ancient commentator on Homer, *Iliad* 18. 191 that when a postposed preposition was elided, it lost its accent.[205] Thus the accentuation at Euripides, *Electra* 574 should be σοῦ μεθ' *soû meth'* ' with you ', not σοῦ μέθ' *soû méth'*. If the scholiast is right, then (*a*) the lack of an accent on ἀντ' *ant'* at A. *Ag.* 1277 is not evidence that the underlying accent was on the last syllable,[206] and (*b*) postposed prepositions had an accent *only* when they were *phonetically* disyllabic. This being so, we have the choice of two analyses:

---

[205] ' Except before a pause ', the scholion says, but this exception may safely be disregarded. It may well signify merely that elided prepositions were pronounced as if unelided when a pause followed, just as ἔρφ' *hérph'* (elided form of ἕρπε *hérpe* ' get a move on ') must surely have been at Sophocles, *Electra* 1502, where it is followed not merely by a pause, but by a change of speaker.

[206] Even supposing we knew that it represented the ancient pronunciation and was not merely a copyist's application of the traditional rule.

(i) that all ' true ' prepositions are lexically atonic, but that at some stage after the rule of Elision postposed disyllabic prepositions are given an accent; or

(ii) that all prepositions are underlyingly accented on the first syllable, and that they lose their accent if preposed, or if monosyllabic.

Of these, (i) is preferable because it requires only one environment for its rule, not two distinct and unrelated ones.[207]

In any event, there is no justification within Attic for giving ἀμφί *amphí* and ἀντί *antí* special status. In spoken usage and prose literature, and quite probably in poetry as well, they never occurred in a position where it was possible to tell what their accent would be if they were not atonic; and we cannot tell what accentuation they were given when they occurred in a Homeric line like *Iliad* 11. 414.

5.2.5. PRONOUNS

The special problem here is that of the accentuation of the extra-emphasis forms of the first person singular pronoun – nominative ἔγωγε *égōge*, genitive ἐμοῦγε *emoûge*, dative ἔμοιγε *émoige* – contrasted with that of the ordinary forms ἐγώ *egó*, ἐμοῦ *emoû*, ἐμοί *emoí*. Vendryes (1929) does not explain why Vendryes' Law, which is evidently responsible for the accentuation of ἔγωγε *égōge* and ἔμοιγε *émoige*, does not apply to ἐμοῦγε *emoûge*. The reason actually is that, as is independently necessary (see note 161), Vendryes' Law must apply before Contraction, and that, as is also independently necessary (to account for its circumflex, rather than acute, accent), ἐμοῦ *emoû* must be regarded as contracted from /ęmę̇+ǫ/ with accent on the last vowel of the stem as in ἐγώ *egó*, ἐμοί *emoí*, and the accusative ἐμέ *emé*. Thus when Vendryes' Law becomes applicable, it duly applies to /ęgǫ̂+gę/ and

[207] Kuryłowicz (1958, 152, note 23) also, for quite different reasons, regards the unaccented form of Greek prepositions as more basic, synchronically speaking, than the accented form.

/ęmộy+ge/,[208] but /ęmę́+ǫ+gę/ fails to meet its structural description, which requires the input to be properispomenon (see p. 187). So two assumptions made for quite different reasons interact to predict the apparently anomalous accentuation of ἐμοῦγε *emoûge*.

5.2.6. ENCLITICS

Whenever possible – that is, whenever there is not a svarita glide on the syllable in question – the syllable immediately preceding an enclitic is accented. The rule for this, in its simplest form, is:

(211) RULE OF ENCLISIS

$$\begin{bmatrix} V \\ -\text{falling} \end{bmatrix} \to [+\text{sharp}] / \underline{\hspace{2em}} C_0 [+\text{WB}] [+\text{enclitic}]$$

There is also a rule that accented word-final syllables which are not circumflex and do *not* immediately precede an enclitic take a grave rather than an acute accent. Making the assumption (to be justified below) that the grave accent-mark denotes a low tone, this second rule may be stated thus:

(212) ACUTE-GRAVE RULE

$$\begin{bmatrix} V \\ -\text{falling} \end{bmatrix} \to [-\text{sharp}] / \underline{\hspace{2em}} C_0 [+\text{WB}]_1 [-\text{enclitic}]$$

If these are indeed the correct forms of the rules in question, and if there is no reason to separate them in the ordering (which it turns out there indeed is not), then they can be combined as one schema:

(213)

$$\begin{bmatrix} V \\ -\text{falling} \end{bmatrix} \to [\alpha \text{ sharp}] / \underline{\hspace{2em}} C_0 [+\text{WB}]_1 [\alpha \text{ enclitic}]$$

---

[208] The [+falling], or circumflex, accent of these forms is due to linking rule (175), which automatically comes into operation when the word boundary between the pronoun and the particle γε *ge* is weakened to formative boundary and a structure is thus created that meets the structural description of (175).

This schema asserts that a word-final syllable which is neither circumflex nor post-acute, whether it was or was not accented before the point of application of the schema, is phonetically high-pitched if and only if it is immediately followed by an enclitic.[209]

Before, though, we can accept the tempting generalization offered by (213), we must show that (211) and (212) are respectively the correct forms of the Rule of Enclisis and the Acute-Grave Rule. And at first sight there seems to be a great deal for which (211) and (212) do not account. They say nothing about the retention of the acute accent on final syllables where a pause follows; they assume that the grave accent-mark, where it appears in our texts, represents a low (or at least non-high) tone; and they say nothing about the accent which, according to the tradition reflected in our texts, appeared on the final syllable of disyllabic enclitics after paroxytone words, as in τρόπον τινά *trópon tiná* ‘ in some way ’.

(*a*) *Prepausal acute*: This phenomenon may well have nothing to do with the Acute-Grave Rule; rather, it may be a feature of sentence intonation, viz. rise at end of phrase. So Trubetzkoy (1949, 258) interpreted it, saying that the rise occurred ‘ avant une pause, si le mot ne possédait aucune autre more aiguë ’; I would observe that we do not know that the rise did not also occur before a pause in other circumstances. Being automatic it would not be marked in writing, except where it fell on a syllable that would otherwise have been marked grave; for while an unmarked vowel would automatically have been pronounced on a high tone before a pause, a grave marking might have been misinterpreted as directing a non-high tone.

(*b*) *Grave as non-high tone*: The strongest evidence for believing that the grave accent-mark means precisely what it seems to say is that it is regularly put on proclitics where these

---

[209] In Warburton’s (1970) treatment, three rules, not counting ‘ boundary erasure ’, are needed to produce the correct output in the case of enclitics alone, without incorporating the Acute-Grave Rule.

appear graphically as separate words. There is overwhelming evidence that proclitics were unaccented; [210] and, especially seeing that most prepositions were not oxytone when they were accented independently, the ancient grammarians would never have regarded proclitics as oxytone if there had not been something in the behaviour of real oxytones to mislead them. The only thing likely to do that would be for the real oxytones also to be sometimes unaccented. The principle on which the traditional graphic practice was based is a reasonable one. A mark is put on the structurally accented syllable, as usual; but it is the grave and not the acute, to show that the accent has in this case no phonetic value.[211]

(c) *The alleged accent on disyllabic enclitics*: It might be thought that this is all but a non-question. As Barrett (1964, 425, note 2) observes, it can make no phonetic difference whether disyllabic enclitics had an accent or not, except before a pause; and in view of the automatic rise at phrase end, it can make no difference before a pause either. And this would be all that needed to be said on the subject if it were not for τινῶν *tinôn*, genitive plural of the enclitic τις *tis* ' some, a '. The traditional accentuation of this word makes the very definite claim that after paroxytone words (but *only* after paroxytone words), its last syllable was phonetically [+sharp, +falling]. The question of this alleged accent will thus have to be discussed in full.

The suggestion I make is that enclitics were *always* unaccented (except before other enclitics – see subsection (d)). There is one major argument against this, and one against the traditional view. Against my suggestion it may be argued that a

---

[210] The most striking points are given by Vendryes (1929, 68–9).

[211] Another language with a system of tonal accent, Japanese, also has, according to McCawley (1968, 134), ' a number of environments in which a final-accented noun *is made unaccented* ' (emphasis mine: AHS), e.g., under certain conditions, before the enclitic *no*. (See further McCawley 1968, 140–1 and 177–9). The syllable which would have been accented is in such cases pronounced exactly as if it had never been accented. This shows that we need not be afraid of concluding that in Greek oxytone words frequently had no accent, phonetically speaking, at all.

phrase like λόγων τινων *lógōn tinōn* ' of some arguments ', which is a single phonological word, violates the Rule of Limitation. But this would not be the only such ' violation '; consider οὕτω που *hoútō pou* ' thus, I suppose ', Βοιωτοῦ τινος *Boiōtoû tinos* ' of a Boeotian ', πόλεως *póleōs* ' of a city ' and βούκερως *boúkerōs* ' with cow's horns '. Moreover, the Rule of Limitation can be said to be ' violated ' only if a form which *at the appropriate stage of derivation* meets its structural description fails to undergo it. To claim that λόγων τινων *lógōn tinōn* violates the Rule of Limitation is to treat that rule as if it were an output condition, and this the other examples given warn us that we cannot do. In point of fact, the Rule of Limitation, in the form (179) in which we have given it, will simply not apply to a combination of an accented word and an enclitic; and if we were to apply it to a phrase like λόγων τινων *lógōn tinōn*, it would, contrary to the traditional rule, accent not the second but the first syllable of the enclitic.

The main objection to the traditional view is that no explanation is usually offered of why the alleged accent is restricted to disyllabic enclitics following paroxytone words: why, that is, οὕτω που *hoútō pou* and Βοιωτοῦ τινος *Boiōtoû tinos* are allowed to ' violate ' the Rule of Limitation, but λόγων τινων *lógōn tinōn* is not. Vendryes (1929, 80–4) suggests that the explanation is that the Rule of Limitation itself should be differently formulated: in particular, that the final syllable of an enclitic should always be treated, for accentual purposes, as if it had a short nucleus. According to him, the only syllables treated by the rule as having long nuclei are those on which there can be a contrast between acute and circumflex ('intonable' syllables, as he calls them); therefore it is crucial to the correctness of Vendryes' hypothesis that no such contrast should be possible on the final syllable of an enclitic; and Vendryes indeed claims that none is possible. Now in this he is either right or wrong. If he is wrong, we are still without an explanation of the alleged facts mentioned at the beginning of this paragraph. If, on the other hand, he is right, what are the consequences ?

It is clear from what Vendryes says in the same passage about another type of syllable which he holds to be 'non intonable' – the final syllable of the word preceding an enclitic – that he considers that 'non-intonable' syllables, if accented, were always pronounced with the acute intonation; only thus can he save *Βοιωτοῦ τινος Boiōtou tinos* from being a 'violation' of the Rule of Limitation. But evidently, if *τινῶν tinôn* was pronounced with this intonation,[212] it would have been subject to the Acute-Grave Rule,[213] and hence phonetically unaccented except before a pause – which is exactly what my hypothesis predicts. Thus in fact Vendryes and I agree, against the ancient grammarians, that *τινων tinōn* was normally unaccented; otherwise, the hypotheses of the ancient grammarians, Vendryes, and myself, are simply alternative attempts at explaining the same facts – with one important exception: Vendryes, since he believes that the final syllable of the word preceding an enclitic was 'non-intonable', is forced to the conclusion that *φῶς ἐστι phôs esti* ' it is light ' and *φώς ἐστι phós esti* ' it is a man ' must have been pronounced alike – for which there is no ancient evidence whatever. My hypothesis is thus more nearly in line with the available data than his.[214]

[212] As Vendryes seems to think it was; at any rate he says, with reference to *τινῶν tinôn* (1929, 81), ' Il n'y a rien à conclure du fait qu'en cette position on distingue dans l'écriture le circonflexe de l'aigu '.

[213] Unless that rule were burdened with an ad hoc and coincidental exception.

[214] A possible further piece of evidence comes from the musical Sicilus epitaph, which I know from Allen (1968, 110). In this, with two exceptions, the syllable which according to the grammatical tradition should bear the accent is always set to the highest note (or one of the equal highest notes) in the word. One of the exceptions is the enclitic *ἐστι esti*, which follows the paroxytone word *ὀλίγον oligon*. Here the highest note is on the unaccented first syllable, and not on the second, which, if the alleged accent on disyllabic enclitics existed, should have borne that accent. Allen (1968, 109, note 2) does indeed mention the possibility that *ἔστι ésti* may be intended, but this would require an existential interpretation, which in the context is most unnatural. The difficulty disappears if we suppose that *ἐστι esti* has no accent – that it is part of an accentual unit *προς-ὀλίγον-ἐστι pros-oligon-esti* which has just one peak. This peak, on the accented syllable of *ὀλίγον oligon*, is indeed set o the highest note in the whole three-word group.

(d) *Successions of enclitics* ('*synenclisis*'): Rule (211) as given preserves the ancient grammarians' rule that the last syllable of an enclitic is accented acute before another enclitic, even when this means that two successive syllables would both be accented acute. Barrett (1964, 427) objects to the grammarians' rule as ' wholly improbable '; but it turns out that the only argument he has against it is that it is ' at variance with the rule that two consecutive syllables cannot both be acute '. We shall have a look at this so-called rule in a moment.

Meanwhile, if we find explicit statements in the ancient grammarians about this rule of ' synenclisis ', we ought, in the absence of compelling reasons to the contrary, to believe them, since this accent, unlike some of the others we have been considering, would be audible, not merely an inference from what happens in prepausal position or from the analogy of ordinary oxytones. And from Apollonius Dyscolus (249, 16 Schneider) we have not merely an explicit statement but what could be an explicit reply to Vendryes (1929, 88) and Barrett. Apollonius was well aware that in most circumstances two consecutive syllables could not both be acute, as appears from what he here says: ' When there are two or three words ' (i.e. successive enclitics) ' there is no bar against a succession of acutes ';[215] after which he proceeds to quote in illustration ἤ νύ σέ που ἔ *nэ́ sé pou* (Homer, *Iliad* 5, 812).

Moreover, this so-called rule of successive acutes does not exist. The other rules of the language are such that if it did exist, it would only be able to apply in two sets of circumstances. One is precisely the set of circumstances with which we are at the moment concerned. The other would be where an acute-accented interrogative word, that is τίς *tís* ' who ' or τί *tí* ' what ', was followed by a word accented acute on the first syllable. In the latter case successive acutes are of course allowed, and nobody has ever contended that they are not; there is

---

[215] δύο λέξεων ἤ τριῶν οὐσῶν ἀκώλυτον τὸ ἐπάλληλον τῆς ὀξείας *dэ́o lékseōn è triôn ousôn akólyton tò epállēlon tês okseiās*.

an instance of this at Euripides, *Hippolytus* 340 τί πάσχεις; *tí páskheis?* ' what is the matter with you ? ' – printed with two acutes by all editors, Barrett included, without apparent qualms, but which would violate the rule of successive acutes, if there were such a rule. And if the ' rule of successive acutes ' is held not to apply to interrogatives, then it does not apply anywhere except just in the case where its applicability is contested and by the ancient grammarians [216] denied. I suggest that the ' rule ' is no rule at all, but simply a false generaliza-tion whose real basis is the undoubted fact that the Rule of Enclisis cannot accent a vowel that has a svarita glide at the stage when the rule becomes applicable.[217]

I conclude that (211) and (212) are justified, and hence also

---

[216] This does not merely refer to Apollonius and other grammarians of later antiquity. Laum (1928, 488) asserts that the Alexandrian grammarians followed the same principles with regard to ' synenclisis ' as their successors, except that pronouns which were enclitic never received an accent; so that the beginning of *Iliad* 5. 812 would be ἤ νύ σε που ἔ νý se pou, not ἤ νν σέ που ἔ ny sé pou as it would be under the system proposed by Barrett (1964, 427). The proviso about pronouns appears to be based, rather weakly, on an *argumentum ex silentio* from the fact that schol. AG on *Iliad* 5. 812 mention the acute on ἤ ē and νν ny but not on σε se (cf. Laum 1928, 243); but if this scholion is to be taken as evidence for the Alexandrian theory, it suggests that that theory did not recognize any ' rule of successive acutes '.

[217] Warburton (1970) shows that if her rules of enclisis are applied cyclic-ally, the output is the same that results from the application of Barrett's principle, whereas she finds that an *ad hoc* rule is needed to derive the repre-sentations that result from the application of the grammarians' rule. But there are other means of deriving the latter set of representations – for example, by the application of (211) simultaneously in every environment in which it will apply. Furthermore, Warburton's rule will only work in the desired manner given a particular constituent structure: all phrases con-sisting of an accented word A plus a string of enclitics E_1, E_2, . . . must have the structure

. . . (((A) E_1) E_2) . . .

– that is, a left-branching structure; and the assumption that this *is* the constituent structure of such phrases is nowhere justified.

Warburton describes the system of synenclisis corresponding to the out-put of her rules as ' given in the manuscripts ' and again as ' the manuscript tradition '. It would be more accurate to say that it is one of a number of traditions reflected in manuscripts; Vendryes (1929, 88), who favours the same system, makes this clear.

(213), which says in effect that (211) and (212) are obverse and reverse of a single phenomenon.

5.2.7. ELISION [218]

When, across a word boundary or a = boundary, a short vowel precedes a vowel or [h], the short vowel is generally dropped. Thus, instead of μετὰ αὐτοῦ *metà autoû* ' with him ', we usually find μετ' αὐτοῦ *met' autou*. If this results in a voiceless stop directly preceding [h], the voiceless stop is aspirated; thus when μετὰ ἡμῶν *metà hēmôn* ' with us ' undergoes elision, the result is μεθ' ἡμῶν *meth' hēmôn*.

Further, elision has consequences for accentuation. When the elided vowel bears an accent, this accent is not lost; it reappears on the preceding syllable. Koster (1962) lists a number of words as not ' throwing back ' their accent, but these words are all proclitics and have no accent to throw back.

---

[218] F. W. Householder (personal communication) has pointed out that the elision rule I propose below will not account for the elision of [ay] and [oy] attested in comedy. I agree, but I notice that in careful speech these diphthongs do not appear to have been elided. The evidence is quite simple: authors who avoid hiatus do not avoid sequences of final short vowel plus initial vowel, but they do avoid sequences of [ay] or [oy] plus initial vowel, The table below shows the frequencies in passages of comparable length from Thucydides (3. 9–13, 37–40. 2, both from speeches) and Demosthenes (18. 1–17, 306–324) of the two kinds of sequence across the boundary between accentual units (this boundary is symbolized by @). That is, sequences where the first vowel was in a proclitic, or the second in an enclitic, or both, were ignored. So also were sequences broken by punctuation.

αι/οι -*ai/oi* @ V		a/ε/o -*a/e/o* @ V (whether or not elided in text)
46	Thucydides	86
1	Demosthenes	82
0·022 : 1	Ratio D : T	0·956 : 1

If Demosthenes could have elided these diphthongs before initial vowels, it is inexplicable that he so carefully avoids placing them there. I conclude that in public speaking, at any rate, they could not be elided. Other styles of speech may well have had a rule, before Elision, deleting final /y/ before vowels.

The following rule accounts for all the facts, to the extent to which the facts are regular.[219]

(214) ELISION

$$
\langle V \quad C_0 \rangle
\begin{bmatrix}
V \\
-\text{long} \\
\left\{ \begin{matrix} -\text{high} \\ -\text{round} \end{matrix} \right\} \\
\langle +\text{sharp} \rangle
\end{bmatrix}
\begin{bmatrix}
-\text{seg} \\
-\text{FB}
\end{bmatrix}_1
[-\text{cons}]
$$

$$
\langle \quad 1 \qquad 2 \rangle \qquad 3 \qquad\qquad 4 \qquad\quad 5 \qquad \Rightarrow
$$

$$
\langle \begin{bmatrix} 1 \\ +\text{sharp} \end{bmatrix} \quad 2 \rangle \qquad \emptyset \qquad\qquad 4 \qquad\quad 5
$$

The rule to aspirate final voiceless stops [220] follows. It is

[219] The rule ensures that [ü] is never elided. There are also certain exceptions; most notably, the rule does not apply when position 3 is filled by the dative morpheme or part of the dative morpheme (so e.g. neither πατρί *patrí* nor πατράσι *patrási* can ever undergo Elision). Note that the specification [−cons] in (214) covers [h] as well as vowels.

As here given, (214) will not call linking rule (175) into operation, since the vowel to which it gives an accent (when it does) is in a final, not a penultimate, syllable, once the rule has applied; so that when the final vowel of δεινά *deiná* ' terrible (things) ' is elided, the remaining syllable is *not* accented circumflex – which, according to the grammatical tradition, is correct.

The tradition also, however, prescribes that the accent assigned by (214) always remains acute – that is, that it is not subject to the Acute-Grave Rule. (So, e.g. Bally 1945). (214) as it stands does not give the desired results in this respect, and it is not open to us to order it after the Acute-Grave Rule, since then oxytone words like δεινά *deiná* would have no accent to throw back. A possible solution might be to modify (214) so that it deletes not only the vowel but also the following boundary or boundaries, thus removing the environment for the Acute-Grave Rule. It would then be necessary, in order to prevent an accent from being incorrectly dropped, to change the cut-off point (see pp. 129–130) for rules (174), (176) and (178) so that they cut off not immediately before the Rule of Enclisis, but before Elision. It is true that on this proposal a sequence like δείν' ἄν *deín' án*, with the boundary deleted, would be subject to (175); this could be avoided by restricting (175) so that it assigned a circumflex accent only where the following syllable was unaccented.

The rule modifications here proposed have been incorporated in the versions of Elision and of the various linking rules that are given in the Summary of Rules.

[220] This rule is responsible for the form οὐχ [ūkʰ] taken by one of the negative particles before [h]. See pp. 49–50.

assumed that the following initial [h] does not emerge from the
rule as an independent segment, but is ' absorbed ' into the
aspiration on the consonant.

(215) ASPIRATION SHIFT

$$
\begin{bmatrix} -\text{cont} \\ -\text{voice} \end{bmatrix} ([-\text{seg}]) \begin{bmatrix} -\text{cons} \\ +\text{hsp} \end{bmatrix}
$$

$$
\begin{array}{ccc}
1 & 2 & 3 \\
\begin{bmatrix} 1 \\ +\text{hsp} \end{bmatrix} & 2 & \emptyset
\end{array} \Rightarrow
$$

5.2.8. ACCENT OF VARIOUS CLASSES OF NOUNS AND ADJECTIVES

For the most part, predictable accentuation on classes of
forms will be assigned by lexical redundancy rules; not all of
these will be exceptionless, but only the exceptions, not the
regular forms, will add to the complexity of the grammar. In
the following discussion only a few of the more interesting
points are touched on.

(a) First-declension feminine nouns of the same form as
feminine adjectives are normally accented on the penultimate,
even if the adjective is oxytone. Under the current theory this
is not capable of being described by a phonological rule; such
a rule cannot refer to more than one set of labelled brackets at a
time,[221] so that a phonological rule can recognize the class
' nouns and adjectives ' (by allowing two sets of labels as
alternatives on the *same* brackets in a structural description [222]), but not the class ' nouns formed from adjectives '.
Rather, a lexical redundancy rule is needed which will say:

(216) If L_1 and L_2 are lexical items phonologically

---

[221] ' A rule of the cycle could not refer to the fact that [a constituent]
contained a smaller constituent which is a noun or ... was part of a larger
constituent which is also a noun ' (McCawley 1968, 47). Perhaps, however,
there is an exception for brackets labelled Stem. It is certainly convenient
for phonological rules to be able to refer to them; see, for instance, Aspirated
Perfect in Summary of Rules.

[222] Numerous examples in Chomsky and Halle (1968).

identical except that L_1 ends in /ǫ/ and L_2 in /ā/; if L_1 is an adjective and L_2 a noun; and if the simultaneous environment of the Gruber [223] lexical entry for L_2 includes as a proper part the simultaneous environment of the Gruber lexical entry for L_1; and if L_2 is feminine – then L_2 is accented on the penultimate syllable.

All the information needed to work (216) can be mechanically derived from lexical entries. If phonological theory is not able to countenance rules that can identify nouns derived from adjectives as such, then rules such as (216) will certainly be needed.[224]

There are various exceptions to (216), among which two classes stand out: names of sciences and of countries ending in *-iké*, e.g. γραμματική *grammatiké* 'grammar', Λακωνική *Lakōniké* 'Laconia'. Evidently a subsidiary lexical rule is needed based on the form of the lexical entries for these words. The lexical entry for γραμματική *grammatiké* may be roughly of the following form: [225]

---

[223] ' Gruber lexical entries ' (introduced in Gruber 1967, which I have not been able to see) are trees like (217); the ' simultaneous environment ' of such an entry is the boxed part, i.e. the part for which a phonological matrix is actually substituted; the remainder of the structure shown in the entry, which merely conditions the substitution, is called the ' peripheral environment '.

[224] Two other devices that might be suggested to account for the facts expressed by (216) will not work. The first is to assign accent in these words by a cyclic rule – one cycle for the contained adjective, another for the noun. This fails because after the first cycle the brackets labelled ' adjective ' are deleted, and it will not be possible to tell on the second cycle which nouns are derived from adjectives.

The second proposal would be to treat the rule as a special case of the ' principe de l'opposition des genres ' mentioned by Vendryes (1929, 151). The difficulty with this is that feminine nouns derived from barytone adjectives are accented in just the same way as those derived from oxytone adjectives; this asymmetry is not typical of the ' principe de l'opposition des genres ', as can be seen from Vendryes' discussion of that principle.

[225] SCIENCE, CONCERN, LANGUAGE, etc., are not, of course, meant to be semantic primitives; they presumably have an internal structure, but we do not know what it is – and for the purposes of the present discussion it does not matter. The subscript integers in (217) show which NPs have to be coreferential.

M

(217)

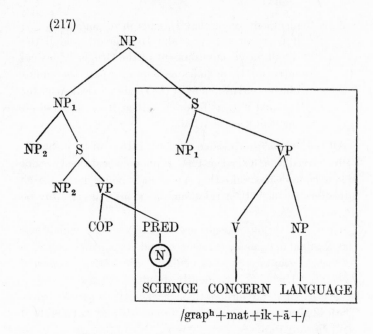

/grapʰ+mat+ik+ā̆+/

Subsidiary to (216), then, we need a further lexical rule:

(218) If, L_1 and L_2 meeting in all respects the specifications of (216), the simultaneous environment for L_2
differs from that for L_1 by the addition of SCIENCE
or COUNTRY to its terminal substring, then not-
withstanding (216) L_2 is accented on the same
syllable as L_1.

Rule (218), as stated, assumes that nouns like γραμματική
grammatikě are in fact introduced by lexical transformations
based on entries like (217), rather than by grammatical
transformations applying to input structures already containing lexical items. This is the preferable analysis: if the
noun γραμματική *grammatikě* were derived not by a lexical
transformation but by the deletion of the noun from an
adjective-noun phrase like γραμματικὴ τέχνη *grammatikè
tékhnē* ' grammatical art ', it would still, after the deletion, be

an adjective,[226] and we could not explain how it comes about that it and other nouns similarly derived are modified by adjectives rather than adverbs.[227] If derived by (217), γραμματική *grammatiké*, etc., can be made to be nouns from the start.[228]

(*b*) There is a general distinction in accent, among nouns formed from verbs without special suffix, between *action* nouns, which have recessive accent if masculine but final accent if feminine, and *agent* nouns, which are oxytone if masculine but have penultimate accent if feminine. (For details see Vendryes 1929). This too can be captured by lexical redundancy rules based on different types of lexical transformation. For example:

[226] To understand why this is so, consider how such a noun-deletion transformation would have to be stated. In the existing theory of transformational grammar, if in an adjective-noun sequence the noun has to be deleted, it can be done in either of the following two ways.

(i) Straight Deletion				(ii) ' Erasure '			
X	A	N	Y	X	A	N	Y
1	2	3	4	1	2	3	4
1	2	∅	4 ⇒	1	∅	2	4 ⇒

In both cases the N node over the noun will disappear completely. In (i) the noun itself (the terminal element) is deleted, so that the N node is left ' dangling ', and, by convention, is deleted also. In (ii) the convention is that the N node and everything it dominates (item 3 of the structural description) is replaced in the tree by the A node and everything *it* dominates (item 2); so that in both cases the adjective will in the end, after the noun has been deleted, be dominated by A, and there will be no N node at all in the relevant part of the tree. For the convention of substitution transformations, such as that included in (ii), see Koutsoudas (1966, 33), especially example (2) at the foot of the page.

[227] As, for example, at Plato, *Gorgias* 517*a*, where we have τῇ ἀληθίνη ῥητορικῇ *têi alēthínēi rhētorikêi* ' (the) true rhetoric ', whereas, if ῥητορική *rhētoriké* ' rhetoric ' were an adjective, we could only have had something like τῇ ὡς ἀληθῶς ῥητορικῇ (sc. τέχνῃ) *têi hōs alēthós rhētorikêi* (sc. *tékhnēi*) ' the art (which is) truly rhetorical '.

[228] A Gruber lexical entry must include a specification of what categorial node or nodes dominate the introduced phonological matrix. Normally this will be one of the nodes present in the simultaneous environment; thus in (217) the phonological matrix is inserted under the N node (ringed in the diagram) dominating SCIENCE, and, by convention, everything else in the simultaneous environment is deleted. Thus, when introduced by (217), γραμματική *grammatiké* ' grammar ' is not an adjective at any stage of derivation.

(219) If lexical item L is of the form $/V_1+\rho/$ or $/V_1+\bar{a}/$, where V_1 is a verb stem, and if L is a noun, and if the simultaneous environment of the Gruber lexical entry for L is

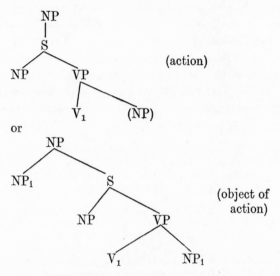

(action)

or

(object of action)

– then L is accented on the last syllable if feminine, and if masculine is unmarked for accent.

It might seem that (219) is useful only for actual verbal derivatives. But there are a great many other nouns, not phonologically relatable to verbs, but semantically action nouns, which are masculine and have recessive accent, and, intuitively, they have this accent *because* they are action (or object) nouns. Vendryes (1929) lists a large number; among those that cannot plausibly be derived from verbs are κόμπος *kómpos* ' boast ', ὅρκος *hórkos* ' oath ', πόθος *póthos* ' yearning', πόλος *pólos* ' axis, pole (of the heavens) ', and τοῖχος *toîkhos* ' wall '. There are various ways in which we can bring these within the compass of (219) so that we can capture the accent-meaning correlation. For example, ὅρκος *hórkos* may be the suppletive object- and action-noun of ὄμνυμι *ómnȳmi* ' swear '; it is noteworthy that ὄμνυμι *ómnȳmi* has no regularly formed noun for either function.[229] A number of other nouns, particularly those with stem vowel /ǫ/, can be treated (like πόλος *pólos*) from verbs attested only in poetry (in this case πέλω *pélō* ' come, be ') or even (like κόμπος *kómpos*) from verbs not attested at all. This is no more unreasonable than was the postulation of a verb *aggress* from which *aggression*, *aggressor*, etc., could be derived.[230]

(c) Compounds whose last element is -ερως *-erōs* ' love ', -κερως *-kerōs* ' horn ' or -γελως *-gelōs* ' laughter ' are always accented as if the [ǭ] of the final syllable was short, e.g. κατάγελως *katágelōs* ' ridicule ' not *καταγέλως *katagélōs*. Only an *ad hoc* solution is possible. One such would be a vowel shortening rule following Contraction [231] and preceding Accent Reassignment, followed by a rule lengthening the vowel again after the word has received the desired accent,[232],[233] resulting in derivations like the following:

[229] The regularly formed nouns would be *ὄμοσις *ómosis* ' a swearing ' and *ὄμομα *ómoma* ' something sworn or sworn by ', neither of which is found.

[230] *Aggress* is not, in fact, unattested, though it is rare. It is in the OED where it is quoted as late as 1882 (only a few years before letter A was published); nor did it then become obsolete, for there is a much more recent example of its use I have come across (Henderson 1940, 277–8): ' In accordance with Hitler's usual technique, everything was then done by the German authorities to prove to the German public that it was the Poles who had been the aggressors, instead of the aggressed '. There are, however, just as good grounds for postulating a verb *aggress* in the lexicon of those idiolects (like mine) which do not use the verb in surface structure as in those which do.

[231] In particular, following the vowel raising rule (130), which must not be given a chance to make these vowels non-low while they are temporarily short, and hence must either be earlier than our shortening rule or later than our lengthening rule. The latter alternative is not possible, since we know that (130), being part of the Contraction schema, precedes Accent Reassignment and therefore precedes our lengthening rule; therefore (130) must also precede our shortening rule.

[232] Since the lengthening rule must be later than (130) (see last note), it need not be confined to the particular low vowels shortened by the shortening rule; it can be simply to the effect that all low round vowels are made long, there being at this stage no low round short vowels except those shortened by the shortening rule.

[233] According to some authorities the minor and highly special shortening rule would have to be made even more special. These claim that the dative singular of words of this type was accented on the penultimate, e.g. that the

(220)   katagélǭs (Special Shortening)   →
        katagélǫs (Accent Reassignment) →
        katágelǫs (Special Lengthening)   →
        katágelǭs
        κατάγελως

dative of βούκερως [bŭkerọs] 'with cow's horns' was βουκέρῳ [būkérǫy].
On inquiring what the evidence is for this, we find that there is no hint of
any such exception in the ancient grammarians (not, at any rate, in any of
those whose works are included in *Grammatici Graeci*), and that the evidence
consists of one passage, Aeschylus, *Agamemnon* 1127, where editors seem to
agree in printing μελαγκέρῳ *melankérōi* 'black-horned' (so Denniston and
Page 1957, Murray 1955, Fraenkel 1950, Thomson 1966). The mss. vary,
some giving the accusative, others the dative; there is, however, on grounds
of sense and style, no doubt that the dative is correct, whatever its accent
may originally have been.

Accounts of the mss. and their relationships are given by the above-
mentioned editors. The three that matter for this passage are M, written
about the 10th or 11th century and carefully corrected by a contemporary
(called below the *diorthotes*), and F and Tr, both of the fourteenth century,
very similar and possibly copied from the same exemplar, but one of them
(Tr) written by the grammarian Demetrius Triclinius, who was very ready
to alter the text when it did not fit in with his grammatical or metrical
expectations.

Now at *Agamemnon* 1127, if Denniston and Page's apparatus is accurate,
the first hand in each of the mss. wrote the accusative. F has μελαγκέρων
melankérōn, Tr μελάγκερων *melánkerōn*; the latter no doubt represents
Triclinius' own correction of an exemplar that had the reading of F. M is
puzzling. According to Denniston and Page, the scribe first wrote the
accusative; then this was altered to the dative; later still a *n* was added
above the line; and the word is accented on both the second and third
syllables (μελάγκερῳ *melánkérōi*). Fraenkel confirms this account, except that
he tacitly assumes that the person who altered the last letter was the same
person who added the superscript – which seems a curious procedure,
especially as the scholiast treats the accusative as the main reading and the
dative as a variant; why erase the main reading only in order to restore it
above the line ? An alternative hypothesis is this: the immediate exemplar
of M had μελαγκέρων *melankérōn*, the last letter being perhaps partly faded.
The scribe read it first as a ν, then, changing his mind, as an ι. Afterwards
the *diorthotes*, checking the scribe's work against his exemplar, found that
the last letter should have been a ν, and rather than erase a second time
in the same place he noted the 'correction' above the line. The paroxytone
accent may be due to him or to a later corrector (the latter, claims Wecklein –
see Fraenkel *ad loc.*). It is thus likely that the accent in the archetype of all
our mss. was paroxytone. It is also, however, likely that the reading of this
archetype was not μελαγκέρῳ *melankérōi* but μελαγκέρων *melankérōn*, since
the accusative appears in both sub-families of the extant mss., the dative

(d) Nouns ending in -τος -tos can be divided into three classes: (i) nouns with the suffix /tǫ/, e.g. ἔμετος émetos ' vomiting' (from ἐμέω eméō ' vomit '), all of which are barytone except κωκυτός kōkȳtós ' wailing '; (ii) nouns where the suffix is /ετǫ/ or /ētǫ/, e.g. πυρετός pyretós ' fever ' (cf. πῦρ pŷr ' fire '), σπορητός sporētós ' sowing ' (cf. σπορά sporā́ ' id.') – these are all oxytone; (iii) nouns from which no suffix can be extracted and which cannot be regarded as derived, e.g. ἀστός astós ' citizen ', καπετός kapetós ' ditch, hole '– for the accent of these no general rule is statable. The facts of (i) and (ii) suggest a pair of lexical redundancy rules, one making all nouns ending in /+ετǫ/ and /+ētǫ/ oxytone, the other specifying that all nouns ending in /+tǫ/ – i.e. all class (i) nouns – are unmarked for accent.[234]

(e) In much the same way, the position of morpheme boundaries, together with a lexical redundancy rule, can account for the distinction between the size-adjectives ending in -ηλίκος -ēlíkos (e.g. πηλίκος pēlíkos ' of what size ? '), which are accented on the penultimate, and the bulk of adjectives ending in -ικός -ikós (e.g. γραμματικός grammatikós), which are oxytone. The former end in /+ēlikǫ/, the latter in /+ikǫ/.

(f) Certain feminine nouns ending in -ις -is, genitive -ιδος -idos, are exceptionally barytone (instead of oxytone like most nouns of this form), e.g. ἔρις éris ' strife ', Ἶρις Îris (name of

only in one (and in peculiar circumstances). If this is so, we have lost the only evidence we had for the accent of the dative singular of these compounds, and there is now no reason to suppose that it was not the same as that of the other cases.

It is possible that editors may have been unintentionally misled by Wackernagel, who, says Fraenkel, ' is inclined to regard the paroxytone as the original accentuation '. Reference to the passage in question, however (Wackernagel 1914, 123), makes it clear that he means by ' original ' something very much earlier than Aeschylus. I can find no other origin for the idea that the dative should be oxytone.

[234] Note that lexical redundancy rules, unlike ordinary phonological rules, can stipulate that morpheme boundary must be absent (Chomsky and Halle 1968, 67); so that although the two redundancy rules mentioned are unordered, ἔμετος émetos is subject only to the second, not to the first. The nouns considered in formulating the above classification are those listed under -τος -tos by Buck and Petersen (1944).

goddess), κάλπις *kálpis* ' pitcher '. It would at first sight seem necessary to regard all these as exceptions. But it proves to be the case, as far as can be determined from extant texts, that all barytone words of this type which are found in the accusative singular at all have the ending -ιν *-in* as well as or instead of -ιδα *-ida* in this case, with the exception of τάπις *tápis* ' carpet ' (Xenophon, *Anabasis* 7. 3. 37); and since this ending is by no means normal for nouns with stems ending in /id/, and remembering that nouns whose stems end in /i/ are mainly barytone, one wonders if these apparently exceptional nouns might not be underlying /i/-stems, /ẹri/, /kalpi/, etc., rather than /ẹrid/, /kalpid/. This would at one blow explain the accent and the form of the accusative singular; it would, however, leave one thing unexplained, namely the /d/ that appears at the end of the stem in all the other cases. This requires one special readjustment rule to add the /d/ in these cases and in derivatives. If the /d/ stem were taken as basic, the rule required would be one to delete it, and the correlation of this with the barytone accent would appear coincidental.[234a]

(*g*) Words of the type of φοῖνιξ *phoïniks* (gen. sg. -ικος *-īkos*) [235] ' dark-red ' have been alleged to be exceptions to rule (175) in that, in the nominative singular, they are accented circumflex on the first syllable although the second (it is said) has a long nucleus. Furthermore, they, as well as other properispomenon words ending in *ks*, are also exceptional in behaving like paroxytones with respect to the Rule of Enclisis, so that we have κλῖμαξ τις *klîmaks tis* ' a ladder ' and κῆρυξ τις *kêryks tis* ' a herald ', not *κλῖμάξ τις *klîmáks tis*, *κῆρύξ τις *kêryks tis*.

To solve this puzzle it does seem to be necessary to posit a

[234a] An exception to the general principle relating barytone accent to acc. sg. ending in -ιν *-in* is that words like ἀγυιᾶτις *agyiâtis* ' of Apollo Agyieus ', that is, feminines of actual or possible nouns or adjectives ending in -ης *-ēs*, have the same syllable accented that is accented in the masculine, whichever that is, and acc. sg. in -ιδα *-ida*.

[235] In the nom. sg. the length of the vowel in the last syllable is disputable; this point will be taken up presently.

rule so framed that it prevents linking rule (175) from operating by explicitly requiring a vowel to be [—falling] in an environment in which (175) would normally make it [+falling]. This rule, operating before the Rule of Enclisis, changes all properispomenon words ending in -*ks* to paroxytones:

(221) PAROXYTONIZATION

$$[+\text{sharp}] \rightarrow [-\text{falling}] / \underline{\quad\quad} C_0 \text{Vks} [+\text{WB}]$$

After the operation of this rule and the Rule of Enclisis, we have both φοίνιξ τις *phoíniks tis* and κλίμαξ τις *klímaks tis*. The correct accents can most easily and generally be restored by a rule like (222) combined with (175):

(222) XI SHORTENING (First Version)

$$\begin{bmatrix} V \\ \alpha \text{ high} \\ -\alpha \text{ low} \\ \beta \text{ long} \end{bmatrix} \rightarrow [-\text{long}] / \underline{\quad\quad} \text{ks} [+\text{WB}]$$

where $\beta = -$ if $\alpha = -$.

The domain of (222) is all words ending in -*aks*, -*iks*, -*īks*, -*yks*, or -*ȳks*. Its application to φοίνῑξ *phoínīks* and κήρῡξ *kērȳks* produces φοίνῐξ *phoíniks* and κήρῠξ *kērȳks* (its application to κλίμᾰξ *klímăks* is vacuous); whereupon linking rule (175) takes over and changes the accent (in the case of κλίμαξ *klímaks* as well as of the others) to circumflex.

This treatment will only work if it is accepted that in the nominative singular of φοῖνιξ *phoîniks* and κῆρυξ *kêryks* the vowel of the last syllable was phonetically short. LSJ s.v. φοῖνιξ *phoîniks* incomprehensibly deny this. Incomprehensibly, because in so doing they go against the only authority they cite on the subject, Choeroboscus *in Theodosii Canones* 1. 292 Hilgard, and yet they say nothing about this disagreement. To paraphrase Choeroboscus' somewhat long-winded exposition, he says that the last vowel of such words as φοῖνιξ *phoîniks* and πέρδιξ *pérdiks* 'partridge', though long by nature in the oblique cases, is long only by position [236] in the nominative singular; that this is unexpected, since nowhere else is a vowel short in the nominative but long in the oblique cases, but that it is due to the fact that [i] and [ü] are never long by nature before [ks], except in the case of the temporal augment. This analysis, Choeroboscus in effect goes on, is confirmed by the fact that the vowel is also short in the dative plural φοίνιξι (*phoíniksi*, etc.), the only other case of these nouns in which the cluster [ks] occurs.[237]

Choeroboscus' testimony suggests that (222) is correct as far as it goes but that nevertheless it is not the whole truth; that would be better expressed by (223).

(223)[238] XI SHORTENING (Final Version)

$$\begin{bmatrix} V \\ \alpha \text{ high} \\ -\alpha \text{ low} \\ \beta \text{ long} \end{bmatrix} \rightarrow [-\text{long}] / \underline{\qquad} ks$$

where, again, $\beta = -$ if $\alpha = -$.

5.2.9. CONCLUSION

With these rules, as well as many others whose content will be found in the works on Greek accentuation I have cited, and which I have not discussed, either because they present no special difficulties and lead to no interesting conclusions, or because apparent irregularities can only be treated as sheer exceptions, how much of accentuation remains unpredictable ? Practically nothing, except in nouns and adjectives; and the

---

[236] I.e. is phonetically short though standing in a rhythmically heavy (in traditional terminology, ' long ') syllable.

[237] The existence of a rule like Xi Shortening is recognized by Kuryłowicz (1958, 122), who speaks of ' un abrègement phonétique ... devant [ks] finale '. It would appear from Choeroboscus' statements that the qualification imported by the word ' finale ' may be omitted.

[238] It is not necessary to complicate (223) to take account of Choeroboscus' proviso that the initial vowel of augmented forms of verbs is not subject to Xi Shortening. Boundary Insertion (see p. 63 always adds a = boundary after that vowel, which will serve to block the application of (223).

accent even of most of these is predictable from their form or their meaning [239] or both.[240] Where it is so predictable, its specification, as we have seen, will not contribute to the complexity of the grammar.

[239] That is, by rules like (218) and (219) referring to the structure of Gruber lexical entries.

[240] A random sample of 240 nouns and adjectives scattered through the lexicon contained, on the most pessimistic estimate, 176 whose accent was predictable by a general rule given above or by Vendryes (1929). It should also be recalled that barytone words do not need to have their accentuation marked in the lexicon.

CHAPTER SIX

GREEK PHONOLOGICAL RULES

6.1. *SUMMARY OF RULES*

SPECIAL LINKING RULES

L1 = (174) (Cuts off before Elision) SLATEWIPING

$$[a \text{ sharp}] \rightarrow [-\text{falling}]$$

L2 = (175) as modified, see note 219: CIRCUMFLEX ACCENT

$$[+\text{sharp}] \rightarrow [+\text{falling}] / \left\{ \begin{bmatrix} \overline{} \\ +\text{long} \end{bmatrix} \atop - \begin{bmatrix} -\text{cns} \\ -\text{syl} \end{bmatrix} \right\} /$$

$$\underline{} C_0 \begin{bmatrix} V \\ -\text{long} \\ -\text{sharp} \end{bmatrix} C_0 [+\text{WB}]$$

L3 = (176) (Cuts off before Elision) NO-DOUBLE-ACCENT CONSTRAINT

$$V \rightarrow [-\text{sharp}] / \# \# X [+\text{sharp}] Y \underline{} Z \# \#$$

Conditions: 1. Mirror-image.
2. X, Y, Z contain no occurrence of $\# \#$.

L4 = (177) SVARITA

$$\begin{bmatrix} V \\ -\text{sharp} \end{bmatrix} \rightarrow \left\{ \begin{matrix} [-\text{falling}] \\ [+\text{falling}] / \begin{bmatrix} +\text{sharp} \\ -\text{falling} \end{bmatrix} C_0 ([-\text{seg}]) C_0 \underline{} \end{matrix} \right\}$$

L5 = (178) (Cuts off before Elision) NO-DOUBLE-SVARITA CONSTRAINT

$$V \rightarrow [-\text{falling}] / \# \# X [+\text{falling}] Y \underline{} Z \# \#$$

Conditions: same as for L3.

MAIN-SEQUENCE RULES [241]

S1 = (102) modified to take account of changes in the proposed underlying vowel system, see pp. 100 ff.:
VOWEL WEAKENING (Minor Rule)

$$\begin{bmatrix} V \\ -\text{high} \end{bmatrix} \rightarrow \left\{ \begin{array}{l} \begin{bmatrix} +\text{back} \\ -\text{round} \end{bmatrix} / \underline{\hspace{1em}} C \left\{ \begin{array}{c} C \\ + \end{array} \right\} X \rrbracket_V \\ \varnothing / \begin{bmatrix} \underline{\hspace{2em}} \\ -\text{back} \end{bmatrix} \end{array} \right\}$$

S2 = (100) METAPHONY (Minor Rule)

$$\begin{bmatrix} V \\ \alpha \text{ back} \\ \alpha \text{ round} \end{bmatrix} \rightarrow \begin{bmatrix} -\alpha \text{ back} \\ -\alpha \text{ round} \end{bmatrix} / \quad \text{in certain irregular verbs, nouns \& adjs. in certain contexts.}$$

S3 = (99) modified, see pp. 129 ff.; VṚDDHI (Minor Rule)

$$\begin{bmatrix} V \\ -\text{high} \\ \alpha \text{ back} \\ \alpha \text{ round} \end{bmatrix} \rightarrow [+\text{long}] / \quad \text{in all endingless non-neuter nominative singulars.}$$

S4 = (103) extended, see p. 81: NASAL VOCALIZATION

$$[+\text{nas}] \rightarrow \begin{bmatrix} +\text{syll} \\ -\text{cons} \\ -\text{nas} \\ +\text{low} \\ +\text{back} \end{bmatrix} / C \underline{\hspace{2em}} \left\{ \begin{array}{c} C \\ \begin{bmatrix} -\text{seg} \\ -\text{FB} \end{bmatrix} \end{array} \right\}$$

S5 = (141) GLIDE VOCALIZATION

$$[-\text{cons}] \rightarrow [+\text{syll}] / [-\text{syll}] \underline{\hspace{2em}} [-\text{syll}]$$

S6 = (83) AUGMENTATION

$$\left\{ \begin{array}{l} V \rightarrow \begin{bmatrix} +\text{long} \\ +\text{AUG} \end{bmatrix} / \begin{bmatrix} -\text{seg} \\ -\text{FB} \end{bmatrix} (h) \underline{\hspace{2em}} \\ \varnothing \rightarrow \begin{bmatrix} e \\ +\text{AUG} \end{bmatrix} / \begin{bmatrix} -\text{seg} \\ -\text{FB} \end{bmatrix} \underline{\hspace{2em}} \begin{bmatrix} -\text{syl} \\ -\text{low} \end{bmatrix} \end{array} \right\} \begin{bmatrix} +\text{past} \\ +\text{indic} \end{bmatrix} X \rrbracket_V$$

[241] All these rules are major and non-iterable, unless otherwise stated.

S7 = (84) BOUNDARY INSERTION

$$\emptyset \rightarrow \; = \; / \, [+\text{AUG}] \underline{\quad\quad}$$

S8 = (181) INITIAL ACCENT RULE

$$V \rightarrow [+\text{sharp}] \, / \, [+\text{WB}] \, C_0 \underline{\quad\quad}$$

S9 = (179) combined with (183): RULE OF LIMITATION

$$V \rightarrow [+\text{sharp}] \, /$$

$$[+\text{sharp}] \, X \left\{ \begin{array}{l} \underline{\quad} C_0 (=) C_0 V C_0 \left(\begin{bmatrix} V \\ -\text{long} \end{bmatrix} C \right)_0 [+\text{WB}] \\ = C_0 \begin{bmatrix} \underline{\quad\quad\quad} \\ \left\{ \begin{array}{l} +\text{infin} \\ +\text{partic} \end{array} \right\} \end{bmatrix} \end{array} \right\}$$

where X contains no word boundary.

S10 = (87) EPENTHESIS

$$\emptyset \rightarrow a \, / \, [+\text{cons}] \begin{bmatrix} +\text{cons} \\ +\text{son} \end{bmatrix} \underline{\quad\quad} [-\text{son}]$$

S11 = (45) EXCRESCENCE

$$\emptyset \rightarrow \begin{bmatrix} -\text{son} \\ -\text{nas} \\ \alpha \text{ features} \end{bmatrix} \, / \, \begin{bmatrix} +\text{nas} \\ \alpha \text{ features} \end{bmatrix} \underline{\quad\quad} \begin{bmatrix} +\text{cons} \\ +\text{son} \\ -\text{nas} \end{bmatrix}$$

S12 = (43) PROGRESSIVE MANNER ASSIMILATION

$$\begin{bmatrix} -\text{son} \\ -\text{cont} \end{bmatrix} \rightarrow \begin{bmatrix} \alpha \text{ hsp} \\ \beta \text{ voice} \end{bmatrix} \, / \, \begin{bmatrix} -\text{son} \\ -\text{cont} \\ \alpha \text{ hsp} \\ \beta \text{ voice} \end{bmatrix} [+\text{strid}] \underline{\quad\quad}$$

S13 = (89) SHORTENING

$$V \rightarrow [-\text{long}] \, / \underline{\quad\quad} \left\{ \begin{array}{l} \begin{bmatrix} -\text{cons} \\ +\text{high} \\ \langle +\text{back} \rangle \end{bmatrix} \left\langle \left\{ \begin{array}{l} C \\ [+\text{WB}] \end{array} \right\} \right\rangle \\ [+\text{nas}] \, [+\text{cons}] \end{array} \right\}$$

S14 = (41) DISSIMILATORY DELETION

$$\begin{bmatrix} -\text{son} \\ -\text{cont} \\ \alpha \text{ ant} \\ \beta \text{ cor} \end{bmatrix} \to \emptyset \; / \; \underline{} \; s \begin{bmatrix} -\text{son} \\ -\text{cont} \\ \alpha \text{ ant} \\ \beta \text{ cor} \end{bmatrix}$$

S15 = (8) with simplified output description: FRICATIVE
           WEAKENING

$$\begin{bmatrix} -\text{son} \\ +\text{cont} \end{bmatrix} \to \left\{ \begin{matrix} \begin{bmatrix} -\text{cons} \\ +\text{low} \end{bmatrix} / \left\{ \begin{matrix} \left\{ \begin{bmatrix} -\text{cons} \\ -\text{seg} \\ -\text{FB} \end{bmatrix} \right\} \underline{} [-\text{cons}] \\ [+\text{cons}] \underline{} ([-\text{seg}]) [+\text{cons}] \end{matrix} \right\} \\ [+\text{nas}] / \underline{} \begin{bmatrix} +\text{nas} \\ +\text{cor} \end{bmatrix} \end{matrix} \right\}$$

S16 = (57) OBSTRUENT DROPPING

$$[-\text{son}] \to \emptyset \; / \left\{ \begin{matrix} \begin{bmatrix} \underline{} \\ -\text{cont} \end{bmatrix} \left(\begin{bmatrix} -\text{son} \\ -\text{cont} \end{bmatrix} \right) [+\text{WB}]_2 \\ \begin{bmatrix} \underline{} \\ \langle -\text{cont} \rangle \\ +\text{cor} \end{bmatrix} + \begin{bmatrix} -\text{son} \\ \left\{ \begin{matrix} -\text{ant} \\ \langle +\text{cont} \rangle \end{matrix} \right\} \end{bmatrix} \end{matrix} \right\}$$

S17 = (9) modified, see note 47: FRICATIVIZATION

$$\begin{bmatrix} -\text{son} \\ +\text{cor} \end{bmatrix} \to \begin{bmatrix} +\text{del rel} \\ +\text{cont} \\ +\text{strid} \end{bmatrix} / \left\{ \begin{matrix} \underline{} \; (\text{h}) \; [-\text{son}] \\ \underline{} + \begin{bmatrix} +\text{nas} \\ -\text{cor} \end{bmatrix} \\ \text{V} \underline{} \text{iV} \end{matrix} \right\}$$

S18 = (15) NASAL ASSIMILATION

$$[+\text{nas}] \begin{bmatrix} \alpha \text{ ant} \\ \beta \text{ cor} \\ \langle +\text{cont} \\ \gamma \text{ features} \rangle \end{bmatrix} / \underline{} \begin{bmatrix} -\text{seg} \\ \langle -\text{FB} \rangle \end{bmatrix} \begin{bmatrix} +\text{cons} \\ \alpha \text{ ant} \\ \beta \text{ cor} \\ \langle +\text{cont} \\ \gamma \text{ features} \rangle \end{bmatrix}$$

S19 = (30) AFFRICATION

$$
\begin{bmatrix} -\text{son} \\ -\text{cont} \\ \alpha\ \text{voice} \end{bmatrix}
\begin{bmatrix} -\text{cons} \\ -\text{syll} \\ -\text{back} \end{bmatrix}
$$

$$
\quad 1 \qquad\qquad 2 \qquad \Rightarrow
$$

$$
\begin{bmatrix} 1 \\ +\text{ant} \\ +\text{cor} \end{bmatrix}
\begin{bmatrix} 2 \\ +\text{cons} \\ -\text{son} \\ +\text{strid} \\ +\text{ant} \\ +\text{cor} \\ \alpha\ \text{voice} \end{bmatrix}
$$

S20 = (37) modified to include the phenomenon mentioned in note 46: REGRESSIVE MANNER ASSIMILA-TION

$$
\begin{bmatrix} -\text{son} \\ \langle -\text{cont} \rangle \end{bmatrix} \rightarrow
\begin{bmatrix} \alpha\ \text{voice} \\ \left\langle \begin{matrix} \beta\ \text{hsp} \\ \gamma\ \text{A} \end{matrix} \right\rangle \end{bmatrix} / ([-\text{seg}])
\begin{bmatrix} -\text{son} \\ \alpha\ \text{voice} \\ \left\langle \begin{matrix} \beta\ \text{hsp} \\ \gamma\ \text{A} \end{matrix} \right\rangle \end{bmatrix}
$$

S21 = (18) NASALIZATION

$$
\begin{bmatrix} -\text{cont} \\ -\text{cor} \end{bmatrix} \rightarrow
\begin{bmatrix} -\text{hsp} \\ +\text{voice} \\ +\text{son} \\ +\text{nas} \end{bmatrix} / \underline{\quad} +
\begin{bmatrix} +\text{nas} \\ -\text{cor} \end{bmatrix}
$$

S22 = (16) and (31) combined: CORONAL CLUSTER SIMPLIFICATION

$$
\begin{bmatrix} -\text{son} \\ +\text{cor} \end{bmatrix} \rightarrow \emptyset /
\left\{ \begin{matrix} [+\text{nas}]\ \underline{\quad} \\ \begin{bmatrix} \underline{\quad} \\ +\text{cont} \end{bmatrix} \end{matrix} \right\}
\langle([-\text{seg}])\rangle
\begin{bmatrix} -\text{son} \\ +\text{cont} \end{bmatrix} \langle[-\text{syll}]\rangle
$$

S23 = (59) GRASSMANN'S LAW

$$\left\{\begin{matrix}[-A]\\ \begin{bmatrix}+\text{cons}\\ \alpha\ \text{ant}\\ \beta\ \text{cor}\end{bmatrix}\\ 1\end{matrix}\right\} \rightarrow \left\{\begin{matrix}[-\text{hsp}]\\ \emptyset\ /\ \begin{bmatrix}\underline{\quad}\\ -\text{syll}\\ +\text{low}\end{bmatrix}\\ 1\end{matrix}\right\} \Big/ \left\{\begin{matrix}[+A]\ V\ \underline{\quad}\\ \underline{\quad}\ C_0 V\begin{bmatrix}+\text{hsp}\\ \left\{\begin{matrix}[-A]\\ \begin{bmatrix}+\text{cons}\\ \alpha\ \text{ant}\\ \beta\ \text{cor}\end{bmatrix}\\ 1\end{matrix}\right\}\\ 1\end{bmatrix}\end{matrix}\right\}$$

S24 = (24) modified, see note 31: RESONANT AORIST RULE

$$\begin{matrix}\begin{bmatrix}V\\ \langle-\text{back}\rangle\end{bmatrix} & \begin{bmatrix}+\text{cons}\\ +\text{son}\end{bmatrix} & + & \begin{bmatrix}+\text{strid}\\ +\text{aorist}\end{bmatrix}\\ 1 & 2 & 3 & 4\\ \begin{bmatrix}1\\ +\text{long}\\ \langle-\text{low}\rangle\end{bmatrix} & 2 & 3 & \emptyset\end{matrix} \Rightarrow$$

S25 = (69) LOW VOWEL RULE

$$\begin{bmatrix}+\text{long}\\ +\text{low}\\ -\text{round}\end{bmatrix} \rightarrow [-\text{back}]\ /\ \left\{\begin{matrix}[+\text{back}]\\ [-\text{high}]\end{matrix}\right\}\ \underline{\quad}$$

S26 = (6) H-PROMOTION

$$\begin{matrix}[+\text{WB}] & V & (=) & h\\ 1 & 2 & 3 & 4\\ 1 & 4+2 & \emptyset & \emptyset\end{matrix} \Rightarrow$$

N

S27 = (80) CRASIS

$$
\begin{bmatrix} V \\ -\text{high} \end{bmatrix} \quad \text{(y)} \; [-\text{seg}] \quad \begin{bmatrix} V \\ \langle +\text{back} \\ -\text{round} \rangle \end{bmatrix}
$$

$$
\begin{matrix} 1 & & 2 & 3 & & 4 \end{matrix} \qquad \Rightarrow
$$

$$
\begin{bmatrix} 1 \\ \langle +\text{low} \\ +\text{back} \\ -\text{round} \rangle \end{bmatrix} \quad 2 \quad \begin{bmatrix} 3 \\ +\text{FB} \end{bmatrix} \quad 4
$$

S28 = (13) GLIDE DELETION

$$
\begin{bmatrix} -\text{cons} \\ -\text{syll} \end{bmatrix} \rightarrow \emptyset \; / \; \left\{ \begin{matrix} [\alpha \text{ syll}] \\ \left\langle \begin{bmatrix} -\text{seg} \\ -\text{FB} \end{bmatrix} \right\rangle \end{matrix} \right\} \; \left[\dfrac{\quad\quad}{\langle +\text{high} \rangle} \right] [\alpha \text{ syll}]
$$

S29 = (64) K-ADDITION

$$
\emptyset \rightarrow k \; / \; \begin{bmatrix} +\text{negative} \\ \langle +\text{factual} \rangle \end{bmatrix} \text{——} \left\{ \begin{matrix} + \\ \langle \# {}_1 \rangle \end{matrix} \right\} [-\text{cons}]
$$

S30 = (81) DIPHTHONG FORMATION

$$
[+\text{high}] \rightarrow [-\text{syll}] \; / \; V \text{——}
$$

S31 = (60) ASPIRATED PERFECT

$$
\begin{bmatrix} -\text{son} \\ -\text{cor} \\ +\text{perfect} \end{bmatrix} \rightarrow \begin{bmatrix} -\text{voice} \\ +\text{hsp} \end{bmatrix}
$$

$$
/ \left\{ \begin{matrix} V \\ [-\text{seg}] \end{matrix} \right\} \begin{bmatrix} C \\ -\text{hsp} \end{bmatrix}_0 \left\{ \begin{matrix} \begin{bmatrix} V \\ -\text{long} \end{bmatrix} \\ \begin{bmatrix} V \\ +P \end{bmatrix} C_0 \end{matrix} \right\} \text{——}]_{\text{Stem}} + V
$$

S32 = (50) GLIDE ASSIMILATION, SPECIAL (Minor Rule)

$$
\begin{bmatrix} -\text{cons} \\ -\text{syll} \end{bmatrix} \rightarrow [+\text{back}] \; / \; \begin{bmatrix} -\text{cons} \\ -\text{syll} \\ +\text{high} \\ +\text{back} \end{bmatrix} \text{——}
$$

S33 = (51) GLIDE ASSIMILATION, GENERAL (Mirror-image)

$$\begin{bmatrix} -\text{cons} \\ -\text{syll} \end{bmatrix} \rightarrow \left\{ \begin{array}{c} \begin{bmatrix} +\text{high} \\ -\text{back} \\ \alpha \text{ features} \end{bmatrix} / \begin{bmatrix} -\text{cons} \\ -\text{syll} \\ +\text{high} \\ -\text{back} \\ \alpha \text{ features} \end{bmatrix} \underline{\quad} \\ \begin{bmatrix} -\text{low} \\ \beta \text{ features} \end{bmatrix} / \begin{bmatrix} -\text{cons} \\ -\text{syll} \\ -\text{low} \\ \beta \text{ features} \end{bmatrix} \underline{\quad} \end{array} \right\}$$

S34 = (207) RULE OF MONOSYLLABLES

$$\begin{bmatrix} \text{V} \\ +\text{accentable} \end{bmatrix} \rightarrow [+\text{sharp}]$$

$$/ [+\text{WB}] \, C_0 V C_0 + \begin{bmatrix} -\text{partic} \\ \alpha \text{ case} \\ 3 \text{ Decl} \end{bmatrix} (\text{V}) C_0 [+\text{WB}]$$

where $\alpha = 4$ or 5.

S35 VENDRYES' LAW

See pp. 126–7 and notes 164 and 195. As here given, the rule, in its application to verbs, includes words with a rhythmically heavy antepenultimate syllable as well as those with a light antepenultimate; this is because verb forms of three or more syllables [242] (unless contracted) are never properispomenon, even if their penultimate syllable contains a diphthong; e.g. λύσοιτο *lýsoito* ' he would ransom ' (3rd sg. future optative middle of λύω *lýō* ' release ') and βούλευσαι *boúleusai* ' take counsel ' (aorist imperative of βουλεύομαι *bouléuomai*).

$$\begin{bmatrix} \text{V} \\ \langle -\text{VERB} \rangle \end{bmatrix} \rightarrow [+\text{sharp}]$$

$$/ \begin{bmatrix} \underline{\quad} \\ \langle -\text{long} \rangle \end{bmatrix} (=) C_0^{<1>} [+\text{falling}] \, C_0 V C_0 [+\text{WB}]$$

[242] Infinitives are an exception, most of those ending in [ay] being always ccented on the penultimate.

S36 = (63) GLIDE REINFORCEMENT

$$\emptyset \to y \ / \ Vy\text{——}V$$

S37 = (131) CONTRACTION (Iterable)

$$
\begin{bmatrix} V \\ -\text{high} \end{bmatrix} \to
\left\{
\begin{matrix}
[-\text{low}] \ / \ \left\{
\begin{matrix}
\left\{ \begin{bmatrix} -\text{seg} \\ -\text{FB} \end{bmatrix} \right\} \\
[-\text{syll}] \\
[-\text{low}]
\end{matrix} \right\}
\begin{bmatrix} \text{———} \\ -\text{long} \\ \alpha \ \text{back} \\ \alpha \ \text{round} \end{bmatrix}
\\
o \ \begin{bmatrix} \text{———} \\ -\text{back} \\ +\text{long} \end{bmatrix} y
\\
\begin{bmatrix} +\text{long} \\ \langle \beta \ \text{round} \rangle \\ \langle \gamma \ \text{back} \rangle \end{bmatrix} \ / \ \begin{bmatrix} V \\ -\text{high} \\ \langle \beta \ \text{round} \rangle \\ \langle \gamma \ \text{back} \rangle \end{bmatrix} \begin{bmatrix} \text{———} \\ \langle -\text{round} \rangle \\ \langle -\text{back} \rangle \end{bmatrix}
\end{matrix}
\right\}
$$

S38 = (73) TRUNCATION

$$
\begin{bmatrix} V \\ -\text{long} \\ -\text{high} \end{bmatrix} \to \emptyset \ / \ \text{——} \begin{bmatrix} V \\ -\text{high} \end{bmatrix}
$$

S39 = (76) DIPHTHONG SHORTENING

$$
\begin{bmatrix} V \\ -\text{high} \\ -\text{low} \end{bmatrix} \to [-\text{long}] \ / \ \text{——} \begin{bmatrix} -\text{cons} \\ -\text{syll} \end{bmatrix}
$$

S40 SPECIAL SHORTENING (Minor Rule; see pp. 227–9)

$$\bar{\text{o}} \to [-\text{long}] \ / \ [+\text{sharp}] \ C_0 \text{——} X]\!]_{NA}$$

S41 = (208) AUXILIARY REASSIGNMENT

$$
\begin{bmatrix} V \\ +\text{back} \\ +\text{sharp} \\ 2\,\text{Number} \end{bmatrix} \to [\alpha \ \text{falling}] \ / \ + \text{——} [\alpha \ \text{seg}]
$$

S42 = (205) ACCENT REASSIGNMENT (Minor Rule)

$$V \rightarrow [+\text{sharp}] \,/\, \underline{} \; C_0(VC_0(\begin{bmatrix} V \\ -\text{long} \end{bmatrix} C_0)) \, [+\text{WB}]$$

S43 = (99) VOCATIVE SHORTENING

$$\begin{bmatrix} V \\ +\text{Vṛddhi} \end{bmatrix} \rightarrow [-\text{long}] \,/\, \left\{ \begin{matrix} \begin{bmatrix} \underline{} \\ -\text{sharp} \end{bmatrix} \\ \underline{} \; s \end{matrix} \right\}$$

S44 = (210) FINAL DIPHTHONG RULE

$$[+\text{sharp}] \rightarrow [+\text{falling}] \,/\, \begin{bmatrix} \underline{} \\ -\text{round} \end{bmatrix} w \, [+\text{WB}]$$

S45 = (52) EPHELCYSIS

$$\emptyset \rightarrow n \,/\, \left\{ \begin{matrix} \text{si} \\ \begin{bmatrix} V \\ -\text{back} \\ -\text{long} \\ 3 \text{ Person} \end{bmatrix} \end{matrix} \right\} \underline{} [+\text{WB}]_1 \quad \begin{matrix} \% \\ [-\text{cons}] \end{matrix} \right\}$$

S46 = (33) LATERALIZATION

$$y \rightarrow \begin{bmatrix} +\text{lateral} \\ \alpha \text{ features} \end{bmatrix} \,/\, V \begin{bmatrix} +\text{lateral} \\ \alpha \text{ features} \end{bmatrix} \underline{}$$

S47 = (34) METATHESIS

$$\begin{matrix} \begin{bmatrix} +\text{cons} \\ -\text{son} \end{bmatrix} & \begin{bmatrix} -\text{cons} \\ -\text{syll} \end{bmatrix} \\ 1 & 2 \\ 2 & 1 \end{matrix} \Rightarrow$$

S48 = (24) NASAL DROPPING

$$\begin{matrix} V & [+\text{nas}] & [+\text{strid}] \\ 1 & 2 & 3 \\ \begin{bmatrix} 1 \\ +\text{long} \end{bmatrix} & \emptyset & 3 \end{matrix} \Rightarrow$$

S49 = (91) LENGTHENING IN IRREGULAR COMPARATIVES

$$V \rightarrow [+\text{long}] \, / \, \underline{\hphantom{xx}} \, C_2 \begin{bmatrix} V \\ +\text{round} \\ +\text{compve} \end{bmatrix}$$

S50 AFFRICATE RESOLUTION [243]

$$\begin{bmatrix} -\text{son} \\ -\text{cont} \\ a \text{ voice} \end{bmatrix} \begin{bmatrix} -\text{son} \\ +\text{cont} \end{bmatrix}$$
$$\quad\;\; 1 \qquad\quad 2 \quad \Rightarrow$$
$$\begin{bmatrix} 2 \\ a \text{ cont} \\ -\text{hsp} \end{bmatrix} \quad 1$$

S51 = (132) HIGH VOWEL FRONTING

$$\begin{bmatrix} +\text{syll} \\ +\text{high} \\ +\text{back} \end{bmatrix} \rightarrow \begin{bmatrix} -\text{back} \\ +\text{round} \end{bmatrix}$$

S52 = (94) QUANTITATIVE METATHESIS

$$\begin{bmatrix} V \\ -\text{back} \\ +\text{low} \\ +\text{long} \end{bmatrix} \begin{bmatrix} V \\ +\text{back} \end{bmatrix}$$
$$\qquad 1 \qquad\quad 2 \quad \Rightarrow$$
$$\begin{bmatrix} 1 \\ -\text{low} \\ -\text{long} \end{bmatrix} \begin{bmatrix} 2 \\ +\text{low} \\ +\text{long} \end{bmatrix}$$

[243] The effect of this rule is the same as that of the previous formulation of Affricate Resolution, given as (32). The version here given, however, has the advantage in formal simplicity, and also brings out the fact that one of the two related changes brought about by this rule is a metathesis (of [dz] to [zd]).

S53 = (36) MONOPHTHONGIZATION

$$
\begin{bmatrix} V \\ -low \\ \alpha\ back \end{bmatrix}
\begin{bmatrix} -cons \\ -syll \\ +high \\ \alpha\ back \end{bmatrix}
\left\{ \begin{matrix} [+cons] \\ [+WB] \end{matrix} \right\}
$$

$$
\begin{matrix} 1 & 2 & 3 & \Rightarrow \end{matrix}
$$

$$
\begin{bmatrix} 1 \\ +long \end{bmatrix} \quad \emptyset \quad 3
$$

S54 SPECIAL LENGTHENING (see pp. 173–4)

$$
\begin{bmatrix} V \\ +low \\ +round \end{bmatrix} \rightarrow [+long]
$$

S55 = (23) ō-RAISING

$$
\begin{bmatrix} V \\ +long \\ +back \\ -low \end{bmatrix} \rightarrow [+high]
$$

S56 = (61) r-DEVOICING

$$
\begin{bmatrix} +cons \\ +son \\ +cont \\ -lat \end{bmatrix} \rightarrow [-voice] \left/ \left\{ \begin{matrix} \left\{ \begin{bmatrix} [+hsp] \\ -seg \\ -FB \end{bmatrix} \right\} - \\ r - \\ -r \end{matrix} \right\} \right.
$$

S57 = (62) r̥-DOUBLING

$$
\emptyset \rightarrow r̥\ /\ V\ [-seg]_0 \longrightarrow r̥
$$

S58 = (221) PAROXYTONIZATION

$$
[+sharp] \rightarrow [-falling]\ /\ \longrightarrow C_0 Vks\ [+WB]
$$

S59 = (214) modified, see note 219: ELISION

$$\langle\ \ V\ \ \ C_0\ \rangle \begin{bmatrix} V \\ -\text{long} \\ \begin{Bmatrix} -\text{high} \\ -\text{round} \end{Bmatrix} \\ \langle +\text{sharp}\rangle \end{bmatrix} \begin{bmatrix} -\text{seg} \\ -\text{FB} \end{bmatrix}_1 [-\text{cons}]$$

$$\begin{array}{ccccc} 1 & 2 & 3 & 4 & 5 \Rightarrow \\ \begin{bmatrix} 1 \\ +\text{sharp} \end{bmatrix} 2 & & \emptyset & \emptyset & 5 \end{array}$$

S60 = (215) ASPIRATION SHIFT

$$\begin{bmatrix} -\text{cont} \\ -\text{voice} \end{bmatrix} ([-\text{seg}]) \begin{bmatrix} -\text{cons} \\ +\text{hsp} \end{bmatrix}$$

$$\begin{array}{ccc} 1 & 2 & 3 & \Rightarrow \\ \begin{bmatrix} 1 \\ +\text{hsp} \end{bmatrix} & 2 & \emptyset \end{array}$$

S61 = (38) ASPIRATION ADJUSTMENT

$$\begin{bmatrix} -\text{cont} \\ \alpha\ \text{ant} \\ \beta\ \text{cor} \end{bmatrix} \rightarrow [-\text{hsp}] / \underline{\hspace{1cm}} \begin{bmatrix} -\text{son} \\ -\text{cont} \\ \alpha\ \text{ant} \\ \beta\ \text{cor} \end{bmatrix}$$

S62 = (213) ACUTE-GRAVE RULE and RULE OF ENCLISIS

$$\begin{bmatrix} V \\ -\text{falling} \end{bmatrix} \rightarrow [\alpha\ \text{sharp}] / \underline{\hspace{1cm}} C_0 [+\text{WB}]_1 [\alpha\ \text{enclitic}]$$

S63 = (223) XI SHORTENING

$$\begin{bmatrix} V \\ \alpha\ \text{high} \\ -\alpha\ \text{low} \\ \beta\ \text{long} \end{bmatrix} \rightarrow [-\text{long}] / \underline{\hspace{1cm}} \text{ks}$$

where $\beta = -$ if $\alpha = -$.

S64 = (170) SVARITA ADJUSTMENT

$$[+\text{falling}] \rightarrow [+\text{sharp}]$$

6.2. INDEX TO RULES

6.3. SPECIMEN PASSAGE IN UNDERLYING REPRESENTATION

Below I give the passage (Andocides, *On the Mysteries*, 17) in three forms. (224) represents what we believe to have been the actual pronunciation. (225) represents a very early stage of derivation, before the application of any of the main-sequence rules of section 6.1. Certain features are not marked in (225). Thus diacritic features are omitted, and so is accent, except where it cannot be predicted by any lexical rule. Further, not all the word boundaries are marked which would be inserted by Chomsky and Halle's convention (1968, 366); since the number

of successive word boundaries, if greater than one, makes no
difference to the operation of any phonological rule, I have
represented all sequences of two or more word boundaries by
two occurrences of the symbol /.

Ἔτι μήνυσις ἐγένετο μία. Λυδὸς ὁ Φερεκλέους τοῦ Θημακέως
ἐμήνυσε μυστήρια γίγνεσθαι ἐν τῇ οἰκίᾳ Φερεκλέους τοῦ
δεσπότου τοῦ ἑαυτοῦ ἐν Θημακῷ. καὶ ἀπογράφει τούς τε
ἄλλους, καὶ τὸν πατέρα ἔφη τὸν ἐμὸν παρεῖναι μέν, καθεύδειν
δὲ ἐγκεκαλυμμένον. Σπεύσιππος δὲ βουλεύων παραδίδωσιν
αὐτοὺς τῷ δικαστηρίῳ. κἄπειτα ὁ πατὴρ καταστήσας ἐγγυητὰς
ἐγράψατο τὸν Σπεύσιππον παρανόμων καὶ ἠγωνίσατο ἐν
ἑξακισχιλίοις Ἀθηναίων, καὶ μετέλαβε δικαστῶν τοσούτων
οὐδὲ διακοσίας ψήφους ὁ Σπεύσιππος. ὁ δὲ πείσας καὶ δεόμενος
μεῖναι τὸν πατέρα ἐγὼ ἦ μάλιστα, εἶτα δὲ καὶ οἱ ἄλλοι συγγενεῖς.

(224)

éti ménūsis egéneto mía.
ludos ho-pʰerekléūs tū-
tʰē̞makéō̞s emḗnūse
müstḗria gígnestʰay en-
tē̞y-oykíāy pʰerekléūs   5
tū-despótū tu-heawtû
en-tʰē̞makō̞y. kay-
apográpʰē tū́s-te állūs
kay-ton-patéra épʰē̞ ton-
emon parḗnay men   10
katʰéwdēn de
eŋkekalümmenon.
spéwsippos de būléwwō̞n
paradídō̞sin awtūs tō̞y-
dikastē̞ríō̞y. kápēta ho-   15
patḗr katastḗsās
eŋgüē̞tās egrápsato ton-
spéwsippon paranómō̞n
kay-ē̞gō̞nísato en-
heksakiskʰīlíoys   20
atʰē̞náyyō̞n kay metélabe

(225)

//éti//mēnū+si+s//gēn+ē̞+tō̞//mi+ya//.
//lūdo̞+s//h+o̞/pʰē̞r+ē̞+klē̞+ē̞s+o̞s//t+o̞+o̞
/tʰē̞mak+ē̞u+o̞s//mēnū+s+ē̞
//mus+tē̞r+i+a//gi+gēn+ē̞+stʰay//ē̞n
/t+ā+ay/o̞ik+i+ā+ay//pʰē̞r+ē̞+klē̞+ē̞s+o̞s
//t+o̞+o̞/dē̞spo̞+tā+o̞//t+o̞+o̞/hē̞+autó+o̞
//ē̞n/tʰē̞mak+ó̞+ay//.//kai
/apo̞=grapʰ+ē̞+i//t+o̞+ns/tē̞//all+o̞+ns
//kai/t+o̞+n/patē̞r+n//pʰā//t+o̞+n
/ē̞m+ó̞+n//para=ē̞s+ē̞+nay/mē̞n
//kata=hē̞ud+ē̞+ē̞n/dē̞
//ē̞n=kē̞+kalub+mē̞n+o̞+n//.
//spē̞ud+s+ipp+o̞+s/dē̞//bo̞ul+ē̞u+y+o̞+nt
//para=di+do̞+si//aut+ó̞+ns//t+o̞+ay
/dik+ad+tē̞r+i+o̞+ay//. /kai/ē̞p+ē̞i+ta//h+o̞
/patér//kata=stā+sa+nt+s
//ē̞ngu+ā+tā+ns//grapʰ+sa+to̞//t+o̞+n
/spē̞ud+s+ipp+o̞+n//para=nē̞m+o̞+an
//kai/agō̞n+id+sa+to̞//ē̞n
/hē̞ks+akis=kʰīli+o̞+is
//atʰē̞nā+i+o̞+an//kai/mē̞ta=lab+ē̞

likastǭn tosûtǭn ūde-   //dik+ad+tā+ǭn//t+ǫss+ǫ+ut+ǫ+an//ǫǫ+de
liākosíās psę̄pʰūs ho-   /di+ā+kǫti+ā+ns//psę̄pʰ+ǫ+ns//h+ǫ
péwsippos. ho-de   /speud+s+ipp+ǫ+s//. //h+ǫ/de//
ǫésās kay-deómenos   25   pę̄itʰ+sa+nt+s//kai/dę̄+ę̄+mę̄n+ǫ+s
nę̄nay ton-patéra egǭ   //mę̄n+s+ay//t+ǫ+n/patę̄r+n//ę̄gǭ
málista êta de kay-   //ę̄s+a//mal+ist+a//ę̄i+ta/de//kai
ɪoy-álloy süŋgenês.   /h+ǫ+y/all+ǫ+y//sun=gę̄n+ę̄s+ę̄s//.

' Then there was yet another information. Lydus, the slave of Pherecles of Themacus, gave information that the Mysteries had been performed in (5) the house of his master Pherecles at Themacus. He listed the names, and in particular alleged that my father (10) was present, but asleep with his cloak over his head. Speusippus, then a councillor, handed them over to the (15) court. After this my father appointed sureties and prosecuted Speusippus for moving an illegal resolution, and in a trial before (20) six thousand Athenians Speusippus got less than two hundred votes out of the whole jury. The one (25) who entreated and finally persuaded my father to remain was chiefly me, but also his other relatives '.

There is one point in (225) that requires special consideration. This relates to the surface structure of coordinate phrases like πείσας καὶ δεόμενος *péisās kai deómenos* ' advising and urging ' (line 25). It might be thought that this structure was

(226)

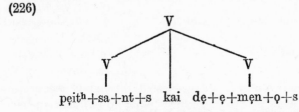

pę̄itʰ+sa+nt+s   kai   dę̄+ę̄+mę̄n+ǫ+s

If, as proposed by Chomsky and Halle (1968, 366), a word boundary is introduced before and after every occurrence of a ' major category ', then, the three V nodes being the only major category nodes in the subtree (226), the result will be

(227)

$$[_V \#[_V \#p\d{e}it^h + sa + nt + s \#_V]$$
$$kai \; [_V \#de + e + men + o + s \#_V] \#_V]$$

But now (227) contains no internal ' word termini ' (Chomsky and Halle 1968, 367), and consequently, by the definition there given, is a single phonological word. The same will happen, just as undesirably, in similar coordinate phrases in other languages. There is no alteration in the conventions on word boundaries that will give the desired results ;[244] what is needed is a different hypothesis about the surface structure. Let us suppose, for example, that the constituent structure is not as in (226), but instead that coordinating conjunctions are Chomsky-adjoined,[245] either to the left or to the right of the first constituent of the second of two conjuncts,[246] by a rule which is in part universal and in part variable – in particular, as regards whether the adjunction is to the left or to the right.

---

[244] Comrie's (1970) hypothesis on word termini does not in itself help. When combined with my Chomsky-adjunction hypothesis it works in the particular case now under discussion, but Comrie shows that in certain slightly more complex cases the conjunction of the two hypotheses will lead to incorrect results. Since both hypotheses are otherwise well motivated – mine as showing why coordinating conjunctions are typically clitic rather than either being independent words or fusing the words they connect into one, and Comrie's for various reasons discussed by him – Comrie is led to suggest that coordination may in the end have to be regarded as an exception to any convention about word termini.

[245] Chomsky-adjunction is a type of elementary transformation with the following effect. Given a node A, a rule Chomsky-adjoining B to the right of A results in the replacement of A, in the derived structure, by a subtree

(in which the lower A dominates whatever the original A node in the input structure dominated), and conversely if the adjunction is to the left. See, e.g. the editorial note to Jackendoff (1969, 14).

[246] This statement may be insufficiently general. I have been told that in some languages the conjunction is a clitic to the *first* conjunct; in these it should be described as Chomsky-adjoined to that conjunct.

In Greek, it is to the left for καί *kaí* and to the right for τε *te*, both of which mean ' and '. Thus (226) as a surface structure should be discarded in favour of (228).

(228)

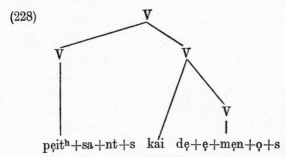

pẹitʰ+sa+nt+s kai dẹ+ẹ+mẹn+ọ+s

The Chomsky-Halle word boundary conventions will make of this

(229)

$$[_V \#[_V \# pẹitʰ + sa + nt + s \# _V]$$
$$[_V \# kai[_V \# dẹ + ẹ + mẹn + ọs \# _V] \# _V] \# _V]$$

which implies that there are two words, *peísās* and *kaì deómenos*, and thus (correctly) makes *kaí* proclitic to the word following.

.4. SAMPLE DERIVATIONS

Underlying Forms			
	pʰẹr+ẹ+klẹ+ẹs+ọs	para=ẹs+ẹ́+nay	dik+ad+tẹ̄r+i+ọ+ay
8	pʰẹ́r+ẹ+klẹ+ẹs+ọs		dík+ad+tẹ̄r+i+ọ+ay
9	pʰẹr+ẹ+klẹ́+ẹs+ọs		dik+ad+tẹ̄r+í+ọ+ay
15	+ẹh+	=ẹh+	
17			+az+
20			+as+
28	+ẹ+	=ẹ+	
37	pʰer+e+klé+e+ōs	para=e+é+nay	dik+as+tẹ̄r+í+o+ọ̄y
38	+kle+ōs	=ể+nay	dik+as+tẹ̄r+í+ọ̄y
	(partial exception)		
55	pʰer+e+klé+ūs		
59		par=ể+nay	
	Φερεκλέους	παρεῖναι	δικαστηρίῳ

Underlying		
Forms	atʰḗnā+i+o̧+an	ȩŋgu+ā+tá̧+ns
S8	átʰḗnā+	
S9	atʰḗnā+í+	
S13	atʰḗna+	+tá+
S18		ȩŋgu+
S25		+ȩ̄+
S30	atʰḗná+y+	
S36	+yy+	
S37	+yy+o+ō̧n	eŋgu+
S38	atʰḗná+yy+ō̧n	
S48		+tá̧+s
S51		eŋgü+
S62		eŋgü+ȩ̄+tā+s
		(no high tone)
	Ἀθηναίων	ἐγγυητὰς

WORKS REFERRED TO

AALTIO, M.-H. (1964), *Essential Finnish.* London : University of London Press.

ALLEN, W. S. (1954), ' Retroflexion in Sanskrit: prosodic technique and its relevance to comparative statement ', *Bulletin of the School of Oriental and African Studies* 16, 556–565.

ALLEN, W. S. (1965), ' On one-vowel systems ', *Lingua* 13, 111–124.

ALLEN, W. S. (1968), *Vox Graeca.* Cambridge: University Press.

BACH, E. (1968), ' Nouns and noun phrases ', in Bach and Harms (1968).

BACH, E. and HARMS, R. T. (ed.) (1968), *Universals in linguistic theory.* New York: Holt, Rinehart & Winston.

BALLY, C. (1945), *Manuel d'accentuation grecque.* Berne: A. Francke S.A.

BARRETT, W. S. (1964), *Euripides: Hippolytos*, edited . . . by W. S. B. Oxford: Clarendon Press.

BOLINGER, D. L. (1967), ' Adjectives in English: attribution and predication ', *Lingua* 18, 1–34.

BUCK, C. D. (1955), *The Greek dialects.* Chicago: University Press.

BUCK, C. D. and PETERSEN, W. (1944), *A reverse index of Greek nouns and adjectives.* Chicago: University Press.

BURROW, T. (1965), *The Sanskrit language.* 2nd ed. London: Faber and Faber.

CAIRNS, C. E. (1969), ' Markedness, neutralization, and universal redundancy rules ', *Language* 45, 863–885.

CHOMSKY, N. and HALLE, M. (1968), *The sound pattern of English.* New York: Harper and Row.

COMRIE, B. S. (1971), ' Some thoughts on defining the word in phonology ', *Papers in Linguistics* 4, 447–461.

DENNISTON, J. D. and PAGE, D. L. (1957), *Aeschylus: Agamemnon*, edited by the late J. D. D. and D. P. Oxford: Clarendon Press.

FRAENKEL, E. (1950), *Aeschylus: Agamemnon*, edited ... by
E. F. Oxford: Clarendon Press.

GONDA, J. (1966), *A concise elementary grammar of the
Sanskrit language* (translated by G. B. Ford jr.) Leiden:
E. J. Brill.

GOODWIN, W. W. (1894), *A Greek grammar*. London:
Macmillan & Co.

Grammatici Graeci, recogniti et apparatu critico instructi. 4
parts. Lipsiae: in aedibus B. G. Teubneri, 1867– .

GREENBERG, J. H. (1966), ' Language universals ', in Sebeok,
ed. (1966).

GRUBER, J. (1967), *Functions of the lexicon in formal descriptive
grammars*. Santa Monica, California : Systems Development Corporation (TM 3 776/000/00).

HAKULINEN, L. (1961), *The structure and development of the
Finnish language*. Bloomington, Indiana: Indiana University (Uralic and Altaic Series, vol. 3).

HALLE, M. (1970), ' Is Kabardian a vowel-less language ? ',
Foundations of Language 6, 95–103.

HALLE, M. (1971a), ' Remarks on Slavic accentology ',
Linguistic Inquiry 2, 1–19.

HALLE, M. (1971b), ' Word boundaries as environments in
rules ', *Linguistic Inquiry* 2, 540–541.

HEESTERMAN, J. C., SCHOKKER, G. H. and SUBRAMONIAM,
V. I. (eds.) (1969), *Pratidānam: Indian, Iranian and Indo-
European studies presented to F. B. J. Kuiper on his sixtieth
birthday*. The Hague: Mouton & Co.

HENDERSON, SIR N. M. (1940), *Failure of a mission: Berlin
1937–1939*. London: Hodder & Stoughton.

HILGARD, A. (1894), *Theodosii Alexandrini canones, Georgii
Choerobosci scholia, Sophronii patriarchae Alexandrini
excerpta*. (Part IV of *Grammatici Graeci*, q.v.)

HOCKETT, C. F. (1955), *A manual of phonology*. (*International
Journal of American Linguistics*, Memoir 11). Baltimore:
Waverly Press.

HOCKETT, C. F. (1958), *A course in modern linguistics*. New
York: The Macmillan Co.

HOUSEHOLDER, F. W. (1971), *Linguistic speculations.* Cambridge: University Press.

HYMAN, L. M. (1970), ' How concrete is phonology ? ', *Language* 46, 58-76.

JACKENDOFF, R. S. (1969), ' Les constructions possessives en anglais ', *Langages* 14, 7-27.

KATZ, J. J. and POSTAL P. M. (1964), *An integrated theory of linguistic descriptions.* Cambridge, Mass.: MIT Press. (Research Monograph No. 26).

KIPARSKY, P. (1967), ' A propos de l'histoire de l'accentuation grecque ', *Langages* 8, 73-93.

KISSEBERTH, C. W. (1969), ' On the role of derivational constraints in phonology '. Bloomington, Indiana: Indiana University Linguistics Club.

KISSEBERTH, C. W. (1970), ' On the functional unity of phonological rules ', *Linguistic Inquiry* 1, 291-306.

KOCK, T. (ed.) (1880-8), *Comicorum Atticorum fragmenta.* 3 vols. Lipsiae: in aedibus B. G. Teubneri.

KOSTER, A. J. (1962), *A practical guide to the writing of the Greek accents.* Leiden: E. J. Brill.

KOUTSOUDAS, A. (1966), *Writing transformational grammars: an introduction.* New York: McGraw-Hill.

KRETSCHMER, P. and LOCKER, E. (1963), *Rückläufiges Wörterbuch der griechischen Sprache.* Göttingen.

KUIPERS, A. H. (1960), *Phoneme and morpheme in Kabardian.* The Hague: Mouton & Co.

KUIPERS, A. H. (1969), ' Unique types and typological universals ', in Heesterman *et al.* (1969).

KURYŁOWICZ, J. (1958), *L'accentuation des langues indo-européenes.* Wrocław and Kraków: Zakład Narodowy imenia Ossolińskich—Wydawnictwo Polskiej Akademii Nauk. (Prace Językoznawcze, No. 17).

LAKOFF, G. (1970), ' Global rules ', *Language* 46, 627-639.

LAKOFF, G. (1971a), ' On generative semantics ', in Steinberg and Jakobovits (1971).

LAKOFF, G. (1971b), *Irregularity in Syntax.* New York: Holt, Rinehart and Winston.

o

LANGACKER, R. W. (1969a), ' Mirror image rules I: syntax ',
Language 45, 575-598.

LANGACKER, R. W. (1969b), ' Mirror image rules II: lexicon
and phonology ', *Language* 45, 844-862.

LASS, R. (1969), ' On the derivative status of phonological
rules: the function of metarules in sound change '.
Bloomington, Indiana: Indiana University Linguistics Club.

LASS, R. (1971), ' Boundaries as obstruents: Old English
voicing assimilation and universal strength hierarchies ',
Journal of Linguistics 7, 15-30.

LAUM, B. (1928), *Das alexandrinische Akzentuationssystem;
unter Zugrundelegung der theoretischen Lehren der Gram-
matiker und mit Heranziehung der praktischen Verwendung in
den Papyri.* Paderborn: Ferdinand Schöningh.

LEES, R. B. (1960), *The grammar of English nominalizations.*
Bloomington, Indiana: Indiana University Research Center
in Anthropology, Folklore and Linguistics.

LEES, R. B. (1961), *The phonology of modern standard Turkish.*
Bloomington, Indiana: Indiana University (Uralic and
Altaic Series, No. 6).

LEJEUNE, M. (1958), *Mémoires de philologie mycénienne: pre-
mière série, 1955-1957.* Paris: Centre Nationale de la
Recherche Scientifique.

LENTZ, A. (ed.) (1867-8), *Herodiani technici reliquiae.* 2 vols.
(Part III of *Grammatici Graeci*, q.v.)

LSJ = LIDDELL, H. G. and SCOTT, R. *A Greek-English lexicon,*
new edn. revised . . . by H. Stuart Jones and R. McKenzie.
Oxford: Clarendon Press, 1925-40.

MCCAWLEY, J. D. (1968), *The phonological component of a
grammar of Japanese.* The Hague: Mouton & Co.

MARTINET, A. (1951), ' Concerning some Slavic and Aryan
reflexes of IE *s* ', *Word* 7, 91-95.

MURRAY, G. G. A. (1955), *Aeschyli septem quae supersunt
tragoediae.* Recensuit G. M. Editio altera. Oxonii: e
typographeo Clarendoniano.

OED = MURRAY, J. A. H. *et al.,* A *new English dictionary on
historical principles.* Oxford: Clarendon Press, 1888-1933.

PAPE, W. (1911), *Wörterbuch der griechischen Eigennamen*. Dritte Auflage, neu bearbeitet von Dr. G. E. Benseler. Braunschweig.

POSTAL, P. M. (1968), *Aspects of Phonological Theory*. New York: Harper & Row.

POSTAL, P. M. (1970), ' On the surface verb " remind " ', *Linguistic Inquiry* 1, 37–120.

PW = *Paulys Real-Encyclopädie der classischen Altertumswissenschaft*. Neue Bearbeitung ... herausgegben von Georg Wissowa [*et al.*] Stuttgart, 1894– .

REIBEL, D. A. and SCHANE, S. A. (eds.) (1969), *Modern studies in English*. Englewood Cliffs, New Jersey: Prentice-Hall.

ROSS, J. R. (1969), ' A proposed rule of tree-pruning ', in Reibel and Schane (1969).

SCHNEIDER, R. and UHLIG, G. (eds.) (1878–1910), *Apollonii Dyscoli quae supersunt*. 2 vols. (Part II of *Grammatici Graeci*, q.v.)

SCHWYZER, E. (1959), *Griechische Grammatik*. 3rd edn. München.

SEBEOK, T. A. (ed.) (1966), *Current trends in linguistics, volume 3: theoretical foundations*. The Hague: Mouton & Co.

SOMMERSTEIN, A. H. (1971), *Phonological theory and Ancient Greek*, unpublished Ph.D. dissertation, University of Cambridge.

SOMMERSTEIN, A. H. (1972a), ' On the so-called definite article in English ', *Linguistic Inquiry* 3, 197–209.

SOMMERSTEIN, A. H. (1972b), ' On the present controversy in transformational grammar ', unpublished paper, King's College, Cambridge.

STANLEY, R. (1967), ' Redundancy rules in phonology ', *Language* 43, 393–436.

STEINBERG, D. and JAKOBOVITS L. (eds.) (1971), *Semantics*. Cambridge: University Press.

STURTEVANT, E. H. (1968), *The pronunciation of Greek and Latin*. 2nd edn. Groningen: Bouma's Boekhuis N.V.

SZEMERÉNYI, O. (1964), ' Structuralism and substratum: Indo-Europeans and Semites in the ancient Near East ', *Lingua* 13, 1–29.

SZEMERÉNYI, O. (1967), ' The new look of Indo-European: reconstruction and typology ', *Phonetica* 17, 65–99.

THOMSON, G. (1966), *The Oresteia of Aeschylus*, edited . . . by G. T. New edn., revised and enlarged. 2 vols. Prague: Czechoslovak Academy of Sciences.

TRUBETZKOY, N. S. (1949), *Principes de phonologie*, traduits par J. Cantineau. Paris: Klincksieck.

VENDRYES, J. (1929), *Traité d'accentuation grecque.* Paris: Klincksieck.

VILBORG, E. (1960), *A tentative grammar of Mycenaean Greek.* Göteborg.

WACKERNAGEL, J. (1914), ' Akzentstudien III ', *Nachrichten von der Königlichen Gesellschaft der Wissenschaften zu Göttingen* (*Philologisch-historische Klasse*), 1914, 97–130.

WANG, W. S-Y. (1967), ' Phonological features of tone ', *International Journal of American Linguistics* 33, 93–105.

WARBURTON, IRENE P. (1970), ' Rules of accentuation in classical and modern Greek ', *Glotta* 48, 107–121.

WARD, R. L. (1944), ' Afterthoughts on *g* as *ŋ* in Latin and Greek ', *Language* 20, 73–77.

WEINGREEN, J. (1959), *A practical grammar for classical Hebrew.* Oxford: University Press.

ZIPF, G. K. (1932), *Selected studies of the principle of relative frequency in language.* Cambridge, Mass.: Harvard University Press.

ZWICKY, A. M. (1970), ' Greek-letter variables and the Sanskrit *ruki* class ', *Linguistic Inquiry* 1, 549–555.

SUBJECT INDEX

Starred entries (*) refer to phonological rules listed in the Summary of Rules.

INDEX OF NAMES AND PASSAGES

INDEX OF GREEK WORDS

Words are generally listed under their dictionary form (nominative singular for nouns ; nominative singular masculine for adjectives ; first person singular present indicative for verbs). Subsidiary entries are given for the more important inflectional forms.